Keyboarding Formatting Communication Skills Document Production

Introductory Course   11th EDITION
COLLEGE KEYBOARDING/ TYPEWRITING

Charles H. Duncan
Professor of Business Education
Eastern Michigan University

S. ElVon Warner
Head, Department of Information Management
University of Northern Iowa

Thomas E. Langford
President, Bay State Junior College
Boston, Massachusetts

Susie H. VanHuss
Professor of Management
University of South Carolina

ISBN: 0-538-20760-4

Library of Congress Catalog Card Number: 84-50474

3 4 5 6 7 8 9 10 11 12 13 14 Ki 2 1 0 9 8 7

Printed in U.S.A.

COVER PHOTO: Aetna Life and Casualty Company

PHOTO, p. 6: Location courtesy of Public Library of Hamilton County,
    Mt. Washington Branch

PHOTO, p. 71: Location courtesy of American Express Travel Related Services Co.,
    Cincinnati Office

Published by

T76 **SOUTH-WESTERN PUBLISHING CO.**

CINCINNATI   WEST CHICAGO, IL   DALLAS   PELHAM MANOR, NY   PALO ALTO, CA

CONTENTS

DIVISION 1

LEVEL ONE

LEVEL TWO

PREFACE

Keyboard-activated equipment, such as typewriters, word processors, and microcomputers, are tools of written personal and business communication. The purpose of learning to operate keyboard-activated equipment is to speed up the communication process. And the function of the instructor, the textbook, and the available learning aids is to facilitate the learning.

Learning to operate keyboard-activated equipment by touch involves training the eyes, ears, mind, and hands to operate simultaneously, but independently. To acquire this skill, students need to learn how to

1 position the body, arms, hands, and fingers correctly
2 assign and use appropriate fingers for specific keyboard reaches
3 strike keys by touch, without hesitation, and release them quickly
4 build keystroking speed early, then drop back slightly to improve control
5 improve their written communication skills

The student must bring to this task a certain amount of self-discipline, patience, determination, willingness to follow directions carefully, and a genuine desire to learn the skill well.

ORGANIZATION

College Keyboarding/Typwriting, Introductory Course. Eleventh Edition, has a threefold purpose: first, to develop the techniques of keyboard operation upon which all applied skills depend; second, to present procedures of copy arrangement and problem solving that are basic to all keyboarding/formatting operations; and third, to provide practice on those forms of communication produced on keyboard-activated equipment that is basic for both personal and business use. This threefold purpose is implemented by 75 carefully planned lessons, a work simulation, and a convenient Reference Guide

to frequently needed keyboarding/formatting information.

The 75 lessons are organized into two levels of closely related activities. Level 1 (Lessons 1-37) focuses on keyboard learning, technique development, speed building, and control of centering, tabulation, and other manipulative operations—the essential foundation for all successful applied keyboarding/formatting activities. Level 2 (Lessons 38-75) emphasizes copy-arrangement concepts and procedures as they apply to such commonly used personal and business papers as letters, tables, outlines, and reports. In addition, composing and supportive communication skills are stressed.

SPECIAL FEATURES

Control. The scientifically structured lessons in *College Keyboarding/Typewriting,* Introductory Course, Eleventh Edition, are built on the findings of scholars who have researched the areas of keyboarding learning and application. The lessons, therefore, have a sound psychological as well as topical base that leads to practical achievement.

Goals. To orient and motivate students, learning goals are stated at the beginning of each section of lessons. Intermediate goals are stated periodically throughout the sections to identify purpose of practice, to indicate how to practice, and to identify expected outcomes.

Skill building. Special sections devoted exclusively to the development and improvement of basic skills are interspersed among application sections. Instructors may use these sections in order of occurrence, group them for intensive emphasis, or select from them to tailor instruction to individual student needs.

Measurement. A section of lessons that focuses on measurement of achievement in basic skill and production power is set at the end of Level 1, and another is set at the end of Level 2. These sections provide ample opportunities to evaluate intensively and appropriately each student's growth.

Controlled copy. Basic skillbuilding and measurement paragraph copy is triple-controlled to insure uniformity of difficulty. Three factors—syllable intensity, average word length, and percentage of high-frequency words—are simultaneously controlled in each paragraph to assure valid and reliable measures of skill growth. Special keyboarding drills are controlled in other ways to assure "loading" of the factors to be emphasized.

Input skills. To provide realism and promote transfer of learning, emphasis is placed on preparing final copy from script and rough-draft source documents.

Directions/illustrations. Complete directions and visual models are used liberally in presenting new learning. The directions-left/copy-right format helps students distinguish operational directions form copy to be typed.

Communication skills. Periodic instruction and review to help students develop basic written communication skills are included in the lessons. This new edition includes the most up-to-date business terminology and gives special attention to new procedures and equipment of electronic offices.

ACKNOWLEDGMENTS

The authors gratefully acknowledge the helpful contributions made by instructors who used prior editions of the text, especially those who responded to the national user survey made just prior to the preparation of this new edition. Special recognition is given, also, to Dr. D. D. Lessenberry, the original author of *College Typewriting*, who for over fifty years set the pattern and pace of typewriting instruction in the United States.

Leaders, a series of alternating
periods and spaces, indicate a re–
lationship between items in col–
umns.

Leaders

Space once after the first item in
the first column and then alternate
a period and a space to a point 2
or 3 spaces short of the next col–
umn. Remember whether you type
the periods on odd or even
line–of–writing scale numbers;
align all other rows by starting
them in the same way.

It has been decided that each Monday
night will be Staff Night. Format and
keyboard a final copy of the program to be
used.

THE COLONY INN

Staff Night in the Elmore Room

Program

Humoresque . . . . Brian Koski, pianist

The Bells of St. Andrews . . . . . Rita Twomey, soprano

Madrid Scenes . . . . Lisa Alvarez, guitarist

The Tramp Escapes . . . . Dale Girt, mime

The Cremation of Dan McGrew . . . . Tom Walker, reader

Do You Dig Clams? . . . . The Old Haven Players

        Little Nell . . . . Judy Askew
        Mother Darling . . . . Tom Walker
        Daniel Dashing . . . . Brian Koski
        Myron Meany . . . . Marty O'Bannion

Babbalou . . . . Rita Twomey, soprano

Master of Ceremonies: Jeff Cleveland

Coffee Courtesy of Chef William

Note: Student should provide
some kind of original
art work.

Tonight's Performers

Lisa Alvarez--senior--business administration--Grambling
Judy Askew--senior--economics--University of Mississippi
Jeff Cleveland--junior--history--Potomac State College
Dale Girt--junior--pre-law--Juniata College
Brian Koski--junior--business education--Ball State University
Marty O'Bannion--sophomore--pre-med--Northern Iowa University
Rita Twomey--junior--music--Duke University
Tom Walker--junior--music--Duke University

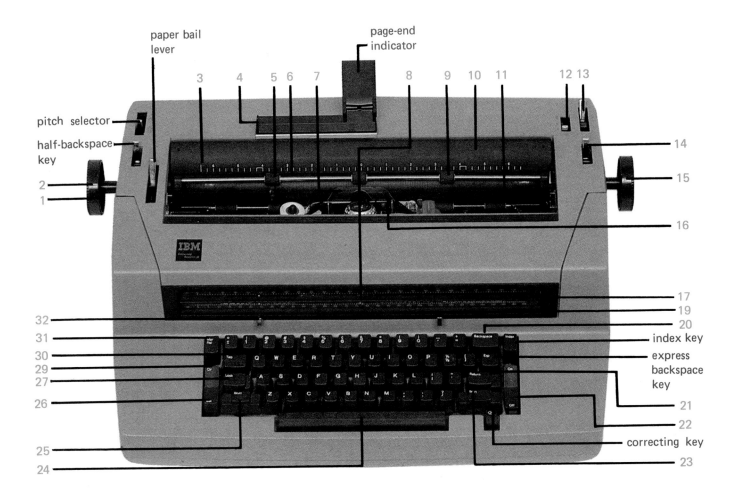

The diagram above shows the parts of an electric typewriter. Since typewriters have similar parts, you should be able to locate the parts of your machine from this diagram. However, if you have the instructional booklet that comes with your machine, use it to identify exact locations of these parts.

If you are learning on a non-electric (manual) typewriter, refer to page 3 for those machine parts and keys that differ in location from an electric machine.

Illustrated on page 2 is an array of data/word processing machines to which your keyboarding skills will transfer.

1 Left platen knob: used to activate variable line spacer

2 Variable line spacer: used to change writing line setting permanently

3 Paper guide scale: used to set paper edge guide at desired position

4 Paper edge guide: used to position paper for insertion

5/9 Paper bail rolls: used to hold paper against platen

6 Paper bail: used to hold paper against platen

7 Card/envelope holder: used to hold cards, labels, and envelopes against platen

8 Printing point indicator: used to position element carrier at desired point

9 (See 5)

10 Paper table: supports paper when it is in typewriter

11 Platen (cylinder): provides a hard surface against which type element strikes

12 Line–space selector: sets typewriter to advance the paper (using carrier return key) 1, 2, or (on some machines) 3 lines for single, double, or triple spacing

13 Paper release lever: used to allow paper to be removed or aligned

14 Automatic line finder: used to change line spacing temporarily, then refind the line

15 Right platen knob: used to turn platen as paper is being inserted

16 Aligning scale: used to align copy that has been reinserted

17 Line–of–writing (margin) scale: used when setting margins, tab stops, and in horizontal centering

18 Ribbon carrier: positions and controls ribbon at printing point (not shown—under the cover)

19 Right margin set: used to set right margin stop

20 Backspace key: used to move printing point to left one space at a time

21 Carrier return key: used to return element carrier to left margin and to advance paper up

22 ON/OFF control: used to turn electric typewriters on or off

23 Right shift key: used to type capitals of letter keys controlled by left hand

24 Space bar: used to move printing point to right one space at a time

25 Left shift key: used to type capitals of letter keys controlled by right hand

26 Tab set: used to set tab stops

27 Shift lock: used to lock shift mechanism so that all letters are capitalized

28 Ribbon control: used to select ribbon typing position (not shown—under cover)

29 Tab clear: used to clear tab stops

30 Tabulator: used to move element carrier to tab stops

31 Margin release key: used to move element carrier beyond margin stops

32 Left margin set: used to set left margin stop

On most electric and electronic machines, certain parts may be used for automatic repeat, such as:

    20—backspace key
    21—carrier return key
    24—space bar

Format/keyboard a personal letter

Job 4

1 Monarch sheet
1 Monarch envelope
(LM p. 94) or plain paper cut to size

You find that you have 20 minutes left of your lunch hour; you decide to write a letter to your instructor who gave you assistance as you searched for summer employment.

Format/keyboard an interoffice memorandum

Although you have not keyboarded an inter-office memo, you have learned the subskills necessary for this format. Use the interoffice memo form provided (LM p. 96).

Job 5

full sheet; 1″ side margins; TS after last line of heading; SS paragraphs; DS between paragraphs; set left margin 2 spaces to the right of the colon in the heading

To: **Summer Staff**

From: **Tom McGriff**

Date: **June 15, 19--**

Subject: **Staff Evening**

(¶ 1) Several members of the summer staff have approached me with the suggestion that they be permitted to provide an evening of entertainment for our guests. Such an event has been staged at several other resort areas near here, and it was done here two years ago with success. I am enthusiastic about the idea if you are.

(¶ 2) I know that some of you have talents and hobbies that might provide entertainment for our guests. For example, do you know that Lisa Alvarez plays classical guitar and sings? Brian Koski plays the piano. Judy Askew and Marty O'Bannion said they would like to do a skit--which, of course, they would write, direct, produce, and stage. While this is hardly a sufficient cast for a whole evening's entertainment, it is a solid beginning.

(¶ 3) Our guests come and go, as you know. However, some of them do not leave The Inn for long periods of time, preferring just to enjoy the surroundings. If we do decide to have a Staff Evening, we can use the Elmore Room for an hour after dinner one evening a week. There is a piano there, good lighting, and hardwood floors.

(¶ 4) What do you say?

xx

Format/keyboard
an unbound report

Job 3
2 full sheets

Reference pages
Prepare an unbound
report: pp. 98, 103

Mr. McGriff asks you to prepare a finished copy of this bulletin in unbound report format. It will be placed in every suite before new guests check in.

Welcome to The Colony Inn → center
TS

Many of our guests come to The Inn for the rest its relaxing comfortable rooms provide; for its friendly, unrushed atmosphere; and for its beautiful walkways and gardens. The management and staff try to maintain an ambiance wherein the most serious decision a guest ever has to make is what to order for breakfast. Some guests, however wish to explore the New Haven area; and we have made arrangements for them to choose from a variety of enjoyable acitivities, such as the following: DS

Golfing. Be our guest at one of three private New Haven Golf Clubs that welcome our guests to their great courses. There are also a number of good public courses nearby. Tee off times should be reserved, and the staff will be happy to make the arrangements.

Sailing. The Inn has made an arrangement with Cap'n Sam's Yacht Club at Morgan Point for the use of sailboats there, weather permitting. Lessons are available for neophytes. Ask Wendy in the our office for information.

Trip to New London and Mystic Harbor. This tow-day trip, available to a limited number of guests, will be long remembered. Our van, with a guide aboard, leaves each Wednesday morning and returns Thursday evening. Overnight reservations are make for trup members. Please give the staff 24 hours notice. advance

Yale Campus and Peabody Museum. Both are within easy reach from The Inn and can be seen in an afternoon. Ask us for maps and maps.

Antique Shops. Connecticut has hundreds of antique shops, and some of the very best are right here in the New Haven area. Whether you are a collector or a looker, we can provide you wish a map showing locations, distances, and typse of shops.

Theater. What is more fun than open-air summer theater? The Summer Stock Theater Company at Indian Neck fits the bill perfectly with a new light comedy every week. Have an early dinner at the Inn, then go to the theater--only 45 minutes away. If you want us to profide transportation our van makes the trip every tuesday evening.

Swimming. Our van goes to Light house Point on Mondays and to Momaguin Beach on Fridays. If you give Chef William a day's notice, he'll pack a picnic lunch for you; or you can dine on hot dogs and soda on you own. your

Judges Cove. A trip to West Rock Park and Judges Cave is a tirp of special interest to history buffs. Ask Brian in our office to tell you the whole sotry--a fascinating one--then go see where til all happened.

Whatever you do, enjoy, enjoy! And let us help you do it.

Yale University, the third oldest institution of higher learning in the United States, and the Peabody Museum are only a short distance from The Inn and can be seen in an afternoon.

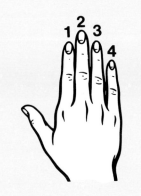

Finger Identification

If you are using a nonelectric (manual) typewriter to learn to keyboard, several of the reaches shown on subsequent pages may be different because of differences in location of the machine part on manual and electric machines. Refer to this page for help in locating these reaches.

Apostrophe

The ' (apostrophe) is the shift of 8. Shift with the left little (fourth) finger; then reach for ' with the right second finger.

```
k'k k'k k'k it's
```

Asterisk

The * (asterisk) is the shift of – (hyphen). Depress left shift; then strike * with the right fourth (;) finger.

```
;–; ;*; ;*; ;*;
*See page 190.
```

Backspacer

Reach to the backspace key with the appropriate little (fourth) finger. Depress the key firmly for each backspace desired.

Carriage return

Move the left hand, fingers bracing one another, to the carriage return lever.

Move the lever inward to take up the slack; then return the carriage with a quick inward flick-of-the-hand motion.

Drop the hand quickly to typing position without letting it follow the carriage across the page.

Carriage release

If your typewriter has a movable carriage, depress the right carriage release to move it freely. When you have finished keyboarding for the day, leave the carriage approximately centered.

Exclamation mark

On most manual typewriters (and some electrics), there is no exclamation mark key. To *make* an exclamation mark, strike ' (apostrophe); then backspace and strike . (period).

```
Oh!   I just won!
```

Quotation marks

The " (quotation mark) is the shift of 2. Shift with the right little (fourth) finger; then reach for " with the left third finger.

```
s"s s"s s"s "so"
```

Tabulator bar

Depress and hold down the tabulator bar with the right first finger until the carriage has stopped.

Tabulator key

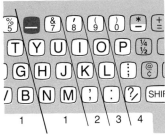

Depress and hold down the tabulator key with the nearest little (fourth) finger until the carriage has stopped.

Underline

The __ (underline) is the shift of 6. Shift with the left little (fourth) finger; then reach for __ with the right first finger.

```
j j j To Yes
```

Format/keyboard a menu

Job 2

full sheet; 1½" top margin; make remaining format decisions

Menu

Chef William asks you to format and keyboard the menu for Friday. He has written it for you and has made some marginal notations to help with the format. He asks you to center all items in the appropriate parts of the page.

THE COLONY INN
Breakfast Menu
Friday Morning, July 7, 19--
(leave 3 blank line spaces)

Fruit Juices

Orange
Pineapple
Grapefruit
Tomato *(leave 3 blank line spaces)*

Fresh Fruit

Minted Orange Slices
Sliced Strawberries
Bay Blueberries
Melon Wedges

From the Range

Fried Eggs
Coddled Eggs
Scrambled Eggs
Eggs Benedict

From the Grill

Sausage Links
Cornmeal Mush
Hashed Browns
Scrapple
Country Bacon

From the Griddle

Griddle Cakes
Waffles
French Toast

Cereal With Milk

Assorted Cold Cereals
Oatmeal with Dates
New Haven Porridge

From the Oven

Toast
Bran Muffins
Croissants
Pecan Coffeecake

Beverages

Coffee
Tea
Cocoa

① Adjust paper guide

Line up paper edge guide (4) with zero on the line–of–writing scale (17).

② Insert typing paper

Take a sheet of paper in your left hand and follow the directions and illustrations at the right and below.

1 Pull paper bail (6) forward (or up on some machines).

2 Place paper against paper edge guide (4), behind the platen (11).

3 Turn paper into machine, using right platen knob (15) or index key.

4 Stop when paper is about 1½ inches above aligning scale (16).

5 If paper is not straight, pull paper release lever (13) forward.

6 Straighten paper, then push paper release lever back.

7 Push paper bail back so that it holds paper against platen.

8 Slide paper bail rolls (5/9) into position, dividing paper into thirds.

9 Properly inserted paper.

③ Set line-space selector

Many machines offer 3 choices for line spacing—1, 1½, and 2 indi–cated by bars or numbers on the line–space selector (12).

Set the line–space selector on (—) or 1 to single–space (SS) or on (=) or on 2 to double–space (DS) as directed for lines in Level 1.

1 Lines 1 and 2 are single-spaced (SS).
2 A double space (DS) separates Lines 2 and 4.
3   1 blank line space
4 A triple space (TS) separates Lines 4 and 7.
5
6   2 blank line spaces
7 Set the selector on "1" for single spacing.

④ Determine type size

Most machines are equipped with pica (10 spaces to a horizontal inch) or elite (12 spaces to a hori–zontal inch) type size.

Marked intervals on the line–of–writing scale (17) match the spacing of letters on the machine. This scale reads from 0 to 110 or more for machines with elite type, from 0 to 90 or more for machines with pica type.

This is elite (12-pitch) type, 12 spaces to an inch.

This is pica (10-pitch) type, 10 spaces to an inch.

inches					
1	2	3	4	5	
centimeters					
1 2	3 4	5 6	7 8	9 10	11 12 13 14 15

Format/keyboard a tabulated report

Congratulations! You have been hired as a keyboard operator at The Colony Inn.
Your work assignments will require you to prepare copy, using keyboarding skills and subskills which you have learned. Many of these assignments will require you to synthesize your knowledge of keyboarding to produce attractive formats for the jobs which you will be assigned.

Job 1

full sheet; 1" top and side margins; decide intercolumn spacing

1 From the journal entry at the right, format/keyboard a 5–column tabulated report.

2 Center secondary headings over the columns.

3 Use an X to indicate point of arrival (Airport or Inn).

Reference pages

Formatting tables: pp. 116, 118

Guest Arrival List

July 3, 19--

Name and Address	Time of Arrival	Airport	Inn	Suite Reservation
Mr. and Mrs. Samuel Craven 235 Bertch Avenue Waterloo, IA 50702-4121	9 a.m.	X		27 E
Capt. E. P. Able 4590 Victoria Drive Ft. Wayne, IN 46815-2111	2 p.m.		X	14 W
Dr. and Mrs. Roy Ellstein 9110 Hillsboro Court Louisville, KY 40207-3817	10 a.m.		X	19 W
Ms. Eleanor Richards 1000 Reed Street Boston, MA 02118-3691	5 p.m.		X	15 E
Mr. and Mrs. Charles Curl 1060 Angeleno Avenue, E. Burbank, CA 91501-8961	9 a.m.		X	11 E
Mr. Glenn J. Tisschler P.O. Box 24 Boise, ID 83702-0124	3 p.m.		X	10 E
Mr. and Mrs. Larry Dearhearst 76 Delaware Avenue Utica, NY 13502-7029	2 p.m.	X		21 E
Mr. and Mrs. John E. Sheard 805 Courtland Avenue Akron, OH 44320-7316	9 a.m.		X	15 W
Miss Kristen Sheard 2277 Darnell Drive Akron, OH 44319-2173	9 a.m.		X	16 W
Mr. and Mrs. David Birsky Danny Birsky Ronny Birsky 45088 Humboldt Street Rochester, NY 14610-2387	1 p.m.		X	17 W 18 W

⑤ Plan margin settings

When 8½– by 11–inch paper is inserted into the typewriter (8½–inch end first) with left edge at 0 on the line–of–writing scale (17), center point is 51 (elite) or 42½ (pica). Use 42 for pica center.

To center typed lines, set left and right margin stops the same number of spaces left and right from center point. Diagrams at the right show margin settings for 50–, 60–, and 70–space lines. When you begin to use the warning bell, 5 or 6 spaces may be added to the right margin.

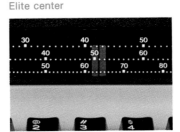

Elite center

Pica center

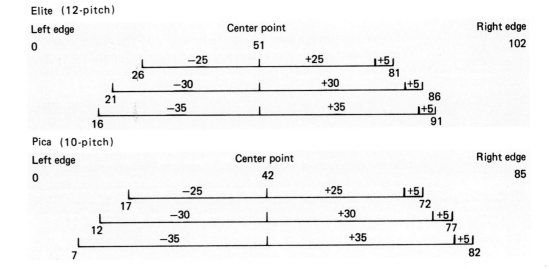

Elite (12-pitch)

Left edge	Center point	Right edge
0	51	102

−25 +25 +5
26   81
−30 +30 +5
21   86
−35 +35 +5
16   91

Pica (10-pitch)

Left edge	Center point	Right edge
0	42	85

−25 +25 +5
17   72
−30 +30 +5
12   77
−35 +35 +5
7   82

⑥ Set margin stops

Type A
Push-button set

Adler, Olympia, Remington, Royal 700/870 manuals, Smith-Corona

1 Press down on the left margin set button.

2 Slide it to desired position on the line–of–writing (margin) scale.

3 Release the margin set button.

4 Using the right margin set button, set the right margin stop in the same way.

Type B
Push-lever set

Single element typewriters, such as Adler, Olivetti, Remington Rand, Royal, Selectric

1 Push in on the left margin set lever.

2 Slide it to desired position on the line–of–writing (margin) scale.

3 Release the margin set lever.

4 Using the right margin set lever, set the right margin stop in the same way.

Type C
Key set

IBM typebar, Olivetti electric

1 Move carriage to the left margin stop by depressing the return key.

2 Depress and hold down the margin set (IBM reset) key as you move carriage to desired left margin stop position.

3 Release the margin set (IBM reset) key.

4 Move carriage to the right margin stop.

5 Depress and hold down the margin set (IBM reset) key as you move carriage to desired right margin stop position.

6 Release the margin set (IBM reset) key.

Type D
Electronic set

To set margins on some electronic machines, such as Xerox and Silver–Reed, space to the desired margin position and strike the appropriate (left or right) margin key.

On other machines, such as IBM, space to the desired margin position and strike the CODE key and the appropriate (left or right) margin key *at the same time*.

> General information for setting margin stops is given here. If you have the manufacturer's booklet for your typewriter, however, use it; the procedure for your particular model may be slightly different.

**Format/keyboard a
personal data sheet**
full sheet; 1″ top and side
margins

Introducing

ADRIAN MAGELLAN
145 Bertram Street
Alexandria, Virginia   22306-3075

Present Career Objective

Desire to participate in and help manage the activities of a modern business office, especially as they involve areas of communications and information processing.

Personal Qualifications

Cheerful, dependable, cooperative; like to work with people
Eager to acquire a variety of early work experiences in an office
Very interested in processing business information
Excellent health; enjoy outdoors, water sports, reading, and gourmet cooking

Experience

1985 (summer)	Software Service Company, 200 Ashton Street, Alexandria, VA 22309-4121
1984 (summer)	Bedore Equipment Rental, 1650 Braddock Road, Alexandria, VA 22302-5381
1983 (summer)	Pet Print and Copy Spot, 4500 Braddock Road, Alexandria, VA 22304-6409

Education

Junior, Office Management and Information Processing, Alexandria College, Alexandria, VA (winner for two years of the Elizabeth Eskildsen Scholarship)
Graduate, North High School, Alexandria, VA (the marching band; president, senior class; secretary, National Honor Society)

References

Mr. George Treader
Software Service Company
200 Ashton Street
Alexandria, VA   22309-4121

Mr. Ed Bedore
Bedore Equipment Rental
1650 Braddock Road
Alexandria, VA   22302-5381

Ms. Lois Joiner
Pet Print and Copy Spot
4500 Braddock Road
Alexandria, VA   22304-6409

Miss Ellen Danzells
Alexandria College
7800 Bellefonte Avenue
Alexandria, VA   22307-1961

LEVEL ONE

Learning to keyboard and to format personal documents

Your decision to learn to keyboard is a wise one. Just as the 1960's were the decade of the computer and data processing, the 1980's are the decade of microcomputers, text editors, and word or information processing. In business, industry, and the professions, the use of electronic input/output devices is growing at lightning speed. Whether you learn to keyboard on a typewriter or a microcomputer, your keyboarding skill will transfer directly to other data/word processing machines because all use the same standard arrangement of the letter and number keys. In addition, some machines have a 10-key numeric pad arrangement which is the same as that on electronic calculators.

Learning to keyboard is only the first step, however. To be able to *use* your skill productively, you must also learn the features of frequently prepared documents (such as letters, reports, and tables) and develop skill in arranging and typing them in their conventional formats.

The purpose of Level 1 (Lessons 1-37), therefore, is to help you develop keyboarding efficiency and to begin teaching you how to format and type documents for personal use. The textbook, like your keyboarding instrument, is only a partner in learning. For your textbook and your machine to help you effectively to learn, you as the third partner must *intend* to learn and must practice intensively to reach your goals.

Format/keyboard a letter of application

1 full sheet; make other format decisions

145 Bertram Street
Alexandria, VA   22306-3075
May 2, 19--

Mr. T. J. McGriff
Manager, The Colony Inn
5828 Artizan Street
New Haven, CT   06511-2578

Dear Mr. McGriff

One of my college instructors, Miss Ellen Danzells, suggests that I write to you about the possibility of summer employment in the office at The Colony Inn. Miss Danzells was a guest at The Colony Inn last summer and enjoyed meeting the college students who were working there.

My practical experience includes working in local business offices during the past three summers, and these companies have agreed to write letters of recommendation for me. This year I should like to spend the summer recess working at a resort away from home, and The Colony Inn seems to be just the kind of place I have in mind.

After three years of academic study at Alexandria College, my grades are well above average in my major area of study, Office Management and Information Processing. Upon your request, I shall be happy to have a copy of my college transcript sent to you.

I enjoy office work and am especially interested in learning how management principles are applied in different settings. I enjoy spending a quiet time with a good book, but I am also an avid outdoors person--hiking, bird watching, swimming, and boating are special pleasures.

A personal data sheet is enclosed. If you believe that I might make a contribution at The Colony Inn this summer, Mr. McGriff, I should be pleased to hear from you.

Sincerely yours

Adrian Magellan

Making application for employment

Learning goals

1 To master alphabetic reaches.

2 To operate keyboard without looking at your fingers or the keys—"by touch."

3 To type easy paragraph copy.

4 To type or keyboard at a rate of 14 or more gross words a minute (*gwam*).

Machine adjustments

1 Set paper guide at 0.

2 Set ribbon control to type on upper half of ribbon.

3 Set left margin stop for a 50–space line (center − 25); set right margin stop at end of line–of–writing scale.

4 Set line–space selector for single spacing (SS).

Prepare for Lesson 1

1 Acquire a supply of 8½″ by 11″ typing paper of good quality.

2 If your chair is adjustable, raise or lower it to a height that is comfortable for you.

3 If your desk is adjustable, raise or lower it until your forearms parallel the slant of the keyboard when your fingers are placed over asdf jkl;.

4 Follow carefully all directions, both oral and written. Therein lies much of the secret for gaining keyboarding skill.

1a
Get ready to keyboard

1 Clear work area and chair of unneeded books and clothing.

2 Place textbook at right of machine, the top elevated for easy reading; stack paper supply at left of machine.

3 Refer briefly to page 1 of this book where typewriter parts are named, illustrated, and described. In these early lessons, frequent reference is made to these parts; you will need to refer to the illustrated typewriter on page 1 at those times.

4 Locate on page 5 the type of margin sets that match those on your machine. Set the left margin stop for a 50–space line (center − 25); move the right stop to the extreme right end of the line–of–writing scale.

5 Study pages 4 and 5 carefully. If necessary, adjust the paper edge guide (at 0) on your machine. Insert paper as illustrated.

6 Set line–space selector for single spacing (SS) as directed on page 4.

Review/improve keystroking technique

60-space line; DS

1st fingers	1	At just about three in the afternoon, the young divers left.
2d fingers	2	Dickie, not Cedric, decided to pack some ice for picnicking.
3d/4th fingers	3	She quizzed, "Will we play jazz?" She owns a sax; we don't.
1st (bottom) row	4	Xavier, can Mrs. Cozman back a van, a black van, as you can?
2d (home) row	5	Jake had a sale last fall; Dad gladly sold half the alfalfa.
3d row	6	Your porter put two pots of purple iris with the ripe fruit.
4th row	7	On May 19, I saw 423 of the 680 stamps; I bought 57 of them.
double letters	8	Anna's committee meets weekly; she calls no summer meetings.
one hand	9	In my opinion, a seafarer union serves only a few in Joplin.
balanced hand	10	Claudian may wish to make the panels for the ancient chapel.
combination	11	He agreed to get the paper from the auditor for Kim to read.
adjacent reaches	12	Buy the silk astors and poinsettias the last part of autumn.
direct reaches	13	Marv, with the grace and ease of a puma, jumped into my car.
left shift	14	Oki Park and Kate Heift left for Las Morales in May or June.
right shift	15	We met Chi, Rita, and Vera in April at the Red City Regatta.
long words	16	Theatrical advertisements announce lavish stage attractions.

| 1 | 2 | 3 | 4 | 5 | 6 | 7 | 8 | 9 | 10 | 11 | 12 |

Improve response patterns

60-space line; DS

Take 1' writings, using Line 1 as a goal sentence. Try to reach the same goal with Lines 2, 3, and 4.

words

1	Did she blend rock with the clay to make the visitor a bowl?	12
2	The men may fuel the flame with a box of oak, fir, and coal.	12
3	it is also his civic duty to fihgt odor problems in teh air.	12
4	In the 1958 census forms, I found 640 names from 273 cities.	12

1b
Take keyboarding position

1 Sit back in chair, body erect.

2 Place both feet on floor to maintain proper balance.

3 Let your hands hang relaxed at your sides. Your fingers will relax in curved position.

4 From this position, raise the left hand and lightly place the fingertips of your left hand on **a s d f** (home keys). Study the location of these keys.

5 Similarly, lightly place the fingertips of your right hand on **j k l ;** (home keys). Study the location of these keys.

6 Your fingers should be curved and upright; wrists should be low, but they should not touch the frame of the machine.

Left Fingers 4 3 2 1 1 2 3 4 Right Fingers

1 Keep fingers curved and upright, wrists low.

2 Keep forearms parallel to slant of keyboard.

3 Keep eyes on copy.

4 Sit back in chair, body erect.

5 Place textbook at right of machine, top raised for easy reading.

6 Keep table free of unneeded books.

7 Keep feet on floor for balance.

1c
Strike home keys, space bar, and return

1 Strike each key with a quick, sharp finger stroke; snap the fingertip toward the palm as the stroke is made.

Type (keyboard):

ffjjffjjfj

2 Strike the space bar with a down-and-in motion of the right thumb.

Type (on same line):

dd kk dd kk dk
space once

3 Keep the fingers well-curved. Concentrate on proper finger action as you keyboard.

Type (on same line):

ss ll ss ll aa ; ;
space once

4 Reach with the little finger of the right hand to the return key and tap it. Then quickly return the little finger to its home position. *Refer to page 3 if your machine is nonelectric.*

Skill measurement: straight copy

3' or 5' writings;
70-space line; DS

Difficulty index

all letters used | A | 1.5 si | 5.7 awl | 80% hfw

| | gwam 3' | 5' |

The ability to express ideas with written and spoken language is   4 | 3 | 44
one of the marks of a civilized nation, states a famed historian. He   9 | 5 | 47
does not state just how sophisticated the use of the language should   14 | 8 | 50
be in order to qualify a nation as civilized, just that enough language   19 | 11 | 53
use be available to provide for some written history of the group.   23 | 14 | 55

We have no question about the significance of language--our ability   27 | 16 | 58
to communicate--for we can't imagine a world in which no one could com-   32 | 19 | 61
municate with anyone else. That's not our problem. Rather, our problem   37 | 22 | 64
lies in the quality of our communication, the extent to which the thoughts   42 | 25 | 67
and images we seek to project are recognized as we want them to be.   47 | 28 | 69

As language is one hallmark of a great civilization, so it is also   51 | 31 | 72
the hallmark of an educated person. Recognizing that fact, most profes-   56 | 33 | 75
sional people exert a direct effort--a lifetime of study really--to   60 | 36 | 78
acquire strong language skills. We are judged by our words; and when   65 | 39 | 80
we can say things well, people believe we can also do things well.   69 | 42 | 83

gwam 3' | 1 | 2 | 3 | 4 | 5 |
5' | 1 | 2 | 3 |

Skill measurement: statistical copy

3' or 5' writings;
70-space line; DS

Difficulty index

all letters/figures used | A | 1.5 si | 5.7 awl | 80% hfw

| | gwam 3' | 5' |

A well-recognized source tells us that about 4 out of 5 American   4 | 2 | 27
families own some sort of life insurance contract. Just about 50 per-   8 | 5 | 30
cent of all life contracts are 1 of the 3 basic kinds of life insur-   13 | 8 | 33
ance sold: (1) straight life, (2) endowment, or (3) term. Over 80   16 | 10 | 35
percent of these contracts are acquired from 1 of 1,500 or so insurance   20 | 12 | 37
firms as a safeguard against loss; but some buyers also invest with their   25 | 15 | 40
life insurance, and about $9.7 billion is held in private life insurance   30 | 18 | 43
reserves. Almost 1 out of 3 life insurance contracts is acquired by a   34 | 21 | 46
buyer between 26 and 43 years of age, and over 60 percent of them pay   38 | 23 | 48
a premium in excess of $260 a year for their coverage.   42 | 25 | 50

gwam 3' | 1 | 2 | 3 | 4 | 5 |
5' | 1 | 2 | 3 |

1d
Learn the home row

1 Strike the return key twice more to leave extra space between the line you have just typed and the lines you will now type.

2 Practice once each line shown at the right. Strike the return key once to single–space (SS) between the two lines of a pair.

3 Strike the return key twice to double–space (DS) between pairs of lines.

4 Strike the return key 3 times to triple–space (TS) after completing Line 6.

5 Repeat the drill.

> **Technique hint:**
> Keep fingers well curved; keep wrists low, but do not allow them to touch the typewriter.

Fingers curved

Fingers upright

```
1  fj fj fj dk dk dk sl sl sl a; a; a; fj dk sl a; a;
2  jf kd ls ;a al ak aj sl sk sj dl dk dj fj fk fl f;
                                        Return twice to double–space (DS)
3  as as ask ask sad sad jak jak fad fad lad lad lass
4  ad ad ads ads jak jak dad dad all all add add fall
                                                              DS
5  a lad; a lass; a jak; all ads; all fall; ask a lad
6  ask dad; all ads; a jak ad; a sad lad; a jak falls
                                        Return 3 times to triple–space (TS)
```

1e
Learn new keyreach: E

1 Find new key on illustrated keyboard; then find it on your keyboard.

2 Study carefully the "Reach technique for **e**."

3 Watch your finger make the *reach* to **e** and back to **d** a few times *without striking the keys.* Keep your fingers curved.

4 Practice the lines once as shown. Keep your eyes on the copy as you keyboard; look only when you "feel lost."

5 If time permits, repeat the drill.

Reach technique for e

Reach *up* with *left second* finger.

Left Fingers   4 3 2   1   1   2 3 4   Right Fingers

all reaches learned

```
1  e ed ed led led lea lea ale ale elk elf eke els ed
2  ed fed fed fled fled kale kale self self lake lake
                                        Return twice to double–space (DS)
3  e elk ekes leek leak sale dale kale lake fake self
4  sell fell jell sale sake jade sled seek leal deal;
                                                              DS
5  a sled sale; a fake jade; see a lake; a kale leaf;
6  sell a safe; a leaf fell; see a leaf; sell a desk;
```

1f
End the lesson
(standard procedure for all lessons)

1 Raise the paper bail (6) or pull it toward you. Pull the paper release lever (13) toward you.

2 Remove paper with your left hand. Push paper release lever back to its normal position.

3 Turn off the power on an electric or electronic machine. See page 3 if you have a movable carriage typewriter.

You are interested in obtaining a job for the summer; you ask your instructor for ideas. She says she knows of a resort in Connecticut where she has been a guest and where a former student has worked. She will make inquiries for you. In the meantime, she suggests that you try to improve your keyboarding skill with drill materials she provides.

Reach for new goals

60-space line; DS

Step 1: Take a 1' writing on the goal sentence below; determine *gwam*.

Step 2: From the columns at the right, choose a goal that will cause you to aim for 2–4 *gwam* more than your rate in Step 1. Note the sentence that accompanies that goal.

Step 3: Take two 1' writings on the chosen sentences. Try to complete the sentence the number of times indicated to reach that goal.

Step 4: If you reach your goal on both 1' writings, choose another sentence which will cause you to increase your rate another 2–4 *gwam*. Take two more 1' writings. If you do not achieve a rate of 2–4 *gwam* higher than your Step 1 rate, try again or choose another sentence.

Step 5: Repeat Step 4 until you decide to end the drill. Then go to Step 6.

Step 6: Repeat a 1' writing on the goal sentence; determine *gwam*.

Straight copy

		Number of times to type line in 1' to reach goal		
		4	5	6
1	I did fix the hem of the gown.	gwam 24	30	36
2	He paid for the rug, so he owns it.	28	35	42
3	It is a blend of turkey, lamb, and fish.	32	40	48
4	They got rid of six or eight keys to the bus.	36	45	54
5	Did they dismantle the worn panel of their sleigh?	40	50	60

| 1 | 2 | 3 | 4 | 5 | 6 | 7 | 8 | 9 | 10 |

Goal sentence

They may go to a town social when they visit the big island.

| 1 | 2 | 3 | 4 | 5 | 6 | 7 | 8 | 9 | 10 | 11 | 12 |

Statistical copy

		Number of times to type line in 1' to reach goal		
		4	5	6
1	He kept 20, or half of the 40.	gwam 24	30	36
2	The 19 men dug the 56 rocks for us.	28	35	42
3	Hang 37 maps and 19 keys from the shelf.	32	40	48
4	They did visit 10 towns on 16 of the islands.	36	45	54
5	The 19 dials on the 20 panels make the robot work.	40	50	60

| 1 | 2 | 3 | 4 | 5 | 6 | 7 | 8 | 9 | 10 |

Goal sentence

I kept 207 fowl: 65 turkeys, 93 hens, 41 ducks, and 8 owls.

| 1 | 2 | 3 | 4 | 5 | 6 | 7 | 8 | 9 | 10 | 11 | 12 |

2a
Prepare to keyboard
Reread procedures described in 1b, 1c, and 1d, pages 8 and 9.

2b
Preparatory practice
each line twice SS (slowly, then faster); DS between 2-line groups

home row 1 `ff jj ff jj dd kk dd kk ss ll ss ll aa ;; aa ;; a;`

e 2 `e el els led ale lea eke lee elf elk eel lake kale`

all reaches learned 3 `as all ask; a jak ad; ask a lad; a fall fad; a fee`
TS

2c
Learn new keyreaches: T and O
Use the standard procedure at the right to learn each new keyreach in this lesson and in lessons that follow.

Standard procedure for learning new keyreaches

1 Find new key on illustrated keyboard; then find it on your keyboard.

2 Study carefully the reach technique illustrated for the key.

3 Watch your finger make the reach to the new key a few times. Keep other fingers curved on home keys. Straighten the finger slightly for an upward reach; curve it a bit more for a downward reach.

4 Practice twice SS the two lines in which the new reach is emphasized. Keep your eyes on the book copy as you keyboard.

5 DS; then learn and practice the next new keyreach according to Steps 1-4.

6 Finally, DS; then practice Lines 5-8 once as shown. If time permits, repeat them. Work for continuity. Avoid pauses.

Reach technique for t

Reach *up* with *left first* finger.

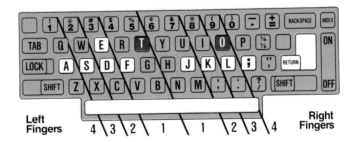

Left Fingers 4 3 2 1 1 2 3 4 Right Fingers

Reach technique for o

Reach *up* with *right third* finger.

t 1 `t tf tf aft aft tall tall talk talk tale tale task`
2 `tf at at aft jet let take tell felt flat slat salt`
DS

o 3 `o ol ol sol sol sold sold of of off off fold folds`
4 `ol old sold sole dole do doe does lo loll sol solo`

t/o 5 `to tot tote told dolt toe toes load toad foal soak`
6 `to too toot lot slot do dot oft loft soft jot jolt`

all letters learned 7 `to do | to do a lot | take a jet | to let a | to do a task`
8 `so to | so to do | to take a | to tell a joke | left off a`
TS

Problem 1

two-column table

half sheet (enter long side first)

Center and type SS the table in vertical and horizontal center; use a 10–space intercolumn.

LEADING AMERICAN MAGAZINES

In 1981

Magazine	Circulation
Reader's Digest	17,926,542
TV Guide	17,670,543
National Geographic Magazine	10,861,186
Better Homes & Gardens	8,059,717
Family Circle	7,427,979
Modern Maturity	7,309,035
Woman's Day	7,004,367
McCall's	6,266,090
Ladies' Home Journal	5,527,071
Good Housekeeping	5,425,790

5
7
15
20
24
32
39
44
49
53
59
65
71

Problem 2

three-column table

full sheet

Center and type DS the table in reading position; decide inter–column spacing.

EARLY AMERICAN COLLEGES

With Dates of Establishment

College	State	Year
Brown	Rhode Island	1764
Columbia	New York	1754
Harvard	Massachusetts	1636
Moravian	Pennsylvania	1742
Pennsylvania	Pennsylvania	1740
Princeton	New Jersey	1746
Rutgers	New Jersey	1766
William and Mary	Virginia	1693
Yale	Connecticut	1701

5
10
15
20
25
30
36
42
47
52
58
62

Problem 3

outline

full sheet

3" top margin; 40–space line; add designation numerals and letters for each order; use correct capitalization and spacing

PLANTING LAWN GRASS

clear the area
    turn over and break up the soil
        hand implements
        power implements
    remove old roots and stems
    spread nutrients over area
prepare the seedbed
    level high and low places
        drag
        light roller
    rake to loosen lumps and clods
plant
    sow seeds
    add protective cover
        straw
        burlap
    wet thoroughly to set seed

4
8
15
19
23
29
36
40
46
48
52
59
61
64
69
71
73
79

2d
Practice keystroking technique

each line twice SS; DS between 2-line groups

Technique hints:

1 Concentrate on copy as you keyboard; work slowly, but continuously.

2 Keep your eyes on the book copy as you keyboard; look up only if absolutely necessary.

home row **1** as ask asks ad ads add jak jaks all fall lass dads

e **2** led lead fee feel ell ells elk elks fee fees leads

t **3** at kat sat tall talk last fast salt slat task tall

o **4** so sol old do ado odd sod of off oaf oak loaf load

all letters learned **5** of a | to do | do so | a joke | to lead | odd leaf | ask a lad

TS

2e
Practice words/phrases

1 Practice the Level 1 lines once SS at an easy pace.

2 DS; then practice the Level 2 lines in the same way.

3 DS; then practice the Level 2 lines again at a faster pace.

4 If time permits, practice the Level 3 lines once, trying to keep the carrier (carriage) moving steadily.

Note: The 3 sets of lines progress gradually in diffi–culty.

Goal: *At least* 1 line per minute (10 *gwam*).

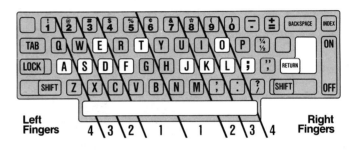

Left Fingers 4 3 2 1 1 2 3 4 **Right Fingers**

all reaches learned

1 a as ask to too foe doe jot jet jak so do sod does

Level 1 **2** ale ask ode old oak let led ade a at kat take told

3 to see; to a set; ask a lad; lot of tea; ate a jak

4 ale oak jet lot all jak doe too off oft odd dot to

Level 2 **5** led doe eat let sol ask add eel sad eke see old of

6 do a loaf; a leaf fell; tell a joke; a lot of talk

7 elf self ask asks jet jets lot lots led lead takes

Level 3 **8** elk elks add adds joke jokes feel feels talk talks

9 to a lake; eat a salad; ask a lass; sell oak desks

2f
End the lesson

(See page 9 if necessary.)

Remove paper

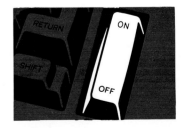

Turn electric off

75a ▶ 5
Preparatory practice

each line 3 times SS (work for smooth, continuous rhythm); DS between 3-line groups; repeat selected lines as time permits

alphabet	1	Meg was not packed to fly to Zanesville to inquire about her next job.
figures	2	Dial 649-4718 or 469-5709 to obtain your copy of this 32-page booklet.
long words	3	Buyers are ordinarily knowledgeable about performance characteristics.
easy	4	Due to the rigor of the quake, the city may dismantle the old chapels.

| 1 | 2 | 3 | 4 | 5 | 6 | 7 | 8 | 9 | 10 | 11 | 12 | 13 | 14 |

75b ▶ 11
Measure skill growth: rough-draft copy

a 3' and a 5' writing; determine *gwam*

Difficulty index

all letters used	A	1.5 si	5.7 awl	80% hfw

	gwam 3'	5'
A lot of people (surprisingly,) measure job potential primarily no	4	3
the basis of the size of the pay check involved. it would be foolish	9	5
to argue that money should play an essential part in job selection and	14	8
career planning, but money along is not an accurate test to use	18	11
when considering a possible career or looking for that first job.	23	14
There is a subtle difference in philosophy between the person who	27	16
is "hunting for a job" and another who is "beginning a career". These	32	19
position itself, however, is not central to this discussion. Rather	36	22
the divergence lies in the approach to the job by each applicant. One	41	25
is attracted by what the job brings; the other, by what it takes.	45	27
we must acknowledge that everybody, or almost everybody, is required	50	30
to work to purchase the necessities of life; money is essential to that	55	33
extent. but when we calculate that we will each spend a third of our life-	60	36
times preforming that work, it follows that whatever we do should be	64	39
enjoyable, allowing us to make a contribution, and help us grow.	68	41

75c ▶ 34
Measure skill application: tables and outlines

Time schedule

Assembling materials .... 3'
Timed production .... 25'
Final check; compute
  g-pram .... 6'

Materials needed

half sheet; 2 full sheets
When the signal to begin is given, insert the paper and begin typing Problem 1 as directed. Type the problems in sequence until the signal to stop is given.

Type Problem 1 again if you finish before time is called. Proofread all problems; circle errors. Compute *g-pram*.

3a
Prepare-to-keyboard checklist

Before you begin to keyboard, check your readiness to begin the lesson.

- ✔ Work area cleared of unneeded clothing and books
- ✔ Book elevated at right of machine

- ✔ Left margin set for 50–space line (center − 25)
- ✔ Right margin set at extreme right end of scale

- ✔ Ribbon control set to type on upper half of ribbon
- ✔ Paper edge guide on correct setting
- ✔ Paper inserted expertly, straightened if necessary

3b
Preparatory practice

each line 3 times SS (slowly, faster, still faster); DS between 3-line groups

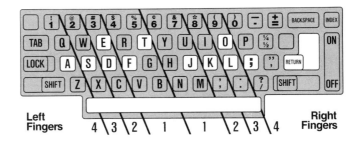

home row 1 `a; sl dk fj a;sl dkfj all lad as ask fall lass add`

e/o/t 2 `ol old sold ed fed led ft oft at dot doe let of to`

all reaches learned 3 `to fold; take a loaf; a lot of; as a joke; at last`
TS

3c
Check position and techniques

As you complete the remainder of the lesson, observe the points of good keyboarding position and techniques listed at the right.

- ✔ Seated erect in chair
- ✔ Both feet on floor
- ✔ Fingers relaxed, curved, upright
- ✔ Fingertips touching home keys
- ✔ Wrists low but not touching the machine

- ✔ Slant of forearms parallel to slant of the keyboard
- ✔ Each key struck with a quick stroke of the fingertip
- ✔ Space bar struck with inward motion of the thumb

3d
Practice keystroking technique

each pair of lines SS as shown; DS between 2-line groups; repeat if time permits

Technique hint:
Strike keys at a smooth pace; avoid pauses.

home row 1 `a jak; ask dad; as a lad; as a lass; add a fall ad`
2 `a fad; as a dad; a fall ad; as all ask; a sad fall`

e 3 `a doe; led a doe; a sea eel; see a lake; jade sale`
4 `a sea; a joke; tell tales; a doe fled; seal a deal`

o 5 `do so; to do so; odd load; lot of old; sold a sofa`
6 `a foe; old oak; jot off a; does a lot; a soft sofa`

t 7 `to let; to talk; tall tale; eat a lot; told a tale`
8 `a tea; to salt; at a late; take a lot; took a seat`
TS

74c, continued

Format and type the prob-
lem as a 2-page report.
Center the heading; use a
1½" (pica) or 2" (elite) top
margin; 1" side and bot-
tom margins.

words

BUSINESSPEOPLE WITH A SENSE OF HUMOR?

8

Is there a place in the hurly-burly world of business for humor? Some 22
businesspeople--perhaps even some successful executives--seem to believe not. 38
Business is a very serious undertaking, they say; and there is not much time to 54
be lighthearted about it. Smiles are all right, but only on the way to the bank. 70

On the other hand, Businesspeople With a Sense of Humor--BWSH we 83
can call them--disagree. They say that the best recipe for business success 99
calls for equal parts of dedication and humor. 108

The BWSH know that business does not thrive on a devil-may-care 121
attitude; they know that it does not thrive on melancholy either. For them, a 137
sense of humor creates a "middle" attitude that tells them how to be con- 151
cerned and smile at the same time. 158

The BWSH are champions of the smile. They know that regardless of how 173
critical things become, a smile helps to ease pain and pressure. A millisecond of 189
life is lived only once, they say; and it can be relived only in retrospect. Nothing 206
will change those spent milliseconds, so the BWSH try to be as positive about 222
the disastrous milliseconds as they are about the more fortuitous ones. 236

A sense of humor is what gets BWSH through such calamities as the 250
last-minute Christmas rush, the over-order for 100 mechanized dolls, and the 265
front door that can't be unlocked on the day of the Big Sale. These problems 280
are truly not laughing matters, but how they are viewed determines how they 296
will be handled. With typical good humor, the BWSH keep business moving 310
positively ahead and on the right track. 319

The BWSH know also that a sense of humor helps build their ability 332
to communicate. To paraphrase a daily newspaper item, 343

> If a business executive can speak to people with a little 355
> warmth and humor, then those people will be more responsive 367
> in listening. If they're paying attention to hear what the speaker 381
> says next, he or she will have a better chance to communicate 393
> effectively.* 396

Businesspeople With a Sense of Humor? Why not? Why not, indeed? 409

413

---

* Detroit Free Press, May 22, 1983, p. 3b. 421

3e
Practice special reach combinations

each line twice SS; DS between 2-line groups

Technique hint:
Do not push for speed; work for smooth, fluid keystroking.

as/sa 1 as ask task fast last lass asks sad salt sale sake

lo/ol 2 lo lot lots lode load loaf old fold sold told sole

ed/de 3 led fed deed seed sled fled ode lode ade deal desk

el/le 4 el els sell felt jell self let leak dale dole lest
TS

3f
Practice phrases

1 Practice the Level 1 lines once SS at an easy pace.

2 DS; then practice the Level 2 lines in the same way.

3 DS; then practice the Level 2 lines again at a faster pace.

4 If time permits, practice the Level 3 lines once, trying to keep the carrier (carriage) moving steadily.

Note: The 3 sets of lines progress gradually in diffi‑culty.

Goal: *At least* 1 line per minute (10 *gwam*).

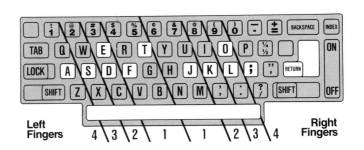

all reaches learned

```
        1 to let; to set; a jak; to do all of; to a sad lad;
Level 1 2 to set; to do a; fed a doe; ask a fee; ask a lass;
        3 ask a lad; a sad ode; to see a foe; a sad old oak;
```
DS

```
        4 to last a; take a jet; tell a tale; take a lot of;
Level 2 5 fall ad; as a set; take a deed; to sell a loaf of;
        6 old jade; to see a; of a sad doll; to seek a deal;
```

```
        7 of a flake; to take a salad; to lose a sales deal;
Level 3 8 too stale; to float a; add a total; of a sad tale;
        9 to a; told jokes; soaks a lot; see a lot of lakes;
```

3g
End the lesson

(See page 9 if necessary.)

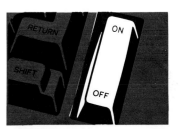

74a ▶ 5
Preparatory practice

each line 3 times SS (work for smooth, continuous rhythm); DS between 3-line groups; repeat selected lines as time permits

alphabet 1 Max queried Parker about having a jewel box for the many huge zircons.

figures 2 Are those last-minute reports on Bill 3657-84 due on October 19 or 20?

shift/lock 3 Ping-ying Fu typed the notations REGISTERED and CERTIFIED in ALL CAPS.

easy 4 The auditor may laugh, but the penalty for such chaotic work is rigid.

| 1 | 2 | 3 | 4 | 5 | 6 | 7 | 8 | 9 | 10 | 11 | 12 | 13 | 14 |

74b ▶ 11
Measure skill growth: statistical copy

a 3' and a 5' writing; determine *gwam*

Difficulty index

| all letters used | A | 1.5 si | 5.7 awl | 80% hfw |

gwam 3' | 5'

According to a special report of NEWSWEEK (January 17, 1983), the   4 | 3
makeup of the American work force is making some sharp adjustments.   9 | 5
Extracting data from the 1980 census, NEWSWEEK says that the median age   14 | 8
of workers dropped from 39 in 1970 to 34 in 1981. Quite a large number   19 | 11
of women have entered the force--67 percent of women between the ages   23 | 14
of 18 and 34 are working. In fact, a total of 46.8 million women--an   28 | 17
amazing 52 percent of the female population--work.   31 | 19

Fewer men are now working, explains the magazine. Consequently,   36 | 21
their portion of the work force has come down since 1951 from 87.3 per-   40 | 24
cent to just 77 percent, due perhaps to better disability benefits and   45 | 27
early retirement. The departure of males begins at the age of 25 and   50 | 30
speeds up at the age of 45. Of males 65 and older, the portion has de-   55 | 33
clined from 44.6 percent in 1955 to 19.9 percent in 1981.   58 | 35

The magazine also quotes some extraordinary figures about the   62 | 37
situation of males and females who are 75 years old and older and who   67 | 40
have continued to work. A total of 451,000 of them remained active in   72 | 43
the 1981 labor force, and the unemployment rate was just 2.8 percent.   77 | 46

gwam 3' | 1 | 2 | 3 | 4 | 5

5' | 1 | 2 | 3

74c ▶ 34
Measure skill application: reports

Time schedule

Assembling materials .... 3'
Timed production .... 25'
Final check; compute
  g-pram .... 6'

Materials needed

2 full sheets

When the signal to begin is given, insert paper and begin typing the problem on page 137, as directed. Type until the signal to stop is given. Begin the problem again if you finish before time is called. Proofread all problems; circle errors. Compute *g-pram*.

4a
Prepare-to-keyboard checklist
Check your readiness to begin Lesson 4.

✔ Work area cleared of unneeded clothing and books

✔ Book elevated at right of machine

✔ Left margin set for 50–space line (center − 25)

✔ Right margin set at extreme right end of scale

✔ Ribbon control set to type on upper half of ribbon

✔ Paper edge guide on correct setting

✔ Paper inserted expertly, straightened if necessary

4b
Preparatory practice
each line twice SS (slowly, then faster); DS between 2-line groups

home row 1 `fj dk sl a; jk fd kl ds l; sa as all fad jak dads;`

e/o/t 2 `ed ol tf led old oft ode dot toe doe foe jets fold`

space bar 3 `to do | do so | a foe | to add | a lot | as a joke | to do so;`

all reaches learned 4 `a jak fell; tell a tale; sold a desk; to a sole ad`
TS

4c
Learn new keyreaches: C and H

Reach technique for c

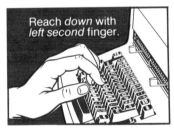

Reach *down* with *left second* finger.

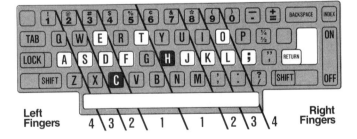

Left Fingers   4 \ 3 \ 2 \ 1 \ 1 / 2 / 3 / 4   Right Fingers

Reach technique for h

Reach to *left* with *right first* finger.

Follow the "Standard procedure for learning new keyreaches" on page 10 (Lines 1–4 twice; Lines 5–8 once; repeat 5–8 if time permits).

Technique hint:
Strike the space bar with a down–and–in motion of the thumb.

c 1 `c cd cd cod cod cot cot call call code codes tacks`
2 `cold clod clad coal cola lack lock dock cool cakes`
DS

h 3 `h hj hj he he she she ah ah ha ha lash dash flash;`
4 `oh ho aha the has had hoe that josh shad hall halt`

c/h 5 `ache echo each cash chat chef hack hock tech check`
6 `a chef; a chat; the ache; all cash; check the hack`

all letters learned 7 `had a look | took the jet | josh the chef | cash a check`
8 `to teach | had the jack | he took half | a cache of food`
TS

Measure skill application: letters

Time schedule

Assembling materials	3'
Timed production	25'
Final check; compute *g-pram*	6'

Materials needed

Letterheads and Monarch sheet [LM pp. 87–91]; copy sheet; carbon paper; large, small, and Monarch envelopes

Format and type as many problems as you can in 25'. Type Problem 1 again if you finish Problem 3 before time has been called. Proofread all problems; circle errors.

Problem 1
Business letter (letterhead)

block style, 1 carbon copy, large envelope; 60-space line; begin on Line 15

Problem 2
Business letter (letterhead)

modified-block style, small envelope; 60-space line; begin on Line 15

Problem 3
Personal letter (Monarch sheet)

modified-block style; Monarch envelope; 50-space line; begin on Line 15

words

June 9, 19-- | Ms. Debra V. Wynn | 80005 Grand Central Pkwy. | Jamaica, NY   14
11435-6071 | Dear Ms. Wynn   19

(¶ 1) Word power! It's important to most people. It's absolutely indispensable   34
to a businessperson like you. Word power commands recognition; it smooths   49
the way to promotion and higher salary; and it brings much personal satisfac-   64
tion.   65
(¶ 2) Vocabulary is a good place to start, of course; but knowing how to choose   80
words, pronounce and spell them, and fit them together to make meaningful   95
sentences is the added knowledge that makes vocabulary work. This is word   110
power. And it can take a lifetime to achieve it.   120
(¶ 3) SPEAK OUT by Guy Hunter brings you a shortcut to word power. This   133
175-page book will help you to build your word power and give you confidence   148
to put your thoughts and ideas to work for you. Your copy of SPEAK OUT is on   164
our "save shelf." You can pick it up at your convenience. It's only $17.95.   180

Sincerely | Cesar J. Strongbow | Manager | xx   188/201

October 28, 19-- | Mrs. L. L. Sangtry, President | United Casings, Inc. | 1600   14
Kirby Street, W. | Shreveport, LA 71103-4923 | Dear Mrs. Sangtry   27

(¶ 1) Last Tuesday afternoon, a shipment of rubber casings from your company   41
arrived at our receiving dock. It had been rushed to us as requested, and we   57
were grateful.   60
(¶ 2) We were not so grateful when we discovered that the shipment was not   74
complete, and I telephoned your sales staff to tell them so. The young lady who   90
answered the telephone listened patiently while I exploded in her ear. Then she   106
went to work.   109
(¶ 3) She asked exactly what was missing and what was happening to our pro-   123
duction schedule. She apologized for the mistake and promised to rush the   138
missing casings to us. I bid her a very doubtful goodbye.   150
(¶ 4) The parts arrived this morning, just 36 hours after I called.   162
(¶ 5) Mrs. Sangtry, I am impressed with the way your firm handled this very   176
serious problem. To have an error handled promptly and courteously was a   191
pleasant surprise. We shall order from you again.   201

Sincerely yours | Ms. Phyllis E. Trerrett | Purchasing Director | xx   214/234

543 El Caprice Avenue | Hollywood, CA 91605-7168 | August 19, 19-- | Miss Felicia   15
Wymore | 278 Fryman Place | Hollywood, CA 91604-4811 | Dear Felicia | 28

(¶ 1) You asked me to write to you about the interviews and tests I took at   42
the Brewer Publishing Company. I spent most of yesterday morning in the   57
company's personnel office. The tests were intensive--mostly keyboarding,   72
composing, editing, spelling, grammar, and vocabulary.   83
(¶ 2) The interviewer asked about my in-school and out-of-school activities,   97
what magazines I regularly read, and what books I had read recently. We also   113
discussed current events.   118
(¶ 3) Frankly, Felicia, I am excited about the prospects of working for Brewer.   133
I'll let you know when I have more news. Thanks for your encouragement.   148

Yours sincerely | Steve Merrewether   151/176

4d
Learn new keyreaches:
R and Right Shift

Reach technique for r

Reach *up* with *left first* finger.

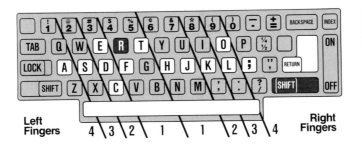

Left Fingers 4 \3 \2 \ 1 \ 1 \2 \3 \4 Right Fingers

Control of right shift key

Reach *down* with *right little* finger; shift, type, release.

Follow the "Standard procedure for learning new keyreaches" on page 10 (Lines 1–4 twice; Lines 5–8 once; repeat 5–8 if time permits).

r

```
1 r rf rf or or for for fro fro ore ore her her ford
2 roe for oar are fork role tore oral soar rode fort
```
DS

right shift
```
3 A; A; Al Al Alf Alf Flo Flo Ed Ed Ted Ted Del Del;
4 Flo Dole; Chad Alte; Alf Slak; Ella Todd; Sol Ekas
```

r/right shift
```
5 Alf Roe; Elke or Rolf Dorr; Rose Salk or Dora Ford
6 Sol Ross asked for Ella; Carl Alda rode for Rhoda;
```

all reaches learned
```
7 Rose Ford told Cora the joke Ross had told to her;
8 Dot Roe has the oar here; Al left the oar for her;
```
TS

4e
Practice words/phrases

1 Practice the Level 1 lines once SS at an easy pace.

2 DS; then practice the Level 2 lines in the same way.

3 DS; then practice the Level 2 lines again at a faster pace.

4 If time permits, practice the Level 3 lines once, trying to keep the carrier (carriage) moving steadily.

Note: The 3 sets of lines progress gradually in diffi-culty.

Goal: *At least* 1 line per minute (10 *gwam*).

all reaches learned

Level 1
```
1 or to do so of he for the she roe toe cod cot coal
2 jak jet hat hot lot jar her car ask lad lass chose
3 Cal had a jar; Rod has a cat; Della has a red hat;
```

Level 2
```
4 cod code jet jets for fore ash cash old hold holds
5 are hare ere here car card ale kale rod rode check
6 Al left; Theo has roe; Flo ate cake; Doc had half;
```

Level 3
```
7 elf self shelf led sled sleds fed feed feeds chose
8 old fold folds she shed sheds hot shot shots jokes
9 Rolf added a cash ad; Flora called here for Chloe;
```

Measurement goals

1 To demonstrate ability to type at acceptable levels average–difficulty writings in straight, rough–draft, and statistical copy for 3' and 5'.

2 To demonstrate ability to type letters, tables, and reports in proper format from semi–arranged copy, according to specific directions.

Machine adjustments

1 Check chair and desk adjustment and placement of copy for ease of reading.

2 Set ribbon control to type on upper half of ribbon.

3 Set paper guide at 0.

4 Set 70–space line.

Materials. Letterheads, full, half, Monarch, and copy sheets; large, small, and Monarch envelopes.

73a ▶ 5
Preparatory practice

each line 3 times SS (slowly, faster, slowly); DS between 3-line groups; repeat selected lines as time permits

alphabet 1 Jack is becoming acquainted with an expert on Venezuelan family names.

fig/sym 2 Our #38065 pens will cost Knox & Brady $12.97 each (less 4% discount).

direct reaches 3 June obtained unusual services from a number of celebrated decorators.

easy 4 It is a problem; she may sue the city for a title to the antique auto.

| 1 | 2 | 3 | 4 | 5 | 6 | 7 | 8 | 9 | 10 | 11 | 12 | 13 | 14 |

73b ▶ 11
Measure skill growth: straight copy

a 3' and a 5' writing; determine *gwam*

Difficulty index

all letters used | A | 1.5 si | 5.7 awl | 80% hfw

gwam 3' | 5'

Clothes do not "make the person." Agree? Still, clothes form an 4 | 3
integral part of impressions we have of others. Whenever we first meet 9 | 6
people, for example, we quickly look them over (and they us), and we 14 | 8
mentally categorize each other. Inexpert as these conclusions may be, 19 | 11
we all justify them in our own minds on the basis that clothing is the 23 | 14
only evidence of personality we have. 26 | 16

Clothes are, of course, quite practical; we need them for modesty 30 | 18
purposes and to protect us from the hazards of extreme weather. Yet, 35 | 21
clothes are also decorative; they should, beyond just looking nice, 40 | 24
reflect a personality, a mood, and a natural coloring--but not a finan- 44 | 27
cial status. Clothes should be part of a picture--a picture of a per- 49 | 29
son--and the person should be the central part of the picture. 53 | 32

Clothes do serve a purpose. They always make a direct statement 57 | 34
about a person; so they should be suitable, and they should be fresh. 62 | 37
High style (but not quality) is out for usual business occasions, as 68 | 40
is excessive jewelry and tantalizing scents. A good mirror and a bit 71 | 43
of common sense can indicate to a person what clothes are appropriate. 76 | 46

gwam 3' | 1 | 2 | 3 | 4 | 5 |
     5' | 1 | 2 | 3 |

5a
Prepare-to-keyboard checklist

Are you ready to keyboard? Check the items listed at the right before you begin. Review 4a, page 14, if you are unsure about any of the items.

- ✔ Work area
- ✔ Book placement
- ✔ Margin stops
- ✔ Ribbon control
- ✔ Paper guide
- ✔ Paper insertion

5b
Preparatory practice

each line twice SS (slowly, then faster); DS between 2-line groups

home row 1 `a; as all lad ask add ash fad jak sad has had lash`

c/r 2 `or ore core jar jars ark lark rock cord lack cross`

h/t 3 `a hat ate hate the that oath heat halt sloth loath`

all reaches learned 4 `Ro has a fake jade; ask Cal to let her do the lot;`
TS

5c
Learn new keyreaches: W and U

Reach technique for w

Reach *up* with *left third* finger.

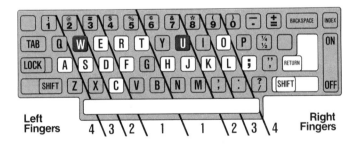

Left Fingers 4 \ 3 \ 2 \ 1 \ \ 1 \ 2 \ 3 \ 4 Right Fingers

Reach technique for u

Reach *up* with *right first* finger.

Follow the "Standard procedure for learning new keyreaches" on page 10 (Lines 1–4 twice; Lines 5–8 once; repeat 5–8 if time permits).

w 1 `w ws ws was was sow sows law laws jaw jaws wow wow`
2 `ow how owl owe woes cow cows row rows sow sows low`
DS

u 3 `u uj uj jut jut cut cut us us use use due due fuse`
4 `cue sue hue rut rude just jute sure lure loud cute`

w/u 5 `how we do; just a duck; we work out our four cues;`
6 `we row; use a wok; our used fuse; Sue wore a tutu;`

all reaches learned 7 `two or four; the cut hurt Wu; a hut for us to use;`
8 `cut two; Duke had a cake; we just saw Dale at two;`
TS

72d ▶ 25
Review tables
and outlines

2 full sheets
1 half sheet

Format and type Problems 1, 2, and 3 for 20 minutes as directed below; compute *g-pram*.

Problem 1
table

half sheet (enter long side first); SS; 6-space intercolumns

Problem 2
outline

full sheet; 1½" top margin; 40-space line; add designation numerals and letters for each order; use correct capitalization and spacing

Problem 3
table

repeat Problem 1; full sheet; DS; reading position; 6-space intercolumns

Reference pages:

Centering
  Vertical: 116
  Horizontal: 116
  Columns: 118
Outlines: 95, 96

			words
BEAUX ARTS CONCERTS			4
Classical Series			7
Date	Presentation	Hall	16
October 1	Elton Kunter, violinist	Harvard Auditorium	27
October 25	Grieg Chamber Group	Harvard Auditorium	37
November 1	Los Angeles Ballet	Cluny Center	45
November 10	Alice Humphrey, pianist	Harvard Auditorium	56
November 16	Marta Ruiz, cellist	Cluny Center	65
February 4	Brett Luxward, tenor	Cluny Center	74
February 15	Minneapolis Players	Harvard Auditorium	84
March 8	John Lo, pianist	Cluny Center	92
March 25	Toledo Symphony	Cluny Center	100
April 4	Rose Kunzel, soprano	Harvard Auditorium	109

	words
COMPENSATION FOR EMPLOYMENT	6
forms of compensation	10
hourly wage	12
regular time	15
overtime	17
straight salary	20
piece rate	22
commission	24
bonus	26
combination	28
deduction from compensation	34
federal income tax	38
federal insurance contributions act	45
other	46
income tax	48
state	49
city	50
dues and assessments	55
health insurance	58
medical	60
dental	61
voluntary items	64

5d
Learn new keyreaches:
Left Shift and . (period)

Control of left shift key

Reach *down* with *left little* finger; shift, type, release.

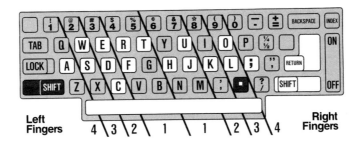

Reach technique for . (period)

Reach *down* with *right third* finger; space twice after . at end of sentence.

Follow the "Standard procedure for learning new keyreaches" on page 10 (Lines 1–4 twice; Lines 5–8 once; repeat 5–8 if time permits).

Period: Space once after a period that fol– lows an abbreviation or an initial, twice after a period that ends a sentence. Do not, however, space after a period at the end of a line.

left shift
1 L La La Lars Lake Ladd Jae Jake Karl Kate Hal Harl
2 Jae or Jake Kale or Lara Karl or Lars Hart or Ladd
DS

. (period)
3 . .1 .1 1 1.1 fl. fl. Dr. E. F. Roe asked for a lot.
4 Dale has left for Soho. Dr. Sorel saw her at two.

left shift and .
5 Hal saw us. He also saw Joe. He was at the lake.
6 J. J. does work for us; he used to work for Laura.

all reaches learned
7 Kae used to read to Joe; she works for the Roe Co.
8 Sr. Jude left for Tulsa; her car was full of food.
TS

5e
Practice words/sentences

1 Practice the Level 1 lines once SS at an easy pace.

2 DS; then practice the Level 2 lines in the same way.

3 DS; then practice the Level 2 lines again at a faster pace.

4 If time permits, practice the Level 3 lines once, trying to keep the carrier (carriage) moving steadily.

Note: The 3 sets of lines progress gradually in diffi– culty.

Goal: *At least* 1 line per minute (10 *gwam*).

all reaches learned

Level 1
1 rf or of uj us sue use ws ow sow cow ol lo low old
2 ed led eke tf to lot dot cd cod doc hj hut hue wok
3 Jeff used the old wok to cook; Lu added the sauce.

Level 2
4 we woe awl cow sow led low for fur let cut our hut
5 for fat law saw how use jet jut the work chew fake
6 Aldo took the saw; Ed has to cut the old jak tree.

Level 3
7 we our was wore were just jade josh take sake hour
8 that lurk wash four keel chew walk crow talk would
9 Suella saw the letter that Cora wrote at the lake.

72a ▶ 5
Preparatory practice

each line 3 times SS (work for errorless lines); DS between 3-line groups; repeat selected lines as time permits

alphabet	1	We have quizzed Joy about a family with whom she is expecting to work.
figures	2	Our store has three locations: 36040 Grand; 6275 Maywood; 1890 Olive.
3d row	3	Perry, you were to type quietly the two erudite reports that were due.
easy	4	He may make a profit on corn, rye, yams, and hay if he works the land.

| 1 | 2 | 3 | 4 | 5 | 6 | 7 | 8 | 9 | 10 | 11 | 12 | 13 | 14 |

72b ▶ 8
Improve keystroking control

each line twice SS; proofread and circle errors before typing the next line; DS between 2-line groups; repeat selected lines as time permits

direct reaches	1	My brother, Mervyn, has my army carbines; Bernice has my breechloader.
adjacent reaches	2	Three guides loped in a column as we stalked over trails after a lion.
double letters	3	Lynn will see that Jill accepts an assignment in the office next week.
long words	4	Governmental departments encourage associations to photocopy booklets.
shift	5	In May, Don, Sonia, and Jason Halls left for Italy, Spain, and Turkey.
quotation marks	6	"Have 'sunglow' all winter," I typed, "with the all-new Polk sunlamp."

| 1 | 2 | 3 | 4 | 5 | 6 | 7 | 8 | 9 | 10 | 11 | 12 | 13 | 14 |

72c ▶ 12
Improve basic skill: straight copy

two 5' writings; proofread carefully; circle errors; compute g-pram

Goal: at least 29 gwam with fewer than 6 errors.

Difficulty index

all letters used	A	1.5 si	5.7 awl	80% hfw

gwam 3' | 5'

I'm a prospective employee. I want to work; indeed, for various   4 | 3

practical reasons, I need to work. I want a job that provides me with   9 | 5

opportunities to earn sufficient income to live a comfortable life.   13 | 8

I want a chance for promotion as quickly as possible. I want to realize   19 | 11

what I believe is my potential for success. Probably of most signifi-   23 | 14

cance, I want a job that I will enjoy doing; I cannot spend a lifetime   28 | 17

dreading Monday mornings.   30 | 18

I'm a prospective employer, but I'm reluctant to hire just one more   34 | 20

worker. I want a team member. I expect to pay well, but I also expect   39 | 23

something in return. I want a person who is promotable and who will   44 | 26

dazzle me to get it. Probably of most significance, I want an employee   48 | 29

who does not add to my absenteeism problems, who takes pride in the   53 | 32

quality of individual output, and who associates personal achievement   58 | 35

with company growth.   59 | 36

gwam 3' | 1 | 2 | 3 | 4 | 5 |
5' | 1 | 2 | 3 |

6a
Prepare-to-keyboard checklist

Are you ready? Check the list at the right.

- ✔ Desk and chair
- ✔ Work area
- ✔ Book placement
- ✔ Paper guide
- ✔ Line–space selector (SS)
- ✔ Margin stops

6b
Preparatory practice

each line twice SS (slowly, then faster); DS between 2-line groups

home row	1	a jak lad as ash ad had add has all fall hash dash
e/o/t/c	2	ed ol tf cd led old cot toe eke due lot colt docks
w/h/r/u	3	ws hj rf uj we raw hut war who haul hawk rule what
all reaches learned	4	Rosela had to cut her rate; Jeff took a weak lead.

TS

6c
Check keystroking technique

each set of lines twice SS; DS between 3-line groups

Technique hint:
Check the list of techniques at the right; use them as you do the drill lines.

- ✔ Seated erect in chair
- ✔ Both feet on floor
- ✔ Fingertips lightly touching home keys
- ✔ Wrists low, but not touching the machine
- ✔ Slant of forearms parallel to slant of keyboard
- ✔ Each key struck with a quick stroke of the fingertip
- ✔ Space bar struck with inward motion of the thumb

all reaches learned

	1	or do he so of el la ow to she for the fur due row
words	2	cue jak foe sod cut doe sow sue all too wood would
	3	alto also hall fall tall rust dust lark dark jowls
	4	to do so | he or she | to do the | of all our | as the doe
phrases	5	had to do | ask the lad | ate the jak | has the fur coat
	6	do the work | saw the show | just as she | take the test
	7	Drew saw the late show. She had to cut law class.
sen-tences	8	Walt was at Olde Lake at two; Joel also was there.
	9	Kate was at the dock at four to see all of us off.

TS

6d
Check spacing/shifting technique

each set of lines twice SS; DS between 3-line groups

- ✔ Space with down–and–in motion of the thumb
- ✔ Shift with quick, 1–2–3/ shift–type–release motions
- ✔ Quiet hands; no pauses before or after spacing or shifting
- ✔ Space once after abbreviation period
- ✔ Space twice after a sentence period
- ✔ Space once after a semicolon

Technique hint:
Check the techniques above right; use them as you do the drill.

all reaches learned

	1	ah so he do la of el us to ha for she due cot work
spacing	2	to do of us do so a jak the fur for the of all the
	3	Ask the lad for the oak. He cut the wood at work.
	4	Ask for Dr. Lor. She took a call. Jae heard her.
shifting	5	Todd has to work. Talk to Jewel; she has the ads.
	6	Laura left for Duluth. She took the jet at three.

71d ▶ 25
Review reports

2 full sheets

Format and type the report at the right in appropriate report form for 20 minutes as directed in Problems 1 and 2 below; circle errors; compute *g–pram.*

Goal: 12 *g–pram* or more.

Problem 1

as first page of a report
margins:
    top: 1½" (pica) 2" (elite)
  sides: 1"
bottom: 1"

Problem 2

as second page of a report; omit main heading; subtract 5 from total word count

Reference pages:

reports: 96, 98
footnotes: 101
second page: 96, 98

	words
THE CONSTANCY OF CHANGE	5

A wise philosopher reflects in one of his books that "There is nothing new   20

under the sun." Form may change, he tells us, but substance does not. Life   35

consists of functions and rituals that are vital parts of living; once we accept the   52

inevitability of these constants, there is, indeed, nothing new under the sun.   68

Changes! Will they never stop? Is there nothing constant we   81
can count on in this world? To the many who are currently asking   94
such plaintive questions, the answer is no; change is the only thing   108
that is permanent.[1]   112

Today, we do all those things that humans have historically done; this   126

is the constancy of life. We have just learned to do them differently; and this is   143

change. We do not change <u>what</u> we do; we change <u>how</u> we do. We tell time by   159

glancing at our digital watches, not at the sun, a candle, a sundial, or an   175

hourglass.   177

Change occurs slowly, persistently. Each generation creates its quota   191

of change--little enough to digest in its lifetime, big enough to revolutionize its   208

way of life. The typewriter, telephone, automobile, airplane, radio, television,   224

and computer are changes that truly exemplify the generations that created   239

them.   241

Change is not always beneficial, it does not always last, and it is not always   257

easy to accept; but it is always taking place. The well-adjusted person expects   273

change, tries it, and adopts from it what seems to serve her or him best in the   289

pursuit of a "way of life." By the way, what are <u>your</u> thoughts about a home   305

robot?   306
  310

—————————

[1] "The Pressures of Change," <u>The Royal Bank Letter</u>, The Royal   322
Bank of Canada 63 (July/August 1982), p. 1.   331

7a ▶ 8
Preparatory practice

each line twice SS
(slowly, then faster);
DS between 2-line groups

Note: Beginning with Lesson 7, each lesson part will include in its headings a suggested number of minutes for practicing that activity.

all letters learned | 1 Doc took just four hours to row to the south lake.

c/u/r | 2 Lou cut the rate cost of our letters to the coast.

w/h | 3 Ask Walt Howe to heat the water to wash the shelf.

all reaches learned | 4 We saw Jack a lot later; he worked for four hours.

TS

7b ▶ 6
Develop keyboarding fluency

two 30″ writings on each line

Goal: To complete each line in 30″ (14 *gwam*).

all letters learned

1 Do the oak shelf for the lake dock.

2 She cut half the fuel for the auto.

3 Throw the kale to the cow for Jake.

4 The autos do the work of the world.

TS

7c ▶ 12
Learn new keyreaches: X and I

Reach technique for x

Reach *down* with *left third* finger.

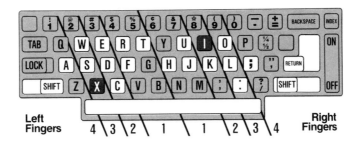

Left Fingers 4 \ 3 \ 2 \ 1 \ 1 \ 2 \ 3 \ 4 Right Fingers

Reach technique for i

Reach *up* with *right second* finger.

Follow the "Standard procedure for learning new keyreaches" on page 10 (Lines 1–4 twice; Lines 5–8 once; repeat 5–8 if time permits).

x | 1 x xs xs ox ox axe axe sox sox fox fox hex hex axle
2 xs ax ox tux lox lax sax flex flax flux crux taxed

i | 3 i ik ik if if is is it it did did kid kid aid aids
4 ik kit sit fit wit sir lid its side cite kick wick

x/i | 5 Felix fixed the six tax rules I asked Exie to fix.
6 I will fix tea for Dixie if she will wax the taxi.

all reaches learned | 7 Sid Cox said it was a lax law; Roxie also said so.
8 Jackie will fix the cut foot of the old fox I saw.

TS

71a ▶ 5
Preparatory practice

each line 3 times SS (work for errorless lines); DS between 3-line groups

alphabet 1 The value of a quality work-experience program has just been realized.

figures 2 Will my summary report on Senate Bill 7635-48 be due the 19th or 20th?

one hand 3 In my opinion, a few plum trees on a hilly acre create no vast estate.

easy 4 The men at the dock may wish to shape the rock in the form of a whale.

| 1 | 2 | 3 | 4 | 5 | 6 | 7 | 8 | 9 | 10 | 11 | 12 | 13 | 14 |

71b ▶ 8
Improve keystroking control

each line twice SS; proofread and circle errors before typing the next line; DS between 2-line groups

Type at a steady rate; concentrate on the copy.

1st row 1 Uncle Xavier mines zinc, cobalt, and silver on vacant land in Bavaria.

2d row 2 As she dashed to Dad's lake last fall, Sarah had half a glass of soda.

3d row 3 Terrie, try to work quietly if you operate our out-of-date typewriter.

4th row 4 A 4-act play, to be given June 17, 26, and 30, will begin at 8:59 p.m.

fingers 1/2 5 Trudy knew by her voice that Martha had broken the hush of the jungle.

fingers 3/4 6 Polly was puzzled by six quaint wax dolls in an antique dealer's shop.

| 1 | 2 | 3 | 4 | 5 | 6 | 7 | 8 | 9 | 10 | 11 | 12 | 13 | 14 |

71c ▶ 12
Improve basic skill: statistical copy

three 3′ writings

Proofread carefully; circle errors.

Goal: at least 28 *gwam* with fewer than 6 errors.

Difficulty index

all letters used | A | 1.5 si | 5.7 awl | 80% hfw

gwam 3′ | 5′

According to a 1984 publication, our 50-state nation is a country 4 | 3
of interesting extremes. First of all, it is a nation of considerable 9 | 5
size, including within its borders approximately 3,623,537 square miles 14 | 8
of land and water. Its largest state, Alaska, alone extends across a 19 | 11
territory of 491,004 square miles, while its smallest, Rhode Island, 23 | 14
has an area of just 1,212 square miles. The lowest town in the country 28 | 17
is Calipatria, California, which is 184 feet below sea level. (Death 33 | 20
Valley, which is uninhabited, is 383 feet below sea level.) If, on the 37 | 22
other hand, we talk of high points, Mount McKinley must be mentioned; 42 | 25
it has a height of 20,320 feet. The rainiest place is an area in Hawaii 47 | 28
that has an annual average rainfall of 480 inches--1.315 inches a day. 52 | 31
The strongest surface wind occurred in New Hampshire, where a measure- 56 | 34
ment of 231 miles an hour is on record. The deepest well, for those who 61 | 37
might be interested in such a figure, is a gas well in Oklahoma that 66 | 40
goes down 31,441 feet. 67 | 41

gwam 3′ | 1 | 2 | 3 | 4 | 5 |
5′ | 1 | 2 | 3 |

7d ▶ 12
Learn new keyreaches:
G and N

Reach technique for g

Reach to *right* with *left first* finger.

Left Fingers 4 \ 3 \ 2 \ 1 \ 1 \ 2 \ 3 \ 4 Right Fingers

Reach technique for n

Reach *down* with *right first* finger.

Follow the "Standard procedure for learning new keyreaches" on page 10 (Lines 1–4 twice; Lines 5–8 once; repeat 5–8 if time permits).

g 1 g gf gf go go fog fog got got rug rug dog dog frog
   2 gf log dug fig wig dig lag tog leg keg jig cog got
DS

n 3 n nj nj an an and and end end hen hen ran ran lend
   4 nj on won wan den tan ten can land want rent sends

g/n 5 Gwen longs to sing a grand song she knew in Genoa.
     6 Gig noted that one swan wing was green with algae.

all reaches learned 7 Leonor left the show to take a cruise to Calcutta.
                     8 Just set a fair goal; then work hard to extend it.
TS

7e ▶ 12
Build keyboarding continuity

1 Practice the Level 1 lines once SS at an easy pace.

2 DS; then practice the Level 2 lines in the same way.

3 DS; then practice the Level 2 lines again at a faster pace.

4 If time permits, practice the Level 3 lines once, trying to keep the carrier (carriage) moving steadily.

Note: The 3 sets of lines progress gradually in difficulty.

Goal: *At least* 1 line per minute (10 *gwam*).

Count typewritten words:

Five characters and spaces are counted as one standard typewritten word. The figures in the scale under the copy show the word–by–word count (5 strokes a word) for each line.

all reaches learned

Level 1 1 I will need four to six weeks to work out the act.
         2 Janet can ask six of the girls to guide the tours.
         3 Ask Nellie to sing one alto aria in our next show.

Level 2 4 He will fix a snack; he will also fix fruit juice.
         5 The four girls will use their auto or hire a taxi.
         6 Gil has asked six girls to a light lunch in Akron.

Level 3 7 Luann wore a ring and long necklace of green jade.
         8 Dixie will send her tax check to the local office.
         9 Lex is an officer of high rank in Jackson Tool Co.

| 1 | 2 | 3 | 4 | 5 | 6 | 7 | 8 | 9 | 10 |

To determine words-a-minute rate:

1 List the figure 10 for each line completed during a writing.

2 For a partial line, note from the scale the figure directly below the point at which you stopped.

3 Add these figures to determine the total gross words typed (the same as *gwam* for a 1' writing).

70c ▶ 31
Review letters

2 letterheads, 1 Monarch sheet [LM pp. 73-77]; 1 large, 1 small, 1 Monarch envelope; carbon paper, copy sheet

Format and type Problems 1, 2, and 3 for 26 minutes as in–structed below; begin each letter on Line 15; circle errors; compute *g–pram*.

Problem 1
business letter

block style; 60–space line; small envelope

words

March 26, 19-- | Mr. Charles Onehawk | 4570 Virginia Avenue, W. | Phoenix, AZ — 14
85035-6231 | Dear Mr. Onehawk — 20

(¶ 1) As a member of a select group of responsible people who have substantial — 35
equity in their homes, you should know about our revolutionary new concept in — 51
homeowner liquidity. Now you can have instant access to large amounts of cash — 67
at low interest rates. — 71

(¶ 2) Our EQUITY LOAN SERVICE can put $10,000 to $100,000 at your instant — 85
disposal, for this line of credit lets you borrow up to 70 percent of the value of — 101
your home at less than current market rates. — 111

(¶ 3) Once your loan application is approved, you'll receive a personalized — 125
checkbook that you can use to write your own loans; you won't even have to go to — 141
the bank. — 143

(¶ 4) I invite you to apply for the EQUITY LOAN SERVICE by returning the en- — 157
closed application blank. Do it now and put your idle assets to work for you. — 172

Sincerely | Amy E. Wilkes | President | xx | Enclosure — 182/**195**

Problem 2
business letter

modified–block style; 60–space line; large envelope

August 30, 19-- | Ms. Barbara B. Brahms | 2457 Washington Avenue | Columbus, — 14
GA 31906-4226 | Dear Ms. Brahms — 20

(¶ 1) Your letter asking for my comments about "easy loan plans" came this — 34
morning. I hope the following information is helpful as you write your paper. — 50
Quote from this letter as you wish. — 58

(¶ 2) It is a well-accepted fact that our economy thrives on credit. Credit replaces — 74
cash and adds to purchasing power, but it leads to inflation if used heavily. Few — 90
of us, however, could live the kind of lives we enjoy if it were not for credit. — 107
Establishing and maintaining a healthy personal credit rating is beneficial to — 122
each of us. — 125

(¶ 3) Credit, however, must be used cautiously; for it enables us to satisfy — 139
wants--and our wants are insatiable. Credit makes getting the things we want-- — 155
from a sink to a mink--easy; paying for them, an eventuality easily dismissed, is — 171
not always easy. — 175

(¶ 4) Have available as much credit as you need; use as little of it as you can. Your — 191
credit rating will be healthier for it--and so will your pocketbook. — 205

Sincerely yours | Andrew W. Mayhouse | President | xx — 214/**228**

Problem 3
personal letter

block style; 50–space line; Monarch envelope

Reference pages

block style letters: 77, 78
modified–block
style letters: 83, 84
personal letters: 57, 58
Monarch/small
envelopes: 62
large envelopes: 81

45 Reed Avenue | Springfield, OH 45505-3971 | October 15, 19-- | Miss J. E. — 14
Murgraff | 545 Saint Johns Lane | New York, NY 10013-2106 | Dear Janelle — 28

(¶ 1) I have some great news. My company has asked me to be in New York on — 42
November 10, 11, and 12 to attend a conference at the St. Regis Hotel. I shall be in — 59
your town for three whole days. — 66

(¶ 2) I am sure my evenings will be free while I am there; and I should very much — 81
like to see a show, dine at some special place, and enjoy a very long chat with you. — 98
Why don't you choose the evening(s), make the reservations, get the tickets-- — 114
whatever--and I'll reimburse you. This time it's my treat. — 126

(¶ 3) Much has happened since I last saw you in July; we have a lot of real — 140
catching up to do. Let me know if your schedule is clear or if it can be cleared for — 157
these days in November. — 162

Very sincerely | Lex Bynum — 166/**179**

8a ▶ 8
Preparatory practice

each line twice SS
(slowly, then faster);
DS between 2-line
groups

all letters
learned

1 Alexi Garcia had gone to San Juan for three weeks.

x/i 2 I next fixed the axle; then I waxed the six taxis.

g/n 3 Ginger is going to England to sing for Jonah King.

all reaches
learned

4 Lex and Rolf saw Luan Ling; Jack had not seen her.

Recall: TS between
lesson parts.

| 1 | 2 | 3 | 4 | 5 | 6 | 7 | 8 | 9 | 10 |

8b ▶ 8
Improve keyboarding technique

each line once as shown;
if time permits, repeat the
drill

all reaches learned

keystroking
and spacing

1 ws ik ed ol nj rf uj tf cd .l xs gf hj ec un rg tf
2 if so is do it of an go he el ha ox ah or eh to us
3 as to | we go | at an | we do | as he | see us | get it | ate an

spacing
and shifting

4 Ken can win if he will set a goal and work for it.
5 Dorn is now in Rio; Janice is to go there in June.
6 Ann and J. D. Fox had seen Lt. Green at the dance.

| 1 | 2 | 3 | 4 | 5 | 6 | 7 | 8 | 9 | 10 |

8c ▶ 12
Learn new keyreaches: V and , (comma)

Reach technique for v

Reach *down* with
left first finger.

Left
Fingers 4 \ 3 \ 2 \ 1 \ 1 \ 2 \ 3 \ 4 Right
Fingers

Reach technique
for , (comma)

Reach *down* with
right second finger;
space once after ,
used as punctuation.

Follow the "Standard procedure
for learning new keyreaches" on
page 10 (Lines 1–4 twice; Lines
5–8 once; repeat 5–8 if time
permits).

v

1 v vf vf vie vie vow vow van van via via five fives
2 vf vf live have dive love vane vain vile view viva
DS

'

3 , ,k ,k kit, kit, Dick, Jane, Nate, and I read it.
4 a rug, a jig, a ski, an igloo, the ring, two songs

Comma: Space once after a
comma.

v/,

5 Vic, Iva, and Viv dived over and over to save Van.
6 Val, Reva, and Vi voted for Eva; even so, Iva won.

all reaches
learned

7 Kevin Nix was a judge at the garden show in Flint.
8 Joan, not Vi, took the jet; Vic also tried for it.

| 1 | 2 | 3 | 4 | 5 | 6 | 7 | 8 | 9 | 10 |

Learning goals

1 To improve keystroking continuity and control.

2 To review principles of typing letters, tables, outlines, announcements, and reports.

3 To improve control of straight, rough-draft, and statistical copy.

Machine adjustments

1 Set paper guide at 0.

2 Set ribbon control to type on upper half of ribbon.

3 Set a 70–space line.

4 SS drills; DS paragraphs.

70a ▶ 5
Preparatory practice

each line 3 times SS (work for errorless lines); DS between 3-line groups; repeat selected lines as time permits

alphabet	1	Place the five dozen gloves in the box quickly before John moves away.
figures	2	The 1984 edition of this book has 5 parts, 30 chapters, and 672 pages.
shift	3	Dora will make a quick flight to La Paz, Bolivia, next March or April.
easy	4	The girls, sick and shaken with dyspepsia, kept to their work in town.

| 1 | 2 | 3 | 4 | 5 | 6 | 7 | 8 | 9 | 10 | 11 | 12 | 13 | 14 |

70b ▶ 14
Improve basic skill

two 3′ writings
one 5′ writing

proofread;
circle errors

Goal: at least 27 *gwam* with fewer than 6 errors on 3′ writing.

Difficulty index

all letters used	A	1.5 si	5.7 awl	80% hfw

	gwam 3′	5′
i remember so well my first encounter in the employment interview	4	3
arena. It was one beautiful morning in early June; but, although when the	9	5
interviewer smiled and shook my hand when we met, I knew at once that I	14	8
was pitted against a strong character who would quickly and zealously	19	11
explore for any chinks in my professional and personal armor.	23	14
The interviewer, who seemed to be totally relaxed, quickly scanned over	27	16
my personal data sheet. The then questions began. What experience had	32	19
I had? Why did I want this specific job? What career goal had I set	37	22
for myself? But I was not caught offguard. I had anticipated many	41	25
questions, and my short answers contained all the data asked for.	45	27
Next, my references came under cold, quiet scrutiny. Had I asked	50	30
permission to use the names? Could they be contacted? Yes, I replied,	55	31
still a step ahead. I relaxed; I had started to enjoy this experience.	59	36
Finally, the interviewer smiled, stood, and took my hand again; and I	64	38
realized the contest was over. she offered me a job. *We both had won!*	69	41

8d ▶ 12
Learn new keyreaches:
Q and Y

Reach technique for q

Reach *up* with *left little* finger.

Left Fingers 4 \ 3 \ 2 \ 1 \ 1 \ 2 \ 3 \ 4 Right Fingers

Reach technique for y

Reach *up* with *right first* finger.

Follow the "Standard procedure for learning new keyreaches" on page 10 (Lines 1–4 twice; Lines 5–8 once; repeat 5–8 if time permits).

q
1 q qa qa qu qu quo quo quit quits quad quads quotes
2 qa qu quo quit quad quick quite equal quilt quarts
DS

y
3 y yj yj jay jay you you yet yet day day yell yells
4 yj eye yes rye dye sky cry sly try joy soy yen toy

q/y
5 Jay says Quay is quite young; he is quiet and shy.
6 Troy, Quent, and I are quite glad that Quinn quit.

all reaches learned
7 Frank Cage enjoyed the novel; Jo can read it next.
8 Next, Jacky Quire will leave; she can go in a day.

| 1 | 2 | 3 | 4 | 5 | 6 | 7 | 8 | 9 | 10 |

8e ▶ 10
Build sustained keyboarding power

1 Practice Paragraph (¶) 1 once SS.
2 DS and practice ¶2 in the same way.

Technique hints:

1 Keep your eyes on the book copy as you keyboard.

2 Do not pause or look up as you return the carrier or carriage (or cursor on a personal computer).

all reaches learned

¶ 1 We often need to choose, and yet it is never easy
to know which of two roads to take. One can look
exactly like another, yet we are never quite sure
what is involved with each journey or each choice.

¶ 2 However, we do have to choose; and, since we will
not know where the unchosen road would have taken
us, we have to trust that we chose the right road.

| 1 | 2 | 3 | 4 | 5 | 6 | 7 | 8 | 9 | 10 |

**Measure skill
application: tables**

Time schedule

Assembling materials .... 3′
Timed production .... 25′
Final check; proofread;
    compute *g–pram* .... 6′

Materials needed

1 full sheet
2 half sheets

Problem 1

full sheet; DS; reading position;
6–space intercolumns

			words
CHIEF JUSTICES OF THE SUPREME COURT			7
as of 1984			9
Justice	State	Term	16
John Jay	New York	1789-1795	22
Oliver Ellsworth	Connecticut	1796-1800	30
John Marshall	Virginia	1801-1835	36
Roger B. Taney	Maryland	1836-1864	43
Salmon P. Chase	Ohio	1864-1873	49
Morrison R. Waite	Ohio	1874-1888	56
Melville W. Fuller	Illinois	1888-1910	64
Edward D. White	Louisiana	1910-1921	71
William H. Taft	Ohio	1921-1930	77
Charles E. Hughes	New York	1930-1941	85
Harlan F. Stone	New York	1941-1946	91
Fred M. Vinson	Kentucky	1946-1953	98
Earl Warren	California	1953-1969	104
Warren E. Burger	Virginia	1969-	111

Problem 2

half sheet (enter long side first);
SS; exact center; decide intercolumn spacing

			words
FAMOUS AMERICAN PAINTINGS			5
Painter	Title	Size	12
Mary Cassatt	After the Bath	26″ × 39″	20
Willem de Kooning	Woman I	76″ × 58″	27
Winslow Homer	The Gulf Stream	28″ × 49″	35
Jackson Pollock	Number 27	11′ × 24′	42
Robert Rauschenberg	Tracer	84″ × 60″	50
John Singer Sargent	Madame X	82″ × 43″	57
Grant Wood	American Gothic	30″ × 25″	65
Andrew Wyeth	Christina's World	32″ × 48″	73

Problem 3

half sheet; make all decisions for
placement of copy

			words
THE UNITED NATIONS			4
Small-Nation Members			8
Country	Admitted	Est. Pop.	18
Belize	1981	146,000	22
Dominica	1978	80,000	26
Grenada	1974	108,000	31
Maldives	1965	150,000	35
St. Lucia	1979	124,000	40
St. Vincent and the Grenadines	1980	120,000	48
Sao Tome and Principe	1975	90,000	55
Seychelles	1976	70,000	60
Vanutu	1981	112,700	64

9a ▶ 8
Preparatory practice

each line twice SS
(slowly, then faster);
DS between 2-line
groups

all letters learned	1	Work quickly, and we can fix the van Janet got us.
v/q/,/y	2	Standing on the quay, Dave, too, felt very queasy.
space bar	3	if it | to do | or he | an ox | for us | to do the | a yen for
easy	4	The city got a quantity of fish for the town lake.

| 1 | 2 | 3 | 4 | 5 | 6 | 7 | 8 | 9 | 10 |

Recall: TS between lesson parts.

9b ▶ 14
Practice keyreaches

1 Practice each line twice SS; DS between 2-line groups.
2 Repeat lines that seem most troublesome.

x	1	Lex next sent six yards of flax to Roxy in a taxi.
g	2	Gwen sang a song as George raised the ragged flag.
y	3	I say Ayn is shy; yet I did enjoy her story a lot.
n	4	For Nana, France was a land of sun, sand, and tan.
v	5	Van ran to visit the levee to view the vast river.
q	6	Quay quickly quoted Queen Arqua. Quent was quiet.

| 1 | 2 | 3 | 4 | 5 | 6 | 7 | 8 | 9 | 10 |

9c ▶ 14
Develop machine parts control

twice as shown; repeat as time permits

Lines 1-4: Practice each short line and return without pausing or looking up.
Lines 5-7: Use space bar efficiently and maintain typing fluency.
Lines 8-10: Shift smoothly and rhythmically.

	1	Finish final stroke in the line.
return	2	Reach quickly to the return key.
	3	Hold your eyes down on the text.
	4	Return; start next line at once.
	5	an key fox van vie own hay can jay coy lay rug any
space bar	6	Vote for Gin; Lu is not a good choice. Tell Quin.
	7	Lex, not Tay, has a wagon; he will hang the signs.
	8	Owen Hays and Lil Young will see Neil in New York.
shift keys	9	Cyd, Rod, Susi, and Don will go on to Vienna soon.
	10	J. C. Wert will see Nel Foyt at the Old City Hall.

| 1 | 2 | 3 | 4 | 5 | 6 | 7 | 8 | 9 | 10 |

9d ▶ 14
Build sustained keyboarding power

1 Practice Paragraph (¶) 1 once.
2 DS and practice ¶2 in the same way.

> **Technique hint:**
> Keystroke smoothly, continuously; avoid pauses.

all reaches learned

¶ 1 There are certain things that each of us wants to own, and we know there are ways to acquire things we want. However, there is a flaw in this design.

¶ 2 As soon as we get the thing we want, it loses its value; so we exchange one want for another. Then we find that just having does not satisfy wanting.

| 1 | 2 | 3 | 4 | 5 | 6 | 7 | 8 | 9 | 10 |

Problem 3

words

CALUMINEX — 2

19-- *Representatives of the Year* — 9

Region	*Representatives*	*Sales*	
Eastern	Polly Murger	$ 357,214	20 / 26
Southern	Brent Ortega	542,168	32
Midwestern	Rick Hyatt	497,135	38
Western	Mika Shibasaki	568,900	44

69

69a ▶ 6
Preparatory practice

each line 3 times SS (slowly, faster, slowly); DS between 3-line groups; repeat selected lines as time permits

alphabet 1 I quickly explained the grave fire hazards of the job to two managers.

fig/sym 2 Order #7849-0 (date 3/16) must be shipped by May 25 to Spahn & Erven.

long words 3 Evaluators ordinarily acknowledge routine performance characteristics.

easy 4 Claudia may make a hand signal to this man with the auditory problems.

| 1 | 2 | 3 | 4 | 5 | 6 | 7 | 8 | 9 | 10 | 11 | 12 | 13 | 14 |

69b ▶ 10
Measure skill growth: straight copy

one 3' and one 5' writing; determine *gwam* for all writings

Difficulty index

all letters used	A	1.5 si	5.7 awl	80% hfw

gwam 3' | 5'

Almost everyone is conscious of a renewed concern about quality-- — 4 | 3
quality of life; of goods; and, yes, of people. Behind this concern, — 9 | 5
which borders on anxiety, lies a realization that we live in a world in — 14 | 8
which we must totally depend on other people to produce the items that — 19 | 11
are essential to our daily living. The quality of such production is, — 23 | 14
justifiably we believe, a matter of some importance to each of us. — 28 | 17

We expect superior workmanship in the goods and services we acquire — 32 | 19
from other people. However, we ought to realize that we are in a real — 37 | 22
sense those "other people." In theory at least, we produce as well as — 42 | 25
consume; and just as we expect excellence from others, we should be pre- — 47 | 28
pared to provide it for them. In an economy wherein people are mutually — 51 | 31
dependent, no one is exempt from making a best-possible contribution. — 56 | 34

The element of quality results from a mixture of skill, judgment, — 60 | 36
knowledge, and energy. These ingredients, however, blend well only — 65 | 39
in the presence of an important catalyst--pride. Pride is the attitude — 70 | 42
that places great value on doing the job, not just on getting the job — 74 | 45
done; the worth of the finished product is viewed in terms of the work — 79 | 47
put into it. The real return for quality work is a very personal one. — 84 | 50

gwam	3'	1	2	3	4	5
	5'	1		2		3

10a ▶ 8
Preparatory practice

each line twice SS
(slowly, then faster);
DS between 2-line
groups

Recall: TS between
lesson parts.

all reaches learned	1	Yes, Clive took a few quarts; Jan had six gallons.
shift keys	2	The Fortune Five will sing at our Lake Youth Hall.
v/y	3	Every year, I have given Yves five heavy old keys.
easy	4	Diane owns the oak shanty; she also owns the land.

`| 1 | 2 | 3 | 4 | 5 | 6 | 7 | 8 | 9 | 10 |`

10b ▶ 8
Reach for new goals

1 Take a 30–second (30″) writing on Line 4 of 10a above; determine *gwam* (total words typed × 2).

2 From the sentences at the right, choose one that will cause you to aim for 2–3 *gwam* more than your rate in Step 1. (30″ *gwam* for each sentence is shown in Column 2 at the right.)

3 Take two 30″ guided writings on the chosen sentence; try to reach the end of the line each time "Return" is called.

4 If you reach your goal in both 30″ writings, take two 30″ writings on the next sentence. (A total of eight 30″ writings will be given.)

5 Take another 30″ writing on Line 4 of 10a above; determine *gwam* (total words typed × 2).

Goal: An increase of *at least* 2 *gwam* from Step 1 to Step 5.

		words in line	gwam 30″	gwam 20″
1	Nan lent the auto to the girl.	6	12	18
2	Iris did throw a rock at the signs.	7	14	21
3	He did work with vigor to land the fish.	8	16	24
4	Hang the keys to the shanty on the oak chair.	9	18	27
5	The girls wish to visit the city to fix the signs.	10	20	30

`| 1 | 2 | 3 | 4 | 5 | 6 | 7 | 8 | 9 | 10 |`

10c ▶ 12
Learn new keyreaches: Z and M

Reach technique for z

Reach *down* with *left little* finger.

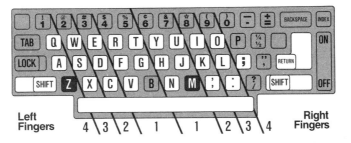

Left Fingers 4 \ 3 \ 2 \ 1 \ 1 \ 2 \ 3 \ 4 Right Fingers

Reach technique for m

Reach *down* with *right first* finger.

Follow the "Standard procedure for learning new keyreaches" on page 10 (Lines 1–4 twice; Lines 5–8 once; repeat 5–8 if time permits).

z	1	z za za az az zoo zoo zed zed jazz jazz lazy crazy
	2	za za haze doze zone cozy zany zing zinc size raze
m	3	m mj mj jam jam ham ham may may yam yam make makes
	4	mj am me ma man men made must fame dome fume major
z/m	5	Zack was amazed when Mazie came home from the zoo.
	6	Lazy Mr. Zym dozed at home in the dim haze of May.
all reaches learned	7	Craving quiet, Jeff mildly dozed; he awoke at six.
	8	Zed will move as quickly next June; why, I forget.

`| 1 | 2 | 3 | 4 | 5 | 6 | 7 | 8 | 9 | 10 |`

68b ▶ 14
Compose at the keyboard
Make all decisions about format.

1 Read carefully the report in 55c, page 102. Then, in a four- or five-line ¶, summarize what you believe to be the main thoughts of the report.

2 Proofread the ¶; make changes with proofreader's marks.

3 Type a final copy. Center a title over the ¶.

68c ▶ 30
Format tables

1 Make all decisions about the format of the two tables below, then type them.

2 Examine each of the tables carefully for correct placement and attractive appearance. Repeat the tables if they do not appear to you to be of high quality.

Guidelines for formatting a table

To format a table attractively, certain questions must be answered appropriately; as:

● Single or double spacing? Double spacing is more attractive and easier to read, but it may require more space than you have available.

● Full or half sheet? Consider how the table will be used and how much space is available. If more than 20 lines are required, use a full sheet.

● Reading position or exact center? Reading position is recommended for a full sheet, exact center for a half sheet.

● Number of intercolumn spaces? Backspace for columns. Then backspace once for each two spaces to be left between columns (leave an even number of spaces between columns). Be sure the body of the table will be wider than the table heading.

Problem 1
Notes:

For Column 3, set the tab for the longest number in the column; then backspace one space to type the dollar sign.

Many electronic typewriters and microcomputers have a decimal tab which automatically aligns copy at the decimal.

			words
THE ALGONQUIN CLUB			4
Operating Budget, 19--			8
Committee	Chairperson	Budget	19
Business Affairs	C. Villeneuve	$310.50	27
Conservation	D. Treece	95.00	33
Finance	A. Perez	8.50	37
International Relations	F. Heckman	85.00	46
Program	I. Breece	375.00	51
Projects	G. Muncey	500.00	56
Youth and Aging	E. Runyan	200.00	62

Problem 2

CALUMINEX			2
Branch Managers' Home Telephones			9
Manager	Branch	Number	14
Gertrude F. Schuyler	Albuquerque	505-821-0147	23
Albert C. Chung	Allentown	215-640-9226	31
Dale T. O'Hargran	Birmingham	413-468-7308	39
F. Samuel Montgomery	Denver	396-386-8469	48
Rose B. Shikamuru	Honolulu	808-104-5580	56
Myrle E. Bragg	New Haven	203-401-5691	63
Margret G. Bredeweg	St. Louis	314-575-3773	72
Trace J. Brecken	San Diego	714-757-4812	80
Jose J. Morales	San Juan	809-039-2934	87
Myrna Lee Targliff	Seattle	846-913-1055	95

Continue with Problem 3, page 126.

10d ▶ 12

**Learn new keyreaches:
B and P**

Reach technique for b

Reach *down* with *left first* finger.

Left Fingers 4 3 2 1   1 2 3 4   Right Fingers

Reach technique for p

Reach *up* with *right little* finger.

Follow the "Standard procedure for learning new keyreaches" on page 10 (Lines 1–4 twice; Lines 5–8 once; repeat 5–8 if time permits).

b 1 b bf bf by by fib fib fob fob bit bit jib jib buff
  2 bf by fib fob but rub job rib rob buy tub bid boff

                                                                    DS

p 3 ; p; p; pa pa pan pan pen pen pad pad pep pep paid
  4 up up; cup cup; sip sip; nap nap; map map; ape ape

b/p 5 Pepe bobbed for an apple; Bo jumped rope; I boxed.
    6 Pablo Paz paid Barb to probe deeply for old bulbs.

all reaches learned 7 Caleb sipped a cup of pink juice at the Boise Zoo.
        8 Five quiet zebus walk up; yet, Drex Marsh jogs on.

| 1 | 2 | 3 | 4 | 5 | 6 | 7 | 8 | 9 | 10 |

10e ▶ 10

Review keyboarding techniques

each line once SS; repeat as time permits

Lines 1-3: Keep wrists low; do not rest palms on machine.

Lines 4-6: Keep unused fingers in home–row position.

Lines 7-9: Move quickly and smoothly from letter to letter and word to word (no pauses).

Spacing review: Strike the space bar with a down–and–in motion of the thumb.

all letters 1 Alice is to speak for the group at the next forum.
       2 Dan joined the squad for spring drills last month.
       3 Denzyl took a short, fast hike; Bev went with him.
                                                                     DS

spacing and shifting 4 If it were up to me, I would go for the top prize.
          5 Vi, Don, and Jo have yet to win a set in the meet.
          6 Ask Dr. Su. She knows O. J.; she once taught him.

easy sentences 7 It is the duty of the firm to fix the eight signs.
        8 This land is held by the city to make into a park.
        9 If you wish to make a big profit, work with vigor.

| 1 | 2 | 3 | 4 | 5 | 6 | 7 | 8 | 9 | 10 |

**Format/type tables
with column headings**

Problem 1

full sheet; reading position; DS;
decide intercolumn spacing

		words
PRINCIPAL WORLD LANGUAGES		5
<u>Language</u>	<u>Millions</u>	12
Arabic	155	14
Bengali	151	16
English	397	19
French	107	21
German	119	23
Hindi	254	25
Japanese	119	28
Malay-Indonesian	115	32
Mandarin Chinese	726	36
Portuguese	151	39
Russian	274	42
Spanish	258	44

Problem 2

half sheet (insert long side first);
exact center; SS; decide inter–
column spacing

THE SPRINGARN MEDAL		4
Selected Winners		7
<u>Recipient</u>	<u>Year</u>	13
Ralph J. Bunche	1948	17
Jack Roosevelt Robinson	1955	22
Martin Luther King, Jr.	1956	28
Edward (Duke) Ellington	1958	33
Leontyne Price	1964	37
Sammy Davis, Jr.	1967	41
Henry Aaron	1974	44
Andrew Young	1977	48
Coleman Young	1980	51

68

68a ▶ 6

**Preparatory
practice**

each line 3 times SS
(work for fewer than
2 errors per group);
DS between 3-line
groups; repeat
selected lines as
time permits

alphabet 1 May the judge quiz the clerks from Iowa about extensive profit-taking?

figures 2 Flight 374 will leave at 10:46 a.m. and arrive in Buffalo at 9:58 p.m.

double letters 3 The school committee will do well to pass on all the Tennessee offers.

easy 4 It is a duty of the civic auditor to aid a city firm to make a profit.

| 1 | 2 | 3 | 4 | 5 | 6 | 7 | 8 | 9 | 10 | 11 | 12 | 13 | 14 |

11a ▶ 8

Preparatory practice

each line twice SS
(slowly, then faster);
DS between 2-line
groups

Recall: TS between
lesson parts.

all letters 1 Have Jeff Pim quickly walk the bridge zone at six.

z/p 2 Pat puzzled Zora; he played a happy piece of jazz.

m/b 3 Bob may remember he was a member of my brass band.

easy 4 The big map firm may make the usual profit for us.

| 1 | 2 | 3 | 4 | 5 | 6 | 7 | 8 | 9 | 10 |

11b ▶ 10

Practice difficult reaches

1 Practice each line once. Place a
check mark on your paper next to
lines that seem difficult for you.

2 Practice at least twice each line
that you checkmarked.

q 1 Quay made a quiet quip to quell a quarrel quickly.

x 2 Knox can relax; Alex gets a box of flax next week.

y 3 Ty Clay may envy you for any zany plays you write.

v 4 Eve and Vera drive the heavy vans every five days.

n 5 Nan danced many a dance, often with Nick and Donn.

| 1 | 2 | 3 | 4 | 5 | 6 | 7 | 6 | 7 | 8 | 9 | 10 |

11c ▶ 12

Learn new keyreaches:
: (colon) and ? (question mark)

Reach technique for : (colon)

Left shift and strike ; key;
space twice after : used
as punctuation.

Left
Fingers   4 \ 3 \ 2 \ 1 \ 1 \ 2 \ 3 \ 4   Right
Fingers

Reach technique
for ? (question)

Left shift; reach *down* with
right little finger;
space twice after ? at
end of sentence.

Follow the "Standard procedure
for learning new keyreaches" on
page 10 (Lines 1–4 twice; Lines
5–9 once; repeat 5–9 if time
permits).

Colon, Question mark:
Hold the left shift key down as
you strike ? and : keys. Except in
rare instances, they are followed
by 2 blank spaces.

: 1 ; :; :; : : To wit: Date: Name: Address: From:

2 Space twice after a colon, thus: To: No.: Time:
DS

? 3 ; ?; ?; ? ? Who? When? Where? Who is? Why not?

4 Did he go? Is she ill? Do I see it? Is it here?

:/? 5 Who is here? I see the following: Joe, Lee, Ray.

6 Have you a pen? Copy these two words: tier, rye.

7 When you are puzzled, ask yourself some questions;

all letters 8 for example: Do I have facts? Can I judge? What

9 options do I have? Who else may be of help to me?

| 1 | 2 | 3 | 4 | 5 | 6 | 7 | 8 | 9 | 10 |

67a ▶ 6
Preparatory practice

each line 3 times SS (work for fewer than 2 errors per group); DS between 3-line groups; repeat selected lines as time permits

alphabet	1	Julie began to study the six chapters on vitamins for her weekly quiz.
figures	2	I will send 2,795 of the 4,680 sets now and the remainder on the 13th.
one hand	3	I refereed only a few cases; I regarded waste water as a greater case.
easy	4	May I also fix the shape of the right hand and elbow of the clay form?

| 1 | 2 | 3 | 4 | 5 | 6 | 7 | 8 | 9 | 10 | 11 | 12 | 13 | 14 |

67b ▶ 12
Improve concentration

1 Type a copy of the ¶. Provide capitalization and terminal punctuation as needed.

2 Compare your typed copy with the ¶ in 63b, page 116. Correct errors.

3 Use the corrected copy for 1' writings as time permits.

Reminder

Type periods inside quotation marks.

Difficulty index

all letters used | A | 1.4 si | 5.4 awl | 80% hfw |

gwam 1'

each of us is quietly building a road that is to lead to some ulti-   13
mate place known as "success" we construct our highway in stages, pass-   28
ing from one objective to another, expecting eventually to reach our   42
goal--to be successful   but how shall we recognize success when we   56
reach it   what is success   when is a person successful   67

| 1 | 2 | 3 | 4 | 5 | 6 | 7 | 8 | 9 | 10 | 11 | 12 | 13 | 14 |

67c ▶ 10
Preapplication drill: center column headings

half sheet; DS; 10 spaces between columns

1 Read the information about centering column headings.

2 Type the drill below; center headings over the columns. Underline the headings.

Guides for centering columnar headings

• A column heading is typed a double space above a column centered over the longest item in the column.

a To determine the center point of the longest item in a column, space forward from the starting point of the column *once* for every *two* strokes or spaces in the longest item. Disregard a leftover stroke.

b The point where the forward spacing stops is the center point of the column. Backspace *once* for each *two* strokes in the heading; disregard a leftover stroke. Starting at the place where backspacing ended, type the heading.

• You may prefer to type column headings after you type the columns. After typing the table headings, space down to the approximate position for the first line of the table, leaving the column heading line vacant. After the columns have been typed, you may enter the column headings.

• If the column heading is longer than its column, use the heading as the longest item in the column for horizontal placement purposes. Then, center the column under the column heading.

Book	Author
Jane Eyre	Bronte
Oliver Twist	Dickens
The Great Gatsby	Fitzgerald
Showboat	Ferber

Key | The Great Gatsby | 10 | Fitzgerald |

11d ▶ 10
Learn to operate the tabulator mechanism

1 Clear all tab stops

1 Move carrier to extreme right (or carriage to extreme left).
2 Depress tab clear (29) and hold it down as you return carrier to extreme left (or move carriage to extreme right).

2 Set tab stops

Move the carrier (or carriage) to the desired position; then depress the tab set (26). Repeat this procedure for each stop needed.

3 Tabulate (tab)*

Tap lightly the tab key (30), using the nearer little finger; or bar, using the right index finger, and return the finger to home position at once.

* If you are using a nonelectric typewriter, refer to page 3 for tabulating technique.

1 Clear all tab stops as directed.
2 Beginning at the left margin, set 3 tab stops at 5–space intervals from the margin stop.
3 Practice the drill once DS as shown. Begin Line 1 at left margin; tab once for Line 2; twice for Line 3; 3 times for Line 4.

1 It is now time for me to learn to use the tab key.

2 <u>tab</u> once ➤ Every tab stop now set must first be cleared.

3 <u>tab</u> twice ➤ After that, I set tab stops that I need.

4 <u>tab</u> three times ➤ Then I touch the tab key to indent.

11e ▶ 10
Check keyboarding skill

1 Practice the two ¶s once DS. Try to type without looking up, especially at the end of lines.
2 Take two 1' writings on each ¶; determine *gwam*.

Goal: At least 14 *gwam*.

Difficulty index

all letters	E	1.2 si	5.1 awl	90% hfw

gwam 1'

¶ 1   Some people like their music fast; some of us   9

do not. Some people have a taste for certain food   19

that others abhor. Some like flying; some do not.   <u>29</u>

¶ 2   Just why we differ should be quite clear. We   9

set our own example. We try a thing, then we make   19

a choice. Decisions others make need not faze us.   29

| 1 | 2 | 3 | 4 | 5 | 6 | 7 | 8 | 9 | 10 |

Key to difficulty index of timed writings

E	= easy
LA	= low average difficulty
A	= average difficulty
si	= syllable intensity
awl	= average word length
hfw	= high–frequency words

To determine words-a-minute rate

1 Note the figure at the end of the last line of the writing that you completed.

2 For a partial line, note the figure on the scale directly below the point at which you stopped keyboarding.

3 Add these two figures to determine the total gross words a minute (*gwam*) you typed.

Format/type columns with main and secondary headings

Problem 1

full sheet; DS; reading position; 20–space intercolumn

A TS usually separates a main heading from a table; when a sec-ondary heading is used, DS after the main heading and TS after the secondary heading.

For columns with dollar signs, use the dollar sign only with the top figure and the total (when one is shown). Keystroke $ one space to the left of horizontal beginning point of the longest line in the col-umn. It should be typed again in the same position when a *total line* appears in the table.

words

CALUMINEX   ℓ
DS
Branch Office Sales for March   8
TS

		words
Albuquerque	$ 32,791	12
Allentown	47,781	16
Birmingham	60,898	19
Denver	4,558	22
Honolulu	8,432	25
New Haven	104,932	28
St. Louis	13,166	32
San Diego	89,005	35
San Juan	113,364	39
Seattle	21,539	43
	$496,466	45

Problem 2

full sheet; DS; reading position; 16–space intercolumn

SOUTH AMERICAN COUNTRIES   5

Approximate Area in Square Miles   12

		words
Argentina	1,072,067	16
Bolivia	424,162	19
Brazil	3,286,470	22
Chile	292,256	25
Colombia	439,512	28
Ecuador	105,685	31
Peru	496,222	34
Uruguay	72,172	37
Venezuela	352,143	40

Problem 3

1 Read the guidelines for deciding intercolumn spacing.

2 Repeat Problem 1. Use a half sheet; exact center; SS. Set a new width for the intercolumn.

Guides for deciding intercolumn spacing

These guidelines will help you decide on the number of spaces to use for inter-columns.

● The body of a table should be wider than its main and secondary headings.

● To center a table, backspace for columns first, intercolumns last.

● Backspace for intercolumns until an ap-propriate place for setting the left margin has been reached. Set the margin stop; space forward as usual.

12a ▶ 8
Preparatory practice
each line twice SS
(slowly, then faster);
DS between 2-line
groups

Recall: TS between
lesson parts.

alphabet	1	Biff was to give the major prize quickly to Dixon.
space bar	2	is it me of he an by do go to us if or so am ah el
shift keys	3	Pam was in Spain in May; Roy Bo met her in Madrid.
easy	4	He may sign the form with the name of the auditor.

| 1 | 2 | 3 | 4 | 5 | 6 | 7 | 8 | 9 | 10 |

12b ▶ 15
Develop keystroking technique

1 Practice each line 3
times SS; DS between
3-line groups; place a
check mark on your
paper next to each line
that was difficult for
you.
2 If time permits, repeat each line that was
difficult.

home row	1	Dallas sadly had a salad as Hal had a large steak.
bottom row	2	Can my cook, Mrs. Zockman, carve the big ox roast?
third row	3	The purple quilt is quite pretty where you put it.
1st/2d fingers	4	I took the main route by the river for five miles.
3d/4th fingers	5	Pam saw Roz wax an aqua auto as Lex sipped a cola.
double letters	6	Ann took some apples to school; Dee, a cherry pie.

| 1 | 2 | 3 | 4 | 5 | 6 | 7 | 8 | 9 | 10 |

12c ▶ 15
Reach for new goals

1 Take a 1' writing on Line 4
of 12a above; determine
gwam (total words typed).
2 From the second column
at the right (*gwam* 30"),
choose a goal that will cause
you to aim for 2–3 *gwam*
more than your rate in Step 1.
Note the sentence that accompanies that goal.
3 Take two 1' writings on
the chosen sentence; try
to reach the end of the
line each time "Return" is
called (each 30").

4 If you reach your goal on both 1'
writings, take two 1' writings on
the next sentence. (A total of eight
1' writings will be given.)

5 Take another 1' writing on Line 4
of 12a above; determine *gwam*
(total words typed).

Goals:
12–14 *gwam*, acceptable
15–17 *gwam*, good
18–20 *gwam*, very good
21+ *gwam*, excellent

		words in line	gwam 30"	gwam 20"
1	I paid for six bushels of rye.	6	12	18
2	Risk a penalty; this is a big down.	7	14	21
3	Did their form entitle them to the land?	8	16	24
4	Did the men in the field signal for us to go?	9	18	27
5	Did she enamel a sign on the auto body with a pen?	10	20	30
6	The ivory emblem is on a shelf in the town chapel.	10	20	30

| 1 | 2 | 3 | 4 | 5 | 6 | 7 | 8 | 9 | 10 |

12d ▶ 12
Check/develop keyboarding continuity

1 Clear tab stops; set a tab for
5-space ¶ indention.
2 Practice ¶ 1 once DS for orientation.
3 Take two 1' writings on ¶1; determine *gwam* on each writing.
4 Use ¶ 2 as directed in Steps 2
and 3.
Goal: At least 14 *gwam*.

Difficulty index
| all letters | E | 1.2 si | 5.1 awl | 90% hfw |

gwam 1'

¶ 1   What is time? Time is the standard needed to 9
fix in sequence each event that makes up the whole 19
fabric of this effort that we like to call living. 29

¶ 2   Time, we realize, means constant pressure for 9
each of us; it must be used. Our minutes are just 19
tiny sums in a book of account. We are the total. 29

| 1 | 2 | 3 | 4 | 5 | 6 | 7 | 8 | 9 | 10 |

65c, continued

Problem 2

half sheet (enter long side first); SS; exact center; 14–space inter–column; SS the heading

		words
TIME DIFFERENCES AT NOON		5
EASTERN STANDARD TIME		9
Albuquerque	10:00 a.m.	14
Allentown	12:00 noon	18
Birmingham	11:00 a.m.	23
Denver	10:00 a.m.	26
Honolulu	7:00 a.m.	30
New Haven	12:00 noon	34
St. Louis	11:00 a.m.	38
San Diego	9:00 a.m.	42
San Juan	12:00 noon	46
Seattle	9:00 a.m.	50

Key |*Albuquerque* | *14* | *10:00 a.m.* |

Problem 3

half sheet (enter long side first); DS; exact center; 12–space inter–column

To align a column of words at the right (as in the second column), backspace as usual to set left margin. When spacing forward, set the tab at the end of the sec–ond column rather than at the be–ginning; backspace once for each character in the second column to position for keyboarding.

		words
PROPOSED BANQUET AGENDA		5
	Tab stop	
Preliminary remarks	Ellen Prater	11
Introductions	Grant Dubin	17
Speaker	Rosalyn Booth	21
Commentary	Drake Eppingham	26
Closing remarks	Ellen Prater	32

Key |*Preliminary remarks* | *12* | *Drake Eppingham* |

66a ▶ 6

Preparatory practice

each line 3 times SS (work for fewer than 2 errors per group); DS between 3-line groups; repeat selected lines as time permits

alphabet	1	Qualified judges will have to analyze our club performances next week.
fig/sym	2	The 7 1/2% interest of $18.68 on my $249.05 note (dated May 3) is due.
1st row	3	Can this excited man, Mr. Zinc, visit the monument to an Indian brave?
easy	4	If he burns the sign, the odor of the enamel may form a toxic problem.

| 1 | 2 | 3 | 4 | 5 | 6 | 7 | 8 | 9 | 10 | 11 | 12 | 13 | 14 |

66b ▶ 14

Compose at the keyboard

Make all decisions about format.

1 Assume that you have agreed to run for president of the student body at your col-lege. Compose a four– or five–line paragraph in which you set forth some of the changes you would attempt to inaugurate.

2 Proofread the ¶; make changes with proofreader's marks.

3 Type a final copy. Center the title **MY PLATFORM.**

66

13

Learning goals

1 To achieve smoother keystroking.

2 To improve use of special machine parts.

3 To develop a relaxed, confident attitude.

4 To increase keystroking speed.

Machine adjustments

1 Set paper guide at 0.

2 Set ribbon control to type on upper half of ribbon.

3 Set left margin for a 50–space line (center point – 25); move right stop to end of scale.

4 Single–space (SS) drills; double–space (DS) paragraphs (¶).

13a ▶ 8
Preparatory practice

each line twice SS (slowly, then faster); DS between 2-line groups

Recall: TS between lesson parts.

alphabet	1	Jacques Lopez might fix the wrecked navy tugboats.
z	2	Liz drove hazardous, zigzag Zaire roads with zeal.
y	3	Kay said you should stay with Mary for sixty days.
easy	4	Their form may entitle a visitor to fish the lake.

| 1 | 2 | 3 | 4 | 5 | 6 | 7 | 8 | 9 | 10 |

13b ▶ 12
Develop keyboarding technique

once as shown; repeat if time permits

Lines 1-2: Reach with fingers; keep hand movement to a mini–mum.

Lines 3-4: Curve fingers over home row.

Lines 5-6: Reach fingers to third–row keys without moving hands.

bottom row	1	Did Cam, the cabby, have extra puzzles? Yes, one.
	2	Do they, Mr. Zack, expect a number of brave women?
home row	3	Gayla Halls had a sale; Jake had a sale last fall.
	4	Gladys had half a flask of soda; Josh had a salad.
third row	5	There were two or three quiet people at our party.
	6	Trudy Perry quietly sewed the four pretty dresses.

| 1 | 2 | 3 | 4 | 5 | 6 | 7 | 8 | 9 | 10 |

13c ▶ 8
Practice difficult reaches

1 Each line once; checkmark any line that you do not keystroke fluently.

2 Repeat each checkmarked line as time permits.

Technique hint:
Work for smoothness and continuity.

v	1	Eva visited every vivid event for twelve evenings.
m	2	A drummer drummed for a moment, and Mimi came out.
p	3	Pat appears happy to pay for any supper I prepare.
x	4	Tex Cox waxed the next box for Xenia and Rex Knox.
b	5	My rubber boat bobbed about in the bubbling brook.

| 1 | 2 | 3 | 4 | 5 | 6 | 7 | 8 | 9 | 10 |

65a ▶ 6
Preparatory practice

each line 3 times SS (work for fewer than 2 errors per group); DS between 3-line groups; repeat selected lines as time permits

alphabet 1 The king and queen brought dozens of expensive jewels from the colony.

fig/sym 2 Check #4690 for $1,375, dated February 28, was sent to O'Neill & Sons.

adjacent reaches 3 As Louise Liu said, few questioned the points asserted by the porters.

easy 4 He may fish for a quantity of smelt; he may wish for aid to land them.

| 1 | 2 | 3 | 4 | 5 | 6 | 7 | 8 | 9 | 10 | 11 | 12 | 13 | 14 |

65b ▶ 9
Preapplication drill: realigning/aligning items

twice as shown DS; 14-space intercolumn

Realigning items at the left
After setting the left margin as usual, adjust it to the right (in this instance 3 spaces) to accommodate the most common line setting. Use the margin release and backspacer for longer lines.

Aligning items at the right
Since spacing forward and backward will be needed to align items at the right, adjust the tab setting for the item length that requires the least forward and backward spacing.

District 9   tab 27

Reset margin ——▶ Almont

Belden   Backspace once ——▶ 150

District 10

Erie   85

Lamberg   Space forward once ——▶ 9

District 11

Orville   46

Racine   9

Key | District 10 | 14 | 150 |

65c ▶ 35
Format/type tables: realign/align columns

Problem 1

full sheet; DS; reading position; 20–space intercolumn (see p. 46 to review reading position, if necessary)

Continue with Problem 2, page 121.

ALLOCATION OF MICROCOMPUTERS

		words
		6
Eastern Region		12
Allentown	51	14
New Haven	112	17
Southern Region		24
Birmingham	65	29
San Juan	121	31
Midwestern Region		38
St. Louis	14	41
Denver	7	43
Western Region		49
Albuquerque	35	52
Honolulu	9	54
San Diego	115	57
Seattle	25	59

Key | Midwestern Region | 20 | 112 |

13d ▶ 10
Control machine parts

once as shown; repeat if time permits

Lines 1-3: From left margin, set two tab stops at 20–space intervals; tab for second and third sentences in each line.

Lines 4-6: Use space bar with down–and–in motion; space correctly after punctuation marks.

Lines 7-8: Use shift–type–release motions.

tab/return	1 Why not us?	Did she ask?	Is it not?
	2 Who was it?	Will he bid?	Why is it?
	3 Can he see?	Is she well?	Was it he?

space bar
4 an any many am ham them by buy bouy ha ah bah bath
5 to buy | for any | the man | did both | by them | the theory
6 I went; Bo did, too. Is it true? To: Ms. Dudley

shift keys
7 Sofie Lamas visits Al and Mae in Denver, Colorado.
8 Tony lives on Elm Court; he works for K. L. Hains.

| 1 | 2 | 3 | 4 | 5 | 6 | 7 | 8 | 9 | 10 |

13e ▶ 12
Develop keyboarding continuity

1 Clear tab stops; set tab stop for 5–space indention.

2 Practice each ¶ once as shown for orientation.

3 Take three 1' writings on each ¶.

Goal: At least 16 *gwam*.

> **Technique hint:**
> Work for smooth, continuous typing, not for high speed.

Difficulty index

| all letters used | E | 1.2 si | 5.1 awl | 90% hfw |

gwam 1'

¶ 1   If we exert great efforts to do something, it   9
could be true that our effort will bring us higher   19
quality returns to match the work that we put out.   29

¶ 2   Is zeal worth the cost? Some people say that   9
maximum efforts will pay off in real results; even   19
others say the joy of hard work is its own reward.   29

| 1 | 2 | 3 | 4 | 5 | 6 | 7 | 8 | 9 | 10 |

14

14a ▶ 8
Preparatory practice

each line twice SS (slowly, then faster); DS between 2-line groups

alphabet 1 Kim Janby gave six prizes to qualified white cats.
shift keys 2 Jay Nadler, a Rotary Club member, wrote Mr. Coles.
y 3 Why do you say that today, Thursday, is my payday?
easy 4 Did the girl also fix the cowl of the formal gown?

| 1 | 2 | 3 | 4 | 5 | 6 | 7 | 8 | 9 | 10 |

			words
CALUMINEX BOARD OF DIRECTORS			6

Margin stop →   Tab stop   TS

Muriel E. Bouhm	President	11
R. Grady Atgood	Vice President	17
Alonzo J. Cruz, Sr.	Secretary	23
Carolyn Lynn Carvere	Treasurer	29
Myron A. Moilion	Member	34
Sara Harley Beck	Member	39

Key | *Carolyn Lynn Carvere* | *10* | *Vice President* |

64c, continued

Center the tables vertically and horizontally on half sheets.

Problem 1

Study the information on page 118 and the illustration above; then format and type the illustrated problem on a half sheet (insert long side first); SS; exact center; 10–space intercolumn.

Problem 2

Format/type the illustrated problem again. Use the same directions as for Problem 1, but change SS to DS.

Problem 3

Format/type the problem at the right on a half sheet (insert long side first); SS; exact center; 14–space intercolumn.

		words
CALUMINEX BRANCH MANAGERS		5
TS		
Gertrude F. Schuyler	Albuquerque	12
Albert C. Chung	Allentown	17
Dale T. O'Hargran	Birmingham	23
F. Samuel Montgomery	Denver	28
Rose B. Shikamuru	Honolulu	34
Myrle E. Bragg	New Haven	39
Margret G. Bredeweg	St. Louis	45
Trace J. Brecken	San Diego	50
Jose J. Morales	San Juan	55
Myrna Lee Targliff	Seattle	60

Key | *Gertrude F. Schuyler* | *14* | *Albuquerque* |

14b ▶ 9
Improve response patterns

once as shown; then re-peat

Lines 1-2: *Say* and type each word as a unit.

Lines 3-4: Spell each word as you type it; work at a steady pace.

Lines 5-6: *Say* and type short, easy words as units; spell and type longer words letter by letter.

word response
1 he of to if ah or by do so am is go us it an me ox
2 The corps may pay for the land when they visit us.

stroke response
3 was pop saw ink art oil gas kin are hip read lymph
4 Sara erected extra seats; Jimmy sat in only a few.

combination response
5 is best | an area | to pump | to join | an acre | he read it
6 My act forms a base for a tax case with the state.

| 1 | 2 | 3 | 4 | 5 | 6 | 7 | 8 | 9 | 10 |

14c ▶ 9
Control machine parts

once as shown; repeat if time permits

Lines 1-4: Clear tabs; set tab at center point. Tab where indicated.

Line 5: Use correct spacing after each punctuation mark.

Line 6: Depress shift key firmly; avoid pauses.

tab and return
1 ——————tab——————►Can you work the parts of
2 your machine?————tab——►Can you work them without
3 looking at them?———tab—►Do you trust your fingers
4 to do the work you have taught them to do?

space bar
5 We did. Was it here? I saw it; Lois saw it, too.

shift keys
6 Jena visited Washington, D.C., to see Kay and Pat.

| 1 | 2 | 3 | 4 | 5 | 6 | 7 | 8 | 9 | 10 |

14d ▶ 10
Improve keyboarding technique

1 Once as shown; checkmark each line that you do not keystroke fluently.

2 Repeat any line that caused you difficulty.

adjacent reaches
1 Bert read where she could stop to buy gas and oil.
2 We three are a trio to join the Yun Oil operation.

direct reaches
3 My uncle and my brother have run many great races.
4 Grace Nurva hunted my canyon for unique specimens.

double letters
5 Jeanne took a day off to see a book show in Hobbs.
6 Jerry has planned a small party for all the troop.

| 1 | 2 | 3 | 4 | 5 | 6 | 7 | 8 | 9 | 10 |

14e ▶ 14
Reach for new goals

1 Take a 1' writing on Line 2 of 14b above; determine *gwam* (total words typed).

2 From the second column at the right (*gwam* 30"), choose a goal that will cause you to aim for 2–3 *gwam* more than your rate in Step 1. Note the sentence that accompanies that goal.

3 Take two 1' writings on the chosen sentence; try to reach the end of the line each time "Return" is called (each 30").

4 If you reach your goal on either 1' writing, take two 1' writings on the next sen-tence. (A total of eight 1' writings will be given.)

5 Take another 1' writing on Line 2 of 14b above; de-termine *gwam* (total words typed).

Goals:
13–15 *gwam*, acceptable
16–18 *gwam*, good
19–21 *gwam*, very good
22+ *gwam*, excellent

	words in line	gwam 30"	gwam 20"
1 The six girls work with vigor.	6	12	18
2 He got the right title to the land.	7	14	21
3 He works a field of corn and rye for us.	8	16	24
4 Row to the big island at the end of the lake.	9	18	27
5 They do their duty when they turn the dials right.	10	20	30

| 1 | 2 | 3 | 4 | 5 | 6 | 7 | 8 | 9 | 10 |

64a ▶ 6
Preparatory practice

each line 3 times SS (work for fewer than 2 errors per group); DS between 3-line groups; repeat selected lines as time permits

alphabet	1	The wizard quickly converted six pert frogs into small bags of jewels.
figures	2	In 1980, their company had 64 drivers; in 1983, 273; and in 1985, 310.
direct reaches	3	Bryce obtained many junk pieces dumped by Marvyn at my service center.
easy	4	Viviana, hand me the element so I may fix the problems with the robot.

| 1 | 2 | 3 | 4 | 5 | 6 | 7 | 8 | 9 | 10 | 11 | 12 | 13 | 14 |

64b ▶ 9
Preapplication drill: tabulation

1 Clear all tab stops. Set a tab stop at center point.

2 Type the drill 3 times as shown SS; DS between drills. Keep your eyes on the book while you keyboard.

———————————— tab ——▶ Centering columns is not a totally

new procedure to you.———— tab ——▶ Center the line for columns as you

center a continuous line.———— tab ——▶ Backspace for blank spaces just as

for typed characters.———— tab ——▶ Backspace for the whole line, then

set the left margin stop.———— tab ——▶ Backspace one for two; set margin;

space forward one for one.——— tab ——▶ Set tab stops as needed.

64c ▶ 35
Center tables

3 half sheets

Guidelines for centering columns horizontally

1 Take preparatory steps

a Move margin stops to ends of scale. Clear all tabulator stops.

b Move carrier (carriage) to center point.

c If spacing is not given, esti–mate spacing for intercolumns (the area between columns)—preferably an even number of spaces (4, 6, 8, 10, or 12, for example).

2 To set left margin stop

Check the longest item in each column. Then from the center point, backspace *once* for each *2* characters and spaces in the longest items in each column then for each 2 spaces to be allowed for the inter-columns. Set the left margin stop at this point.

If the longest item in one column has an extra character, combine the extra character with the first letter in the next column. If one stroke is left over after back-spacing for all columnar items, disregard it.

Study the illustration below used to center two items and a 10-space intercolumn for the first table on p. 119.

3 To set tabulator stops

After setting the left margin stop, space forward once for each character in the longest item in the first column, then for each space to be allowed for the first intercolumn. Set tab stop at this point. Follow this procedure for each sub-sequent column and inter-column.

backspace once for each two characters ——▶ | Ca | ro | ly | n | Ly | nn | C | ar | ve | re | Vi | ce | P | re | si | de | nt | 1-2 | 3-4 | 5-6 | 7-8 | 9-10 |

15a ▶ 8
Preparatory practice

each line twice SS (slowly, then faster); DS between 2-line groups

alphabet	1	Max Jewel picked up five history quizzes to begin.
space bar	2	Did she say she may copy the form in a day or two?
z	3	Liz Zahl saw Zoe feed the zebra in an Arizona zoo.
easy	4	They risk a penalty if he signs their usual forms.

| 1 | 2 | 3 | 4 | 5 | 6 | 7 | 8 | 9 | 10 |

15b ▶ 14
Improve response patterns

1 Once as shown; checkmark three most difficult lines.

2 Repeat the lines you checked as difficult.

3 Take a 1' writing on Line 2, next on Line 4, and then on Line 6. Determine *gwam* on each writing.

word response	1	with they them make than when also work such right
	2	Diana did key work for the city dock for half pay.
stroke response	3	were only date upon ever join fact milk care nylon
	4	Milo acted on only a few tax rebate cases in July.
combination response	5	with were they only them upon than ever when plump
	6	Julio paid the tax on six acres of rich lake land.

| 1 | 2 | 3 | 4 | 5 | 6 | 7 | 8 | 9 | 10 |

15c ▶ 14
Reach for new goals

1 Using your best rate in 15b as a base, choose from the sentences at the right one that will raise your goal by 2–3 *gwam*.

2 Beginning with that sentence, take a series of 1' writings as directed in 14e, page 31.

Goals:

13–15 *gwam*, acceptable
16–18 *gwam*, good
19–21 *gwam*, very good
22+ *gwam*, excellent

		words in line	gwam 30"	gwam 20"
1	This is an authentic ivory antique.	7	14	21
2	Did the cowhand dismantle the worn auto?	8	16	24
3	Is the body of the ancient dirigible visible?	9	18	27
4	If they wish, she may make the form for the disks.	10	20	30
5	Did they mend the torn right half of their ensign?	10	20	30

| 1 | 2 | 3 | 4 | 5 | 6 | 7 | 8 | 9 | 10 |

15d ▶ 14
Check/develop keyboarding continuity

1 Clear tab stops; set a tab for 5–space ¶ indention.

2 Practice ¶1 once DS for orientation.

3 Take two 1' writings on ¶1; determine *gwam* on each writing.

4 Use ¶2 as directed in Steps 2 and 3.

Goal: At least 15 *gwam*.

Technique hints:
Keep the carrier moving at a fairly steady pace. Avoid looking up, especially at line endings.

Difficulty index

all letters used	E	1.2 si	5.1 awl	90% hfw		gwam 1'

¶1 To learn to keyboard requires that you simply 9
allow the skill to form day by day. You may often 19
be concerned as a result of doubt that the fingers 29
will do just what you have been told they will do. 39

¶2 So the secret is revealed. Typing is not the 9
hard job it once may have seemed. Now you realize 19
that what you must do is simply relax and read the 29
copy carefully; your hands should do all the rest. 39

| 1 | 2 | 3 | 4 | 5 | 6 | 7 | 8 | 9 | 10 |

63c, continued

Problem 1

Use a half sheet (insert long side first). Center the problem vertically; center each line horizontally; DS.

words

ARS MUSICA	2
under the direction of Serge Chomentikov	10
will present its	14
Annual Spring Concert	18
Friday evening, April 24, at eight o'clock	27
Taer Recital Hall	30

Problem 2

Follow directions given for Problem 1. The left margin will not be even, as shown.

Dr. Grace G. Gregory	4
announces the relocation of her	11
dental practice	14
to the Professional Arts Building	21
2300 Plymouth Avenue	25
541-8500	27
Effective August 1	30

Problem 3

Follow directions given for Problem 1.

Ambassador and Mrs. Jorge Samoya	7
request the honor of your presence	14
at dinner	16
Wednesday, October 15, at seven	22
1424 Hemlock Road	26
R. S. V. P.	28

Learning goals

1 To learn figure keyreaches.
2 To proofread/revise copy.
3 To type statistical copy.
4 To type handwritten copy.
5 To improve stroking continuity.

Machine adjustments

1 Set paper edge guide at 0.
2 Set ribbon control to type on upper half of ribbon.
3 Set left margin for a 50–space line (center point − 25); move right stop to end of scale.
4 SS drills; DS paragraphs.

16a ▶ 7

Preparatory practice

each line twice SS (slowly, then faster); DS between 2-line groups; repeat selected lines if time permits

alphabet	1	We got six quaint bronze cups from heavy old junk.
q/?	2	Did Marq Quin go? Did Quent Quin go? Did Quincy?
z/:	3	To: Zane Mozel, Tempe, AZ From: Ezra A. Lazzaro
easy	4	She may do the work when she signs the right form.

| 1 | 2 | 3 | 4 | 5 | 6 | 7 | 8 | 9 | 10 |

16b ▶ 16

Learn new keyreaches: 3 7 1

Follow the "Standard procedure for learning new keyreaches" on page 10 (Lines 1–6 twice; Lines 7–10 once; repeat 7–10 if time permits).

Under certain circumstances, the small letter l can be used to type the figure 1. Your instructor will tell you which reach to use for daily work.

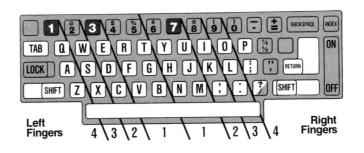

Left Fingers   4 3 2 1   1 2 3 4   Right Fingers

Reach technique for 3

Reach *up* with *left second* finger.

Reach technique for 7

Reach *up* with *right first* finger.

Reach technique for 1

Reach *up* with *left little* finger.

NOTES ON ABBREVIATIONS

Space once after a period (.) following an initial. Abbreviations such as M.D., B.C., Ph.D., U.S., N.Y., C.O.D., a.m., and p.m. may be typed solid (without internal spacing).

Abbreviations such as mph, rpm, and mg are usually expressed without caps, periods, or internal spacing.

Abbreviations such as ERA, AMA, and TVA are typed in ALL CAPS (without internal spacing).

3	1	d 3d 3d 3 3; 3 did, 3 days, 3 deals, 3 dozen, 3 33
	2	The 33 girls and 3 boys met at 3 p.m. near Gate 3.
7	3	j 7j 7j 7 7; 7 jobs, 7 jets, 7 jacks, 7 jeeps, 7 7
	4	She wrote 7, 7, 7, not 777. She wrote it 7 times.
1	5	a la la l l lla; l arm, l aide, l awl, ll ayes, ll
	6	He bought ll tons of No. l coal on May l at l p.m.
3/7/1	7	Page 371 of Volume 31 states the date as 1737 B.C.
	8	Flight 173, a 737 jet, left on May 31 at 1:31 p.m.
all figures learned	9	Only 3 of the 7 cars clock 71 to 73 mph or better.
	10	Read pages 7, 17, and 37; copy Lines 3, 7, and 31.

| 1 | 2 | 3 | 4 | 5 | 6 | 7 | 8 | 9 | 10 |

Learning goals

1 To type tables in exact center and in reading position.
2 To type main, secondary, and column headings.
3 To align figures, decimals, and dollar signs in columns.
4 To center announcements horizontally and vertically.

Machine adjustments

1 Set paper guide at 0; remove tab stops.
2 Set ribbon control to type on upper half of ribbon.
3 Use a 70–space line.
4 SS drills; DS paragraphs.

63a ▶ 6
Preparatory practice

each line 3 times SS (work for fewer than 2 errors per group); DS between 3-line groups; repeat selected lines as time permits

alphabet 1 Jack may provide a few extra quiz questions or problems for the group.

figures 2 We can try to add these fractions: 2/3, 3/4, 4/5, 5/6, 7/8, and 9/10.

shift/lock 3 THE LAKES TODAY, published in Dayton, Ohio, is issued in June or July.

easy 4 Enrique may fish for cod by the city docks, but he may risk a penalty.

| 1 | 2 | 3 | 4 | 5 | 6 | 7 | 8 | 9 | 10 | 11 | 12 | 13 | 14 |

63b ▶ 16
Compose at the keyboard

Make all format decisions.
1 Read the ¶ thoughtfully.
2 Compose a second ¶ of five or six lines in which you express your ideas about success. Begin with the word **Personally**.
3 Proofread your ¶.
4 Type a final copy of both ¶s. Center a title over the ¶s.

Each of us is building a road that is to lead to some ultimate place known as "success." We construct our highway in stages, passing from one objective to another, expecting in time to reach our goal--to be successful. But how shall we recognize success when we reach it? What is success? When is a person successful?

Personally, (Compose the remainder of the second paragraph.)

63c ▶ 28
Format/type centered announcements

3 half sheets

Review centering procedures shown at the right, then type the three announcements on page 117.

Vertical centering

1 Count the lines to be centered.
2 Subtract counted lines from total lines available (66 for a full sheet and 33 for a half sheet).
3 Divide the remaining lines by 2 and distribute these lines as top and bottom margins. Ignore fractions.
4 Space down from the top edge of the paper 1 more line than the number of lines figured for the top margin.

Horizontal centering

1 Move margin stops to ends of the scale.
2 Clear all tab stops.
3 From the center point, backspace *once* for each 2 letters, figures, spaces, or punctuation marks in the line to be centered. Do not backspace for a leftover stroke at the end of a line.
4 Begin to keyboard where you complete the backspacing. If all lines are of the same length, set a margin stop; if not, repeat Steps 3 and 4 for each subsequent line.

16c ▶ 12
Reach for new goals

Follow the directions given for 12c on page 28. Use Line 4 of 16a to determine beginning and ending *gwam*.

Goals:

12–14 *gwam*, acceptable
15–17 *gwam*, good
18–19 *gwam*, very good
20+   *gwam*, excellent

all figures learned

		words in line	gwam 30"	gwam 20"
1	Did the girl hang the 37 maps?	6	12	18
2	She paid Jane to turn the 71 dials.	7	14	21
3	I got 73 burlap panels to make the form.	8	16	24
4	Kent kept 17 worn keys to work the 17 panels.	9	18	27
5	Did they augment the 371 bushels of corn with rye?	10	20	30
6	I did visit a neighbor at 1737 Iris Lane on May 7.	10	20	30
7	Dismantle the 37 chairs in the shanty at 173 Palm.	10	20	30

| 1 | 2 | 3 | 4 | 5 | 6 | 7 | 8 | 9 | 10 |

16d ▶ 7
Improve figure response patterns

each line once DS; repeat Lines 2, 4, and 6

Technique hint:
Control your reading speed. Read only slightly ahead of what you are typing.

all figures learned

1 Flight 371 left Miami at 3:17 on Monday, March 31.

2 *Bill 731 was for 71 boxes of No. 33 bailing brads.*

3 Rico counted 3,711 cartons containing 7,317 tools.

4 *Send Nan 731 No. 3 nails for her home at 771 Anne.*

5 On May 31, Eva drove 373 miles to Denver in Van 7.

6 *Max put 71 extra boxes in the annex at 3731 Parks.*

16e ▶ 8
Improve keystroking technique

once as shown; repeat if time permits

all letters used

1st finger
1 Bob Mugho hunted for five minutes for your number.
2 Juan hit the bright green turf with his five iron.

2d finger
3 Kind, decent acts can decidedly reduce skepticism.
4 Kim, not Mickey, had rice with chicken for dinner.

3d/4th fingers
5 You will write quickly: Zeus, Apollo, and Xerxes.
6 Who saw Polly? Max Voe saw her; she is quiet now.

| 1 | 2 | 3 | 4 | 5 | 6 | 7 | 8 | 9 | 10 |

17

17a ▶ 7
Preparatory practice

each line twice SS (slowly, then faster); DS between 2-line groups; repeat selected lines if time permits

alphabet
1 Roz Groves just now packed my box with five quail.

b
2 Barb, not Bob, will buy the new bonds at the bank.

figures
3 Try Model 3717 with 7 panels or Model 1733 with 3.

easy
4 Their problems may end when they audit the profit.

| 1 | 2 | 3 | 4 | 5 | 6 | 7 | 8 | 9 | 10 |

62c ▶ 16
Review/improve communication skills: spelling

full sheet, DS, 1½" top margin; 70-space line

1 Clear tab stops; set two new tab stops, one 28 spaces from left margin and one 56 spaces from left margin.

2 Type the first word at left margin; tab and type the word again; then tab and type it a third time—this time, do not look at the word in the book or on the paper.

3 Repeat this procedure for each word on the list.

4 Study your completed copy; correct errors.

SPELLING DEMONS

			words 3
accommodate	accommodate	accommodate	10
acknowledgment			19
argument			25
congratulate			33
conscience			39
description			46
eligible			52
grammar			57
irresistible			64
license			69
miscellaneous			78
pamphlet			83
questionnaire			91
ridiculous			98
similar			103
usable			107
whether			112

62d ▶ 18
Proofread/revise as you keyboard

full sheet

1 Use the copy at the right as the body for a personal letter. (See page 58 if needed.)

2 Make changes as marked and those needed changes that have not been marked. Proofread carefully.

3 Incorporate the additional information below.

Return address:
485 Burgundy Drive
Flint, MI 48506-4789
Date: **January 15, 19—**
Letter address:
Mr. Guy Baggett
1845 Berent Street
Flint, MI 48529-2973
Salutation: **Dear Guy**
Complimentary close: **Cordially**
Signer: **Terri Vreede**

opening lines 25

¶ Congradulations on your superb talk. The fact you gave us 37

from the Ph. D. questionnaire were not at all similar to those 49

we heard last year. You make an interesting Argument that 61

both women and men should must be eligible for the jobs that you 73

describe. it is ridiculous to beleive otherwise, and people 85

of good conscience will find your logic irrefutable. ¶A pam- 97

phlet about the research would be very useable, beleive me. 109

Would you consider publishing sucha pamphlet? If so, may I 121

help? Would it be advantageous to work for us in the office 133

in my basement? or in Buell Hall? or in your study at home? 146

I wonder if Mrs. Shewerr would help us with grammer and punc- 158

tuation. ¶Let me hear from you soon, Guy. 166

closing line 168

17b ▶ 16
Learn new keyreaches: 8 4 0

Follow the "Standard procedure for learning new keyreaches" on page 10 (Lines 1–6 twice; Lines 7–10 once; repeat 7–10 if time permits).

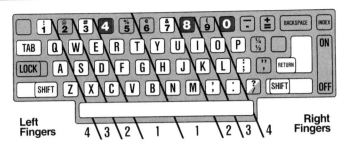

Left Fingers 4 3 2 1 1 2 3 4 Right Fingers

Reach technique for 8
Reach *up* with *right second* finger.

Reach technique for 4
Reach *up* with *left first* finger.

Reach technique for 0
Reach *up* with *right little* finger.

Note: Capitalize nouns that are identified by a number except for certain ones such as *page* and *verse* with*in* a sentence.

8	1	k 8k 8k 8 8; 88 keys, 8 kegs, 8 kits, 888 kwh, 8 8
	2	I took 8 keys to lock 8 kits in Truck 8 on Dock 8.
4	3	f 4f 4f 4 4; 4 fans, 4 fobs, 44 folk, 4 forks, 4 4
	4	Tour 44 leaves at 4 p.m. to see 4 bays in 4 lakes.
0	5	; 0; 0; 0 0; 30 paid, 70 posts, 30 pages, 10 plays
	6	Send 30 palms to 30730 East 30th Street on May 30.
8/4/0	7	Page 10 of the program listed 48, not 84, members.
	8	In 1840, the 84 men and 80 women walked to Toledo.
all figures learned	9	On June 30, we sent Check 184 to pay Invoice 7403.
	10	In 1830, 14 feet of snow fell; in 1831, almost 18.

| 1 | 2 | 3 | 4 | 5 | 6 | 7 | 8 | 9 | 10 |

17c ▶ 7
Improve figure response patterns

each line once DS; repeat Lines 2, 4, and 6

all figures learned

1 I live at 418 East Street, not at 418 Easy Street.
2 *Memorize pages 137 to 148; omit pages 140 and 141.*
3 Tours 478 and 4781 travel to 10 cities in 30 days.
4 *Cy will be 18 on May 30; Jo, 17 on May 4 or May 7.*
5 English 348 meets in Room 710 at 10 a.m. each day.
6 *Memo 7481 says 7 pads and 8 pens were sent May 30.*

17d ▶ 8
Improve keystroking technique

each line twice SS; DS between 3-line groups; repeat if time permits

adjacent reaches	1	Teresa knew well that her opinion of art was good.
direct reaches	2	Herb Brice must hunt for my checks; he is in debt.
double letters	3	Anne stopped off at school to see Bill Wiggs cook.
long words	4	Debate concerned parochialism versus universalism.

| 1 | 2 | 3 | 4 | 5 | 6 | 7 | 8 | 9 | 10 |

61c ▶ 10
Measure straight-copy skill

two 3' writings; proofread; determine *gwam*; circle errors

Difficulty index

all letters used | A | 1.5 si | 5.7 awl | 80% hfw

	gwam 1'	3'
Just recently an acquaintance of mine was complaining about how	13	4	50
quickly papers accumulated on her desk; she never seemed able to reduce	27	9	54
the load down to ground zero. There appeared to be some law working,	41	14	59
she explained, that continued to increase the stack each day by exactly	56	19	64
the amount she had reduced it the day before.	65	22	67
My friend ought to be better organized. She should schedule activi-	14	26	72
ties so that work is attended to daily. Any paper that requires only a	28	31	76
glance, a decision, and swift, final action should get just that. Any	42	36	81
paper that must for some reason get closer attention should be subject	56	40	86
to a fixed schedule for completion. Self-discipline is the key to order.	71	45	91

gwam 1' | 1 | 2 | 3 | 4 | 5 | 6 | 7 | 8 | 9 | 10 | 11 | 12 | 13 | 14 |
3' | | 1 | | 2 | | 3 | | 4 | | 5 |

61d ▶ 17
Make decisions: format a business letter

plain full sheet

1 Make decisions about the style and placement of the letter, then keyboard it.

2 Examine the letter carefully when you have finished it. Correct errors. Note your comments about your deci–sions at the bottom of the page.

If necessary, refer to pages 78 or 84 for assistance.

	words
August 1, 19--	Mr. Frederick K. Barnum	4748 Jarvis Drive	Corpus Christi,	15
TX 78412-2346	Dear Mr. Barnum	21
(¶) Thank you for your letter requesting information about one of our personalized	37
Name Pictures for your grandson. I hope the following description will be	52
helpful.	54
(¶) The Name Picture is an original hand-painted design featuring the name of a	69
child--in this case your grandson's name--in bold artist's print. Three or four	85
little boys or girls in colorful outfits are portrayed in playful situations as a part	102
of each picture. As a finishing touch, each picture is matted and framed in a	118
12″ by 16″ anodyzed aluminum frame. It sells for $30.	129
(¶) The enclosed order form specifies clearly the information we need to complete	145
the picture for you. Please allow us six weeks for delivery.	158
Sincerely yours	Miss Brenda Weaster	Sales Manager	xx	Enclosure	170

62

62a ▶ 6
Preparatory practice

each line 3 times SS (slowly, faster, still faster); DS between 3-line groups; re-peat selected lines if time permits

alphabet 1 Max perhaps realized that jet flights can quickly whisk us to Bolivia.

figures 2 Our latest inventory includes 958 rings, 3,064 pins, and 172 brooches.

hyphen 3 Oki thinks we have an up-to-the-minute plan for our out-of-town sales.

easy 4 Clement and eight neighbor girls wish to visit this cornfield at dusk.

| 1 | 2 | 3 | 4 | 5 | 6 | 7 | 8 | 9 | 10 | 11 | 12 | 13 | 14 |

62b ▶ 10
Measure straight-copy skill

Repeat 61c, above.

17e ▶ 12
Improve keyboarding continuity

1 Practice the ¶ once for orientation.

2 Take three 30" writings (30" *gwam* = words typed × 2).

3 Take three 1' writings.

4 Determine *gwam*.

Goal: *At least 14 gwam.*

Difficulty index

all letters/figures learned | E | 1.2 si | 5.1 awl | 90% hfw

```
                  .        2        .        4        .        6        .        8        .
Why did we not all realize that July 17 was a
    10       .       12        .        14       .        16        .       18
hot day?  For 30 days, still summer air had closed
    20      .        22       .       24        .        26      .        28
in on us.  Just to move was an effort; but here we
       30    .        32       .        34       .        36       .       38      .
stood, 48 quite excited people, planning our trek.
```

18

18a ▶ 7
Preparatory practice

each line twice SS (slowly, then faster); DS between 2-line groups; repeat selected lines if time permits

alphabet	1	One judge saw five boys quickly fix the prize elm.
p/x	2	Dixie, please have Pam fix the tax forms Hope has.
figures	3	Is it Channel 3, 8, or 10? Was the score 14 to 7?
easy	4	The girl may enamel the chair for the town chapel.

```
|  1  |  2  |  3  |  4  |  5  |  6  |  7  |  8  |  9  | 10  |
```

18b ▶ 16
Learn new keyreaches: 6 2 / (diagonal)

Follow the "Standard procedure for learning new keyreaches" on page 10 (Lines 1–6 twice; Lines 7–10 once; repeat 7–10 if time permits).

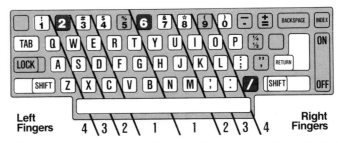

Left Fingers 4 3 2 1 1 2 3 4 **Right Fingers**

Reach technique for 6

Reach *up* with *right first* finger.

Reach technique for 2

Reach *up* with *left third* finger.

Reach technique for /

Reach *down* to / with *right little* finger.

6	1	j 6j 6j 6 6; 6 jobs, 6 jugs, 66 jays, 6 jokes, 6 6
	2	On July 6, 66 jumpers made 6 jumps of over 6 feet.
2	3	s 2s 2s 2 2; 2 skis, 2 sons, 22 sites, has 2 signs
	4	On May 2, Car 222 delivered 22 tons of No. 2 sand.
/	5	; /; /; / /; 1/3; and/or; 4/7/84; 4/14; 8 1/3; / /
	6	Type these mixed fractions: 1 3/8; 4 4/7; 1 3/14.
6/2/diag.	7	On May 26, I ordered 2 2/6 yards, not 6 2/6 yards.
	8	The recorder, Model 226/62, Serial 626/A, is mine.
all figures learned	9	Aida was 21 on 3/7/80. Bill will be 21 on 4/6/87.
	10	The terms for Invoice 7867/3 are 4/10, 2/30, n/60.

```
|  1  |  2  |  3  |  4  |  5  |  6  |  7  |  8  |  9  | 10  |
```

61a ▶ 6
Preparatory practice

each line 3 times SS
(slowly, faster, still
faster); DS between
3-line groups; re-
peat selected lines
as time permits

alphabet 1 Pamela Becker recognized the excellent quality of this silver jewelry.

figures 2 Walford reported on the following rooms: 6, 10, 25, 37, 129, and 148.

double letters 3 Will Scott attempt to sell his three bookkeeping books to Ellis Leeds?

easy 4 Orlando did vow to fight for his right to work as an auditor for them.

| 1 | 2 | 3 | 4 | 5 | 6 | 7 | 8 | 9 | 10 | 11 | 12 | 13 | 14 |

61b ▶ 17
Review/improve communication skills: suffixes

1 Set for 70–space line. Use a 1½″ top margin.

2 Center the heading, TS, and keyboard the first column as shown. Indent examples 5 spaces from left margin.

3 Reset left margin 4 spaces to the right of center point. Keyboard the second column. Indent examples 5 spaces from left margin.

4 Study carefully your finished copy. Correct errors.

ADDING SUFFIXES TO WORDS ENDING IN E OR Y

1. The e is usually dropped if the suffix begins with a vowel.

    like--likable
    pursue--pursuant
    sue--suing
    drive--drivable

2. The e is usually retained if the suffix begins with a consonant.

    care--careful
    nice--nicely
    rare--rareness
    case--casement

3. The e is usually retained before the ous or able when the root word ends in ce or ge.

    change--changeable
    notice--noticeable
    outrage--outrageous
    advantage--advantageous

4. The e is usually retained when the word ends in oe.

    shoe--shoeing
    canoe--canoeing
    hoe--hoeing

5. When a word ends in y preceded by a consonant, the y is usually changed to i before adding a suffix.

    lovely--loveliness
    economy--economical
    plenty--plentiful
    drowsy--drowsiness

6. Of course there are always exceptions that have to be remembered.

    oboe--oboist
    malice--malicious
    judge--judgment
    argue--argument

Compare skill: sentences

1 Take a 1' writing on Line 1; de-termine *gwam* and use this score for your goal as you take two 1' writings on Line 2 and two on Line 3.

2 Take a 1' writing on Line 4; de-termine *gwam* and use this score for your goal as you take two 1' writings on Line 5 and two on Line 6.

Goal: To have rates on Lines 2 and 3 and Lines 5 and 6 equal those on Lines 1 and 4.

words in line

1 Did the men enamel emblems on big panels downtown?   10

2 Pay the men to fix a pen for 38 ducks and 47 hens.   10

3 *They blame the chaos in the city on the big quake.*   10

4 Did the amendment name a city auditor to the firm?   10

5 He owns 20 maps of the 16 towns on the big island.   10

6 *Dian may make cocoa for the girls when they visit.*   10

18d ▶ 5

Proofread/revise as you keyboard

each line once DS; correct circled errors as you keyboard; read carefully

1 Court will not (ve) in session again until (august) 6.

2 Put more grass (sede) on the lawn at 307 Elm (Strett).

3 A team is (madeup) of 11 men; 12 were on (t he) field.

4 Liza and/or Dion (willldirect) the choir on (Tuseday).

5 (Theer) were (abuot) 10 or 11 pictures in the gallery.

18e ▶ 9

Improve keyboarding continuity

1 Practice the ¶ once for orienta-tion.

2 Take three 30" writings.

3 Take three 1' writings.

4 Determine *gwam*.

Goal: At least 14 *gwam*.

Difficulty index

all letters/figures learned | E | 1.2 si | 5.1 awl | 90% hfw

Volume 27 is quite heavy. Its weight must be
in excess of 10 pounds; yet I realize the only way
to complete this type of job is to study 164 pages
of Chapter 183 and all of the art in the big book.

60c ▶ 10
Improve keystroking technique

70-space line; keyboard each line 3 times SS; DS between each 2-line group

1st/ fingers 1 Those 456 heavy black jugs have nothing in them. Fill them by June 7.
2 A youth of just over 6 or 7 years of age ran through the orange grove.
2d/ fingers 3 Mike Deak, who was 38 in December, likes a piece of ice in cold cider.
4 Eddie decided to crate 38 pieces of cedar decking behind the old dock.
3d & 4th/ fingers 5 Polly made 29 points on that quiz; Wex made 10 points. Did they pass?
6 Zone 12 was impassable; we quickly roped it off. Did you wax Zone 90?

| 1 | 2 | 3 | 4 | 5 | 6 | 7 | 8 | 9 | 10 | 11 | 12 | 13 | 14 |

60d ▶ 20
Review/improve communication skills: period and question mark

1 Make decisions about place-ment of the copy. A full sheet and a 1½" top margin are suggested.
2 Proofread carefully; correct errors.
3 Note your comments about your placement decisions at the bottom of the page.
4 Study the rules and examples from your copy.

THE PERIOD AND THE QUESTION MARK

1. Use a period after a complete sentence; follow the period with two blank spaces.

    Examples: Buy the books. She will use them later.
                  I know Don. He is a member of our club.

2. Use a period after an abbreviation. Space once after periods used after abbreviations unless the abbreviation is made up of letters that are combined to represent more than one word; in that case, space only after the final period.

    Examples: Mr. Ogden will be graduated with a Ph.D.
                  Mrs. Sipe arrived at 6 a.m. last Monday.

3. Use periods to form an ellipsis. Ellipsis periods, commonly three in number, represent the omission of words from quoted data. Use four periods when an ellipsis ends a sentence. Space once between ellipsis periods.

    Examples: The economy . . . has not yet responded.
                  We agree the general won the war . . . .

4. Use a question mark after a direct question--not after an indirect question. Space twice after a question mark that is used to terminate a question.

    Examples: Where is he? I wonder if he had dinner.
                  Did she go? I asked if she had tickets.

5. A request that is phrased as a question is usually terminated with a period.

    Examples: Will you please bring me a glass of tea.
                  Will you kindly mail that letter for me.

6. Use a question mark after each of a series of short questions that are related to a single thought. Capitalize the first word of each of the questions only if it is a complete sentence. Space once after all but the final question mark.

    Examples: Was it birds? squirrels? rabbits? ducks?
                  Who wrote this? Was it Lee? Was it Dale?

19a ▶ 7
Preparatory practice

each line twice SS (slowly, then faster); DS between 2-line groups; repeat selected lines if time permits

Space once after a question mark when the question is incomplete.

alphabet 1 Mavis Zeff worked quickly on the next big project.

q/? 2 Can you spell queue? quay? aqua? quavered? acquit?

figures 3 If 24 of the 87 boys go on May 10, 63 will remain.

easy 4 Fit the lens at a right angle and fix the problem.

| 1 | 2 | 3 | 4 | 5 | 6 | 7 | 8 | 9 | 10 |

19b ▶ 16
Learn new keyreaches: 9 5 - (hyphen) -- (dash)

Follow the "Standard procedure for learning new keyreaches" on page 10 (Lines 1-6 twice; Lines 7-11 once; repeat 7-11 if time permits).

Hyphen, dash: The hyphen is used to join closely related words or word parts. Striking the hyphen twice results in a dash--a symbol that shows sharp separation or interruption of thought.

Left Fingers   4 \ 3 \ 2 \ 1   1 \ 2 \ 3 \ 4   Right Fingers

Reach technique for 9

Reach *up* with *right third* finger.

Reach technique for 5

Reach *up* with *left first* finger.

Reach technique for –

Reach *up* to - with *right little* finger.

9 1 l 91 91 9 9; 9 left, 9 lost, 9 loans, sell 99 lots
   2 On May 9, 99 buyers offered 99 bids for 999 lambs.

5 3 f 5f 5f 5 5; 5 fish, 5 fans, 5 forms, for 55 firms
   4 At 5 p.m., the 55 cars, 55 vans, and 5 jeeps left.

– 5 ; -; -; - -- co-op; top-rate; in-depth; up-to-date
   6 Use a 5-inch line--50 pica spaces--for lines 1-10.

9/5/– 7 We--all 59 of us--have read pages 59, 95, and 595.
       8 All 95 girls--5 did not attend--voted on Item 599.

           9 Of 13,687 ex-workers, 2,481--or 9/50--had retired.
all figures/ 10 Invoice 347/8--it is dated 2/9, not 2/10--is here.
symbols learned 11 Do Problems 2-27, 8-35, and/or 16-42 before May 9.

| 1 | 2 | 3 | 4 | 5 | 6 | 7 | 8 | 9 | 10 |

Learning goals

1 To gain skill in improving data input.

2 To strengthen ability to spell.

3 To understand better the functions and usage of the period and the question mark.

4 To improve ability to format materials.

Machine adjustments

1 Set paper guide at 0; remove all tab stops.

2 Set ribbon control to type on upper half of ribbon.

3 Unless otherwise appropriate, use a 70–space line.

60a ▶ 6

Preparatory practice

each line 3 times SS (slowly, faster, still faster); DS between 3-line groups; repeat selected lines if time permits

alphabet	1	Please have Dorothy get four dozen quarts of lemon juice by next week.
fig/sym	2	Duggan & Ford's catalog lists Item #93276 at $845 (less 10% for cash).
shift/lock	3	Send Marshall & Filarb ten copies of THE NEW LOOK by Hahn and Ostgard.
easy	4	Theodosia paid them to go downtown to bid on the authentic enamel owl.

| 1 | 2 | 3 | 4 | 5 | 6 | 7 | 8 | 9 | 10 | 11 | 12 | 13 | 14 |

60b ▶ 14

Improve keystroking continuity

1 Take two 1′ writings on each ¶, then two 3′ writings on both ¶s.

2 Proofread; circle errors; determine *gwam*.

3 Try to add one additional word to your *gwam* on each successive writing.

Difficulty index

all letters used	A	1.5 si	5.7 awl	80% hfw

	gwam 1′	3′
It has been said that human intelligence is the ability to acquire	13	4 | 60
and retain the kind of knowledge that will permit a person to respond	27	9 | 64
quickly and successfully to new and different problems. It is also the	42	14 | 69
ability to use mental power and sound judgment to recognize problems	56	19 | 74
we face and resolve them. In other words, it is the driving force that	70	23 | 79
moves our bodies from place to place, like moving game-board pieces.	84	28 | 83
Education teaches us to use intelligence. How shall we use it?	13	32 | 88
That question is partly answered for us when we realize that we need to	27	37 | 92
be bright enough to earn a livelihood, coexist with others, and make	41	42 | 97
contributions to our society and our environment. Beyond that, we must	56	46 | 102
decide for ourselves just how we use our intelligence, how different we	70	51 | 107
want to be from the other moving pieces on the game board.	82	55 | 110

gwam 1′ | 1 | 2 | 3 | 4 | 5 | 6 | 7 | 8 | 9 | 10 | 11 | 12 | 13 | 14 |
3′ | | 1 | | 2 | | 3 | | 4 | | 5 |

19c ▶ 7
**Improve figure
response patterns**

each line twice SS; DS between 2-line groups

Technique hint:
Work for continuity. Avoid
any pause before or after
figures.

all figures used

1 Send immediately *30* Solex cubes, Catalog No. *2748*.

2 As of *6/28*, your new extension number will be *375*.

3 Reserve for me Tape *640*. My identification: *819* .

4 Date of call: *2/7* . Time: *3:30* p.m. No message.

5 Top individual score: *87* . Top team average: *46* .

19d ▶ 5
**Proofread/revise
as you keyboard**

each line once DS; correct
circled errors as you
keyboard; read carefully

1 Erin had ⓢ size 11/12 dress, but it was (two) large.

2 The figure he wrote--475-⓪is not a correct answer⓪

3 All that snow--(mroe) than 5 (feaⓣ--kept her at home.

4 Edna says 936 Valley (Rode) is (here) new home address.

5 He scored 80 on the first (test;he) must do (bet ter).

19e ▶ 5
**Improve keystroking
technique**

each line twice SS; DS
between 2-line groups

bottom row 1 Zach, check the menu; next, beckon the lazy valet.

home row 2 Sal was glad she had a flashlight; Al was as glad.

third row 3 Powell quit their outfit to try out for our troop.

| 1 | 2 | 3 | 4 | 5 | 6 | 7 | 8 | 9 | 10 |

19f ▶ 10
**Improve keyboarding
continuity**

1 Practice the ¶ once for orienta–
tion.
2 Take three 30″ writings.
3 Take three 1′ writings.

Goal: *At least* 14 **gwam**.

Technique hint:
Work with confidence. Set
your own "comfortable"
rate and try to maintain it.

Difficulty index

all letters/figures used	E	1.2 si	5.1 awl	90% hfw

Think with me back to a quite cold morning in

1984. It was just 7:50; I opened my door to leave

for work. Little did I realize that snow had been

expected--2/3 foot of it. I live at 6 Summer Way.

59c, continued

Problem 2

Outline

50–space line: 1½" top margin; spread heading; use standard outline format

words

M E X I C O

2

I. LAND AREA 5

    A. Approximately 761,600 Square Miles ... 13

    B. Temperate to Tropical Climate 19

II. HISTORY 22

    A. Early Advanced Indian Cultures 29

        1. Mayans 31

        2. Toltecs 34

        3. Aztecs 36

    B. Conquered by Spanish in 1521 43

    C. Independence from Spain in 1821 50

III. GOVERNMENT 53

    A. Federal Republic (President Elected) . 61

    B. Federal District and 31 States 68

    C. Capital: Mexico City 73

Problem 3

Unarranged outline

Use Problem 2 format with a solid (not spread) heading; add designation numerals and letters for each order; use correct capitalization and spacing.

WORD PROCESSING SYSTEM

5

origination 8

  thoughts reduced to some communicable form ... 17

    written 20

    spoken 22

  transmitted into system 27

production 31

  placed in semi-final form 37

    formatted 39

    keyboarded 42

  placed in final form 47

    edited 50

    printed 52

reproduction 56

  number of desired copies produced 63

  photocopy or mechanical process 71

distribution 74

  dissemination of data as planned/directed ... 83

  hard copy or electronic mail medium 91

retention 94

  hard copy file 98

  soft copy file 102

    floppy diskette 106

    archival disk 109

    winchester disk 113

Learning goals

1 To set margins.

2 To determine line endings using the warning bell.

3 To center copy horizontally and vertically.

4 To divide words at line endings.

5 To type short reports and an–nouncements.

Machine adjustments

1 Set paper guide at 0.

2 Set ribbon control to type on upper half of ribbon.

3 Use a 60–space line (center point −30; center point +30).

4 SS drills; DS paragraphs; indent first line of ¶ 5 spaces.

5 Insert half sheets long side first, unless otherwise directed.

20

20a ▶ 7
Preparatory practice

each line twice SS (slowly, then faster); DS between 2-line groups; repeat selected lines if time permits

alphabet 1 Freda Jencks will have money to buy six quite large topazes.

o/i 2 We take action from our position to avoid spoiling our soil.

figures 3 The 26 clerks checked Items 37 and 189 on pages 145 and 150.

easy 4 She bid by proxy for eighty bushels of a corn and rye blend.

| 1 | 2 | 3 | 4 | 5 | 6 | 7 | 8 | 9 | 10 | 11 | 12 |

20b ▶ 15
Learn to establish margin widths

study copy at right; then do the drills below

Margin release (31)
If the carrier locks, depress the margin release key with the little finger and complete the line.

Know your machine: margin stops

Typewriters (and other keyboarding machines) are usually equipped with one of two type sizes: pica or elite (some with both). Pica (10-pitch) is the larger—10 pica spaces fill a horizontal inch. Paper 8½ inches wide will accommodate 85 pica characters and spaces. Center point for pica type is 42 when left edge of paper is inserted at 0 on line-of-writing scale.

Elite (12-pitch) type is smaller—12 elite spaces fill a horizontal inch. Paper 8½ inches wide will accommodate 102 elite characters and spaces. Center point for elite type is 51 when left edge of paper is at 0 on line-of-writing scale.

Equal margin widths can be had either by (1) setting margin stops an equal distance in inches or spaces from extreme right and left edges of paper or by (2) setting the margin stops an equal distance right and left from center point. In lessons that follow, the second procedure will be used.

Drill 1

exact 60–space line (center − 30; center + 30); DS; make one copy, line for line

Note: A warning bell will sound as you approach the end of each line; listen for it.

If the margins are set correctly, if the paper guide is set at 0, and if you have made no mistakes which affect line length, each of these paragraphs can be typed with right and left margins which are exactly equal in width to each other.

| 1 | 2 | 3 | 4 | 5 | 6 | 7 | 8 | 9 | 10 | 11 | 12 |

Drill 2

exact 50–space line (center − 25; center + 25); DS; make one copy, line for line

If it is not already obvious to you, you will soon find that, while the left edge of a paragraph is even, the evenness on the right edge depends on your ability to decide where and how to end lines.

| 1 | 2 | 3 | 4 | 5 | 6 | 7 | 8 | 9 | 10 |

Problem 1

Second page of an unbound report

Use standard unbound report format; number as page 2; place footnotes on foot of page.

words

2 0

adds to profits. To be profitable, Cecil says that business offices must "aim for   17

the most efficient method to generate, record, process, file, and distribute in-   33

formation."[2] It is in the quest for this goal that word processing has developed.   50

Word processing involves people, procedures, and highly technical   63

equipment, all of which are scientifically interposed between originating   78

thoughts (in words) and the production of the same thoughts in some physical,   93

functional form.   97

People. The people involved in word processing need specialized training.   113

They should be able to manipulate a keyboard with facility; be sure in their   129

knowledge of language, especially spelling and grammar; have managerial   143

skills; and /or understand word processing concepts, procedures, vocabulary,   158

and equipment.   163

Procedures. The procedures of word processing are not really new, but   178

they have new importance. They include such operational tasks as formatting,   193

or giving form to documents; editing and proofreading copy; and keyboarding,   209

or activating equipment.   214

Equipment. Types of word processing equipment vary; Anderson reports   230

that there are more than a hundred companies manufacturing word processing   245

equipment and supplies.[3] A list of recent equipment, though, will likely include   261

stand-alone display text editors, optical character readers, central dictation   277

systems, intelligent printers, electronic typewriters, and sophisticated storage   293

media.   295

298

[2] Paula B. Cecil, Word Processing in the Modern Office, 2d ed. (Menlo   320
Park: The Benjamin/Cummings Publishing Company, 1980), p. 3.   332

[3] Ruth I. Anderson, "Word Processing," The Changing Office Environ-   351
ment (Reston: National Business Education Association, Yearbook No. 18,   365
1980), pp. 56-57.   369

20c ▶ 5
Learn to use the backspacer and the margin release

exact 50-space line

Backspacer (20)

Use a quick, light stroke with the little finger. Depress the key firmly for repeated backspace action on an electric or electronic typewriter.

1 At the left margin of your paper, type the first word as it appears in the list at the right.

2 After typing the word, backspace and fill in the missing letter v.

3 Return, then repeat the procedure with each of the remaining words on the list.

lea e

har est

o ens

oli es

sa ings

Margin Release (31)

1 Before typing the sentence below, depress the margin release with the little finger and backspace 5 spaces into the left margin.

2 Type the sentence. When the carrier locks, depress the margin release and complete the line.

My typed work should be done neatly, correctly, and quickly.

20d ▶ 13
Learn to end lines

study copy at right; then do Drills 1 and 2

Know your machine: line ending warning bell

Margin stops cause the machine to lock at the point at which they are set. To bypass the lock, you must use the margin release (31), a time-consuming operation if used often.

Lines of a paragraph automatically align at the left margin, but they do not automatically align at the right margin. It is necessary, therefore, that the operator or typist ends lines at the right as evenly as possible.

To help you know when to end a line, a warning bell sounds 7 to 12 spaces before the margin stop is reached. Most typists find that a warning of 5 or 6 spaces (a half inch) is adequate to maintain a fairly even righthand margin. Thus, after setting margins for an exact line length, they move the right margin set 5 or 6 spaces farther to the right.

To use this procedure, set margin stops for an exact line length (50, 60, or 70 spaces); then move the right margin set another 5 or 6 spaces to the right. Doing so allows you to: (1) end a short word or (2) divide a longer one within 5 or 6 spaces after the bell rings.

Drill 1

full sheet; begin on Line 10; DS copy

1 Set exact 60–space line.

2 Move right margin stop 5 or 6 spaces farther to the right.

3 Read the ¶ at the bottom of this page. Then, as you type it, listen for the bell. When it sounds, complete the word you are typing; return immediately. If the machine locks on a long word, operate the margin release, complete the word, and return.

Your typed line endings will not match those in the textbook.

Drill 2

1 After typing Drill 1, return twice.

2 Set machine for a 50–space line with appropriate right margin bell adjustment.

3 Retype the ¶; follow the directions in Step 3 of Drill 1.

When the bell sounds, you must decide just where to end that line and begin a new one. If the word you are typing as the bell rings can be finished within 5 letters, finish it. If it takes more, you may need to divide it. You will learn soon how and when to divide words.

59a ▶ 6
Preparatory practice

each line 3 times SS (work for fewer than 3 errors per group); DS between 3-line groups; repeat selected lines as time permits

alphabet 1 June Wilcox printed five dozen banquet tickets for my seventh meeting.

figures 2 Please turn to page 350 and answer Questions 2, 4, 6, 7, 8, 9, and 17.

double letters 3 Lynn's committee supplied food and coffee for the Mississippi meeting.

easy 4 We may augment with an eighth element the fuel for the busy dirigible.

| 1 | 2 | 3 | 4 | 5 | 6 | 7 | 8 | 9 | 10 | 11 | 12 | 13 | 14 |

59b ▶ 10
Measure skill growth

Take one 3' and one 5' writing; determine *gwam*; proofread and circle errors.

Difficulty index

all letters used | A | 1.5 si | 5.7 awl | 80% hfw |

gwam 3' | 5'

Usually, writing a report does not seem quite so difficult if the   4 | 3
writer breaks the task down into smaller jobs. Before even starting to   9 | 5
write, for example, a writer must know exactly what is to be written,   13 | 8
for whom, and why; and a request for a report ought to have specific   18 | 11
directions with it. The next step is to build a working outline that   23 | 13
summarizes the report. The outline can later be changed to a skeleton   28 | 17
report with statements of purpose and main headings, subheadings, and   32 | 19
paragraph headings that will in time grow into a completed report.   37 | 22

Solutions to the problem under study must be found and analyzed;   41 | 25
and supporting data can be found, among other sources, by observation,   46 | 28
by experimentation, in books, with a questionnaire, with interviews,   50 | 30
and by examining all kinds of records. Each bit of data can be jotted   55 | 33
on a file card, along with a complete citation of its source. As a   60 | 36
last step, these data are added to the skeleton report; the citations   65 | 39
are the footnotes. Then all that is needed are the final touches that   69 | 41
produce a report that is usable, complete, to the point, and readable.   74 | 44

gwam 3' | 1 | 2 | 3 | 4 | 5 |
5' | 1 | 2 | 3 |

59c ▶ 34
Measure skill application

Time schedule

Assembling materials .... 2'
Timed production .... 26'
Final check; compute
  g–pram .... 6'

Materials needed

3 full sheets

When the signal to begin is given, insert paper and begin Problem 1. Format/type the problems in sequence until the signal to stop is given. Do Problem 1 again if you have finished Problem 3 and time

has not been called. Proofread all problems; circle errors. Calculate *g–pram*.

$$g–pram = \frac{\text{total words typed}}{\text{time (26')}}$$

20e ▸ 10
Learn to divide words

half sheet; insert (with long side up) to Line 9

1 Read the ¶; it explains basic rules for dividing words.

2 Use a 60–space line, ad–justed for bell warning.

3 As you type, listen for the bell. Complete or divide words as appropriate for a fairly even right margin.

As long as certain guides are observed, words may be divided in order to keep line lengths nearly even. For example, always divide a word between its syllables; as, care-less. Words of one syllable, however long, may not be divided, nor should short words --such as often--of five or fewer letters. The separation of a one- or two-letter syllable, as in likely or across, from the rest of a word must also be avoided.

21a ▸ 7
Preparatory practice

60-space line; each line twice SS (slowly, then faster)

Note: Line 3 has two ALL–CAP items. To type them, find the shift lock (27); depress the key with the left little finger; type the item; release the lock by striking either shift key.

alphabet	1	Jessie Quick believed the campaign frenzy would be exciting.
figures	2	The 2 buyers checked Items 10, 15, 27, 36, and 48 on page 9.
shift/lock	3	Titles of reports are shown in ALL CAPS; as, DIVIDING WORDS.
easy	4	Did they fix the problem of the torn panel and worn element?

| 1 | 2 | 3 | 4 | 5 | 6 | 7 | 8 | 9 | 10 | 11 | 12 |

21b ▸ 9
Learn to use the warning bell

half sheet; DS; begin on Line 9; 60-space line

Listen for the bell as you type. Make decisions about line endings. Avoid looking at the paper or typewriter as you type.

Learning to use a keyboard is worth our efforts. Few of us do so for the sheer joy of it. When most people type, they have a goal in mind--they want something in return. If we send a letter, we expect a reply--at least a reaction. If it is a job that we are doing for someone, we want approval--maybe payment. If it is for school, we hope for a top grade. What we get, though, will depend on what we give.

21c ▸ 9
Learn to center lines horizontally (side to side)

Drill 1

half sheet; DS; begin on Line 16

1 Insert paper (long side up) with left edge at 0.

2 Move each margin stop to its end of the scale. Clear all tab stops; set a new stop at center point of the page (elite, 51; pica, 42).

3 From center point, backspace once for each two letters, figures, spaces, or punctuation marks in the line.

4 Do not backspace for an odd or leftover stroke at the end of the line.

5 Begin to type where you com–plete the backspacing.

6 Complete the line; return; tab to center point. Type subsequent line in the same way.

Drill 2

half sheet; DS; begin on Line 14; center each line

Drill 1

LEARN TO CENTER LINES

Horizontally--Side to Side

Drill 2

You are invited

to attend the opening

of the new

JONES PUBLIC LIBRARY

Monday, May 3, 10 a.m.

Introducing

SALLY ANN DUPOIS
123 Poinciana Road
Memphis, Tennessee 38117-4121
(901-365-2275)
TS

Present Career Objective

Eager to accept part-time position that provides opportunities for
additional training and potential for full-time employment.
TS

Personal Qualifications

Cheerful, outgoing personality; dependable, cooperative worker
Very interested in retailing work; find it challenging
Excellent health; participate in golf, racquetball, and tennis

Experience

1985--present   The Toggery, 100 Madison Avenue, Memphis, TN 38103-
                  4219; Assistant Manager
1984 (summer)   Chobie's, 1700 Poplar Avenue, Memphis, TN 38104-
                  2176; Inventory Clerk and Cashier
1983 (summer)   Todds, 1450 Union Avenue, Memphis, TN 38104-5417;
                  Clerk and Assistant to the Buyer
1982 (summer)   Chobie's, 1700 Poplar Avenue, Memphis, TN 38104-
                  2176; Salesperson and Utility Helper

117
122
135
141
154
161
174
181

Education

Junior, Marketing, Memphis State University, Memphis, Tennessee
AA degree (associate degree/advertising; honors), State Technical
Institute, Memphis, Tennessee
Graduate (honor student), East High School, Memphis, Tennessee

References

Mrs. Evelyn J. Quinell   Professor Aldo R. MacKenzie
Manager, Chobie's   Department of Marketing Management
1700 Poplar Avenue   Memphis State University
Memphis, TN 38104-2176   Memphis, TN 38114-3285

Ms. Lanya Roover   Mr. Robert E. Tindall, Jr.
The Toggery   Attorney-at-Law
100 Madison Avenue   1045 Quinn Avenue
Memphis, TN 38103-4219   Memphis, TN 38106-4792

21d ▶ 25
Format a short report on dividing words

full sheet; 60-space line; DS body; begin on Line 10; TS below heading; proofread and circle errors

To TS when machine is set for DS: DS, then by hand turn cylinder (platen) for- ward one space.

1 Read the report care- fully.

2 Center heading on Line 10; then type the report.

3 Listen for the warning bell; decide quickly about line endings. Avoid looking up.

4 When finished, exam- ine the margins criti- cally; proofread your copy and circle errors.

Proofreading. Con- scientious keyboard operators always check carefully what they have keyboarded before they remove the paper from the machine. They *proofread* para- graphs; that is, they read them for *mean- ing*, as if they had not read them before. They double–check figures, proper names, and uncer- tain spellings against the original or some other source.

words

DIVIDING WORDS · 3
TS

A word may be divided at the end of a line in order to keep · 15
the margins as nearly equal in width as possible. Divided words, · 28
of course, tend to be more difficult to read than undivided words; · 41
so good judgment is needed. The following guides can help you · 54
make sound decisions about word division. · 62

Words that contain double consonants are usually divided be- · 74
tween consonants; as, bal-lots. However, if a word that ends in · 87
double letters has a suffix attached, divide after the double let- · 100
ters; as, dress-ing or stuff-ing. · 107

Words that contain an internal single-vowel syllable should · 119
be divided after that syllable; as, miti-gate. If two internal · 132
one-letter syllables occur consecutively in a word, divide between · 145
them; as, situ-ation or gradu-ation. · 153

Compound words that contain a hyphen should be divided only · 165
at the hyphen; as, second-class. Compound words written without a · 178
hyphen are best divided between the elements of the compound; as, · 191
super-market. · 194

Two final suggestions: Once you have decided to divide a · 205
word, leave as much of that word as you can on the first line; that · 219
way, a minimum of guesswork is required of the reader. Further, · 232
when in doubt about how to divide a word, remember that a dictio- · 245
nary is still the best friend a writer can have. · 254

22a ▶ 7
Preparatory practice

60-space line; each line twice SS (slowly, then faster); DS between 2-line groups

alphabet 1 Roxy waved as she did quick flying jumps on the trapeze bar.
shift keys 2 Yang Woerman hopes Zoe Quigley can leave for Maine in March.
figures 3 Buy 25 boxes, 147 bags, 39 sacks, 68 cartons, and 10 crates.
easy 4 Did the girl make the ornament with fur, duck down, or hair?

| 1 | 2 | 3 | 4 | 5 | 6 | 7 | 8 | 9 | 10 | 11 | 12 |

57d ▶ 15
Format/type footnotes as a bibliography

full sheet; 1½" top margin; 1" side margins

I. Center the heading **BIBLIOGRAPHY.**

2 Adapt the copy in footnote format at the right to appear as entries in a bibliography.

Refer to 57c, page 105, as necessary.

[1] Chicago Manual of Style, 13th ed., (Chicago: The University of Chicago Press, 1982), p. 40.

[2] Irvin Y. Hashimoto, Barry M. Kroll, and John C. Schafer, Strategies of Academic Writing: A Guide for College Students, (Ann Arbor: The University of Michigan Press, 1982), p. 1.

[3] William C. Himstreet and Wayne M. Baty, A Guide to Business Communication, (Homewood: Learning Systems Company, 1981), p. 161.

58

58a ▶ 6
Preparatory practice

each line 3 times SS (work for fewer than 3 errors per group); DS between 3-line groups; repeat selected lines as time permits

alphabet	1	Melva Bream required exactly a dozen jackets for the long winter trip.
fig/sym	2	Carter & Unter's check for $679.20 (Check #1348) was cashed on June 5.
one hand	3	You deserved, in my opinion, a reward after you started a faster race.
easy	4	Did he sit in a chair and do sleight of hand for the prudish visitors?

| 1 | 2 | 3 | 4 | 5 | 6 | 7 | 8 | 9 | 10 | 11 | 12 | 13 | 14 |

58b ▶ 12
Improve concentration

1 Make a copy of the ¶ DS.
2 Where a blank space occurs, insert a common 4–letter word that fits the context.
3 Using your corrected copy, take 1' writings as time permits.
Key: that, more, must, from, know

Difficulty index

all letters used	A	1.5 si	5.7 awl	80% hfw

gwam 1'

Men and women who succeed seem to realize _____ genuine success is   13
much _____ than just turning in one star performance after another. To   27
acquire actual success, they tell us, we _____ measure our achievements   42
by our own standards of excellence. Success truly stems _____ a belief   56
in ourselves and a determination to do well what we _____ we can do.   69

gwam 1' | 1 | 2 | 3 | 4 | 5 | 6 | 7 | 8 | 9 | 10 | 11 | 12 | 13 | 14 |

58c ▶ 32
Format/type a personal data sheet

full sheet; 1" top and side margins; set tab stop at center point

1 Read the information about data sheets at the right.
2 Keyboard a copy of the data sheet on page 107.

Developing personal data sheets

A personal data sheet is a summary of pertinent, personal facts, organized for quick reading. Data can be categorized in a number of ways, and the writer should use a form that will best display her or his qualifications. Note the following suggestions:

• The data sheet is accompanied by a well-worded letter of application.

• The appearance of the data sheet is as important as what it says.
• Complete sentences are rarely used.
• The data sheet should stress capabilities, not just aspirations.
• The data sheet should be as brief as possible but as long as necessary. Try not to exceed one page.

22b ▶ 13

Review procedure for horizontal centering

half sheet (long side up); begin on Line 13; DS body; TS below heading; proofread and circle errors

1 Review steps for centering lines horizontally (see 21c).
2 Center each line of the announcement shown at right.

EASTERN HILLS GOLF CLUB
TS
Annual Awards Banquet
The Nineteenth Hole
October 10, 6:30 p.m.

22c ▶ 30

Learn to center copy vertically

half sheet

Study the guides for vertical centering given at the right; then format and type Problem 1 below and Problem 2 on p. 45.

Guides for vertical centering

1 Count all lines and blank line spaces required by the problem (1 blank line space between DS lines; 2 blank line spaces between TS lines).

Note. Both pica and elite type require 1" for 6 lines of copy.

2 Subtract the total lines required by the problem from the number of lines on the paper (33, half sheet; 66, full sheet).

3 Divide the resulting number by 2 to determine number of lines to be left in top margin. *Disregard any fraction that may result from the division.*

4 From the top edge of the paper, space down 1 more than the number of lines figured for the top margin; begin typing on that line.

5 Center each line of the problem horizontally.

Calculation check

Lines available:	33
Lines required:	12
Lines remaining:	21
Top margin: (20 ÷ 2)	10

(Begin on Line 11)

This procedure places copy in what is called "exact center."

Problem 1

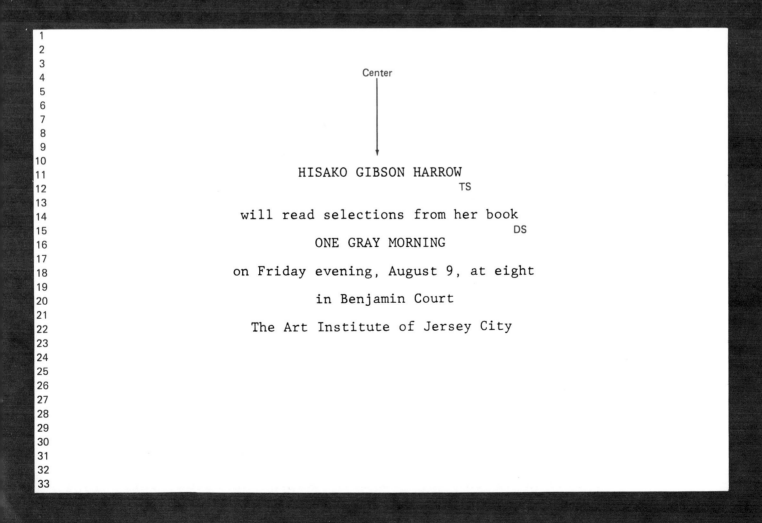

57a ▶ 6
Preparatory practice

each line 3 times SS (work for fewer than 3 errors per group); DS between 3-line groups; repeat selected lines as time permits

alphabet   1   Wilma thinks freezing prices at fixed levels for July is questionable.

fig/sym   2   A grant of $12,367.50 won't fund 10% of the studies; it is $948 short.

direct reaches   3   No doubt my brother Cecil served as an umpire on that bright June day.

easy   4   A fox lay in an island lair; a girl dug a quantity of pale lake worms.

| 1 | 2 | 3 | 4 | 5 | 6 | 7 | 8 | 9 | 10 | 11 | 12 | 13 | 14 |

57b ▶ 14
Compose at the keyboard

full sheet; 1½" top margin; DS; 1" side margins

1 Compose a four- or five-line paragraph in which you describe one or two hobbies you enjoy or wish you could enjoy.

2 Proofread the ¶; make changes with proofreader's marks.

3 Type a final copy. Center a spread heading H O B B I E S over the ¶.

57c ▶ 15
Format/type a bibliography

full sheet; use standard unbound report format; 1½" top margin recommended

1 Read the guides at the right; study the illustrated bibliography.

2 Keyboard the bibliography; make one carbon copy.

Guidelines for preparing a bibliography

A bibliography is a list of works cited or used in some way in the preparation of a report. Bibliographical entries are distinctive from footnotes, as can be noted in the following items:

• A bibliography is the final part of a report.

• The first surname of an entry is identified first, allowing the list to be arranged in alphabetic order.

• The first line of an entry is placed flush left; all succeeding lines of the entry are indented five spaces.

• Reference characters are not used.

• Items are made more incisive with the elimination of most parentheses and commas.

• Specific page numbers used in a footnote may be omitted.

BIBLIOGRAPHY

pica type

Langford, Floyd. "Systems Concept." The Changing Office Environment. Reston: National Business Education Association. Yearbook No. 18, 1980.

Lesikar, Raymond V. Business Communication: Theory and Application. 4th ed. Homewood: Richard D. Irwin, Inc., 1980.

Will, Mimi, and Donette Dake. Concepts in Word Processing: The Challenge of Change. Boston: Allyn and Bacon, Inc., 1981.

22c, continued

Problem 2

half sheet; DS; center each line horizontally and the entire an–nouncement vertically; proofread; circle errors

Calculation check

Lines on half sheet	33
Lines in announcement	12
Unused lines	21
Top margin	10
(Begin on Line 11)	

THE RUGBY SHOP

TS

invites you to attend

a special unadvertised sale

of sweaters, slacks, and shirts

one day only

Saturday, March 13, from 9 to 9

23a ▶ 7
Preparatory practice

60-space line; each line once DS; two 1' writings on Line 4

alphabet 1 Merry will have picked out a dozen quarts of jam for boxing.

d/s 2 Eddie Deeds sold daisy seeds to a student from East Dresden.

figures 3 Your 3:15 p.m. show drew 49 men, 72 women, and 680 children.

easy 4 As usual, Len bid and paid for a quantity of big world maps.

| 1 | 2 | 3 | 4 | 5 | 6 | 7 | 8 | 9 | 10 | 11 | 12 |

23b ▶ 10
Measure straight-copy skill

two 1' writings
two 3' writings

Difficulty index

all letters used | E | 1.2 si | 5.1 awl | 90% hfw |

gwam 3'

By this time, you must realize that there are many rules   4

you should learn about line endings and word division. Add   8

to your store of rules those that explain when you ought to   12

avoid dividing a word at the end of a line. Unless you must,   16

for example, you should not divide a figure, a proper name, a   20

date, or the last word on a page. If you learn these rules   24

and combine them with just a little common sense, you will be   28

able to handle problems of word division quickly and wisely.   32

| 1 | 2 | 3 | 4 |

words

2   314

Reference characters. To keystroke a superior figure, 329

turn the platen back half a line and type the figure. Aster- 341

isks and other refrence symbols requires no such adjustment. 353

Keyboards equipped with special symbol keys for report writing are also 367

available for regular use. 369

Page endings. A few very simple guides become important when- 383

ever a report has more than one page. For example, never end a 396

page with a hyphenated word. Farther, do not leave a single 408

line a of paragraph at the bottom of a page or at the top of a 420

page (unless the paragraph has only one line, of course.) 432

Footnote content. Underline titles of complete publica- 446
tions; use quotation marks with parts of publications. Thus, 460
the name of a magazine will be underlined, but the title of an 472
article within the magazine will be placed in quotation marks. 485
Months and locationla words, such as volume and number, may be 500
abbreviated. 503

Penciled guides. A light pencil mark can be helpful to 517

mark approximate page endings, planned placement of page numbers, 530

and potential foot note locations. When the report has been 542

finished, of course, erase any visable pencil marks. 553

Conclusion 557

With patience and skill, the keyboard operator can give a 569

well-written report the porfessional appearance it deserves. Says 582

Lesikar, 584

    Even with the best typewriter available, the fin- 594
ished work is no better than the efforts of the typist. 605
But this statement does not imply that only the most 616
skilled typist can turn out good work. Even the the 626
inexperienced typist can produce acceptable manuscripts 637
simply by exercising care. 642

646

Raymond V. Lesikar, Basic Business Communcation (Homwood: 657
Richard D. Irwin, Inc., 1979), p. 364. 665

23c ▶ 15
Center announcements

Problem 1

half sheet; DS; use exact vertical center; center each line hori–zontally (not aligned as shown); proofread/circle errors

Problem 2

full sheet; DS; use directions for Problem 1, but center in *reading position*

Reading position

Reading position places data slightly higher on a page than exact vertical center. Find top margin for exact center, then subtract 2 lines. Reading position is generally used only for full sheets (or half sheets with short side up— long edge at the left).

THE ELMIRA CONCERT SOCIETY
TS
proudly presents

the eminent Latin American pianist

Jorge Cabrara

in concert

Saturday afternoon, April 30, at 4:00

Carteret Auditorium

23d ▶ 9
Center data on special-size paper

half sheet, short side inserted first; DS; begin on Line 22; center information requested for each line

---

Finding horizontal center

To find the horizontal center of special-size paper or cards

1 Insert the paper or card into the machine. From the line-of-writing scale, add the numbers at the left and right edges of the paper.

2 Divide this sum by 2. The result is the horizontal center point for that size paper or card.

Your name

Your street address

Your city and state

The name of your college

Current date

23e ▶ 9
Center on a card

use a 5″ × 3″ card or paper cut to size; insert to type on 5″ width; center the data vertically and horizontally DS; proofread/circle errors

Calculation checks

There are 6 horizontal lines to a vertical inch. A 3″ card, therefore, holds 18 lines.

Lines available	18
Lines required	9
Lines remaining	9
Top margin	4
(Begin on Line)	5

John and Mary Dexter
DS
announce the arrival of

Meredith Anne

Born December 8

7 pounds 8 ounces

56b ▶ 44

**Format/type a
two-page report
with footnotes**

2 full sheets;
standard unbound
report format; SS
and indent enu-
merated items 5
spaces from each
margin; number
second page in
upper right corner

1 Review unbound re-
port format on page 96
for placement of un-
bound report.

2 Format and type the
report at right as an
unbound report.

3 Proofread; correct
errors.

	words
preparing REPORTS: THE PROFESSIONAL TOUCH < TS	9
Both the writer and keyboard operator, or compositor, share	21
a mutual concern for the preparation and for the ultimate suc-	30
cess of a report, but usually the writer must accept final	42
accountability. The compositors contribution, however, is an	54
extremely vital one; and she or he should porceed with great	62
caution. For example, even before they start to prepare a	73
final copy of a report, the compositor should proceed with	82
determining	84

1. the specified purpose of the report and whether some par-   96
ticular format is required;   102

2. the number, kind, and grade of cpies required and   113

3. deadliens for completion.   119

The keyboard operator should be prepared to word from the   130
script, rough-draft, or printed copy and yet give the report a   143
final presentation that is as professional as it is functional.   156

< TS before a side heading

"Tricks of the Trade"   164

Those with experience in preparing reports have found that   176
there are special procedures they can use to simplify their   188
tasks. The following paragraphs contain samples of some pro-   200
cedures that can be especially ehlpful to a person who had not   212
prefiously keyboarded reports. (Anyone who plans to prepare   224
more that a few reports, however, should read several good books on the subject.)   241
Right margins. Attractive right margins result result when   254
good judgment is exercised used. Using the warning bell judiciously   267
ensures right margins that approximate left margins in width.   279

SS _____   283

[1]For further information see The Chicago Manual of Style,   300
13 th ed. (Chicago: The University of chicago Press, 1982),   312
p. 40.   314

(continued on page 104)

Lesson **56** | Section **12** | Formatting/typing outlines, reports, and data sheets   **103**

Learning goals

1 To learn symbol keystrokes.

2 To improve facility on figure keyreaches.

3 To improve proofreading and revision skills.

4 To learn proofreader's marks and their uses.

5 To improve keyboarding con–tinuity.

Machine adjustments

1 Set paper edge guide at 0.

2 Set ribbon control to type on upper half of ribbon.

3 Use a 60–space line (adjusted for bell) unless otherwise directed.

4 SS drills; DS paragraphs.

5 Space problems as directed.

24a ▶ 6
Preparatory practice

each line twice SS (slowly, then faster); DS between 2-line groups; repeat selected lines as time permits

alphabet **1** John Quigley packed the zinnias in twelve large, firm boxes.

n/m **2** Call a woman or a man who will manage Minerva Manor in Nome.

figures **3** Of the 13 numbers, there were 4 chosen: 29, 56, 78, and 90.

easy **4** An auditor may handle the fuel problems of the ancient city.

| 1 | 2 | 3 | 4 | 5 | 6 | 7 | 8 | 9 | 10 | 11 | 12 |

24b ▶ 12
Learn new keyreaches: $ &

$ = dollars
& = ampersand (and)

Technique hint

Pace your shift–type–release technique when practicing the symbol reaches. Straighten the appropriate finger; avoid as much as you can moving the hands and arms forward.

Reach technique for $

Shift; then reach *up* to $ with *left first* finger.

Left Fingers   4 \ 3 \ 2 \ 1   1 \ 2 \ 3 \ 4   Right Fingers

Reach technique for &

Shift; then reach *up* to & with *right first* finger.

Follow the "Standard procedure for learning new keyreaches" on page 10 (Lines 1–4 twice; Lines 5–7 once; repeat 5–7 if time permits).

$ **1** $ $ $4 $4, if $4, 4 for $44, her $444 fur, per $4, $4 tariff

2 The items cost them $174, $184, and $54. They paid $14 tax.

& **3** & & J & J, Jory & Jones, Bern & James, H & U Co., Foy & Hope

4 We buy pipe from Smith & Jones, Li & Hume, and Clay & Young.

all fingers/ new symbols **5** The $185 check is from J & J. The $192 check is from B & B.

6 Send $274 to Fish & Heath; deposit $300 with Booth & Hughes.

7 Hecot & Ryne charged us $165; Carver & Hunt charged us $340.

| 1 | 2 | 3 | 4 | 5 | 6 | 7 | 8 | 9 | 10 | 11 | 12 |

Format/type the second page of a report

full sheet; refer to pages 96 and 98 for format directions if necessary

words

line 4   2   0

line 7   Today, much of the movement for technological change involves the   14

search for efficiency; that is, shortcutting time and energy, especially as they   30

touch upon the flow of information. Langford says, "Society today is an infor-   45

mation society. Information is what office operations produce."[1] In today's   61

highly competitive business world, accurate information must be readily avail-   76

able; and it is this need, of course, that has given us word processing.   91

Sociologists say that society does not adopt new technology until con-   105

ditions, always changing, make it ready to do so; then it assimilates change very   121

rapidly. The automobile, for example, was invented years before its acceptance   137

as a popular method of transportation. It seems, therefore, that as technology   153

becomes available, society needs pioneers with foresight who will work for its   169

acceptance. Speaking of word processing, Will and Dake say,   181

> In order to keep up with technological change and at the same   194
> time address human factors, those involved in setting up and run-   206
> ning word processing systems must be change agents. Change   218
> agents know where to find information on the constant changes in   231
> the industry and how to utilize it advantageously.[2]   242

Other "agents of change" must function to prepare a consuming society   256

to trust change; to support it financially; and, above all, to use it. Perhaps the   273

greatest challenge involving technology is not to create change, but to learn to   289

live with it.   292

   296

[1] Floyd Langford, "Systems Concept," The Changing Office Environ-   314
ment (Reston: National Business Education Association, Yearbook No. 18,   329
1980), p. 31.   332

[2] Mimi Will and Donette Dake, Concepts in Word Processing: The Chal-   353
lenge of Change (Boston: Allyn and Bacon, Inc., 1981), p. v.   368

56a ▶ 6

Preparatory practice

each line 3 times SS (work for fewer than 3 errors per group); DS between 3-line groups; repeat selected lines as time permits

alphabet 1   Jenny Saxon left my squad a week after giving back the disputed prize.

fig/sym 2   I paid $1.95 for 2% milk and $3.87 for 60 rolls at J & D's on June 14.

long words 3   A probability study is particularly helpful for effective forecasting.

easy 4   At a signal, he may sign a name and title at the end of the amendment.

| 1 | 2 | 3 | 4 | 5 | 6 | 7 | 8 | 9 | 10 | 11 | 12 | 13 | 14 |

24c ▶ 8
Reach for new goals

1 Two 30" writings on each line; try to pace yourself to end each writing just as time is called.

2 Three 1' writings on Line 4; de–termine *gwam* on each writing.

1 The six girls paid $81 to visit the old city. 18

2 Lana paid the man the $94 due for the work he did. 20

3 Coe & Wu may sign the form for the auditor of the firm. 22

4 If Torke & Rush paid $730, then Corlan and Aldorn paid $637. 24

| 1 | 2 | 3 | 4 | 5 | 6 | 7 | 8 | 9 | 10 | 11 | 12 |

24d ▶ 7
Use the warning bell/ divide words

two half sheets; begin on Line 12; once with 70-space line, once with 60-space line

Take time to evaluate your completed work. Look carefully at what you have done. Would you be impressed with it if you were a reader? Is it attractive in form and accurate in content? If it does not impress you, it will not impress anyone else.

24e ▶ 9
Proofread/revise as you keyboard

each line twice SS; DS be-tween 2-line groups; identify and correct the circled errors *as you keyboard*

1 He chose 12 to 14 dozen (carda) for my all-(prupose) card shelf.

2 The expert (quick ly) listed 23 sources of information (forher).

3 I drove my new jeep at an average (ratt) of 56 miles per hour(?)

4 Minimum (spedd) on that part of Route 789 is 35 miles an (horu).

5 The (whit) pine frame is 15 x 20 inches;◯there is no picture.

24f ▶ 8
Improve keyboarding continuity

1 Practice the ¶ once for orienta-tion.

2 Take three 30" practice writings on the ¶. Determine *gwam*: words typed × 2.

3 Take three 1' speed writings on the ¶. Determine *gwam*: total words typed = 1' *gwam*.

Goal: 20 or more *gwam*.

Difficulty index

| all letters used | E | 1.2 si | 5.1 awl | 90% hfw |

We purchased our computer from the Jeff & Zorne Company for $500. That is quite a lot of money; but I think it will be a good investment if I can use the machine and all of the parts--figures and symbols, for example--in the correct way.

25

25a ▶ 7
Preparatory practice

each line twice SS (slowly, then faster); DS between 2-line groups; repeat selected lines if time per-mits

alphabet 1 Why did the judge quiz poor Victor about his blank tax form?

t/r 2 Bart had trouble starting his truck for a trip to Terrytown.

figure/ symbol 3 Buy 103 ribbons and 45 erasers from May & Muntz for $289.67.

easy 4 Did she rush to cut six bushels of corn for the civic corps?

| 1 | 2 | 3 | 4 | 5 | 6 | 7 | 8 | 9 | 10 | 11 | 12 |

**Preapplication drill:
format/type
source footnotes**

1 Study carefully the guides and models for preparing footnotes.

2 Using the appropriate model (pica or elite) below, type the final lines of a page and its source footnotes. Use 1″ side margins. (Note: Since 19 typed and blank lines are needed to complete the 66-line page, begin typing on Line 48.)

3 Compare the appearance and content of your finished product with the model in the textbook.

Format/type source footnotes

Preparing footnotes correctly takes skill, knowledge, and careful planning. The guidelines below will help you to plan and type the footnotes in Section 12.

• Footnotes should be placed at the foot of the page on which reference to them is made.

• Use a superior figure (raised a half line) in the text as reference to the footnote; repeat the superior figure with the footnote.

• Separate footnotes from the body of the report with a single underline 1½″ (18 elite or 15 pica spaces); SS before the line and DS after it.

• SS footnotes; DS between them if more than one occurs on a page.

• When one or more footnotes must appear at the foot of a page, allowances must be made for a 1″ (6 lines) bottom margin, 3 or 4 lines for each footnote, and 2 lines for the dividing line. As can be seen, it is important to know when to stop keyboarding and when to begin the footnotes.

---

pica   formats as discussed by Guffey and Erickson[1] (business reports)   48

and Hashimoto, Kroll, and Schafer[2] (academic reports).   49 50

SS   _____   51

DS   [1]Mary Ellen Guffey and Lawrence W. Erickson, Business Office   52
Practices Involving the Typewriter with Implications for Business   53
Education Curricula, Monograph 136 (Cincinnati: South-Western   54
Publishing Co., 1981), pp. 17, 27, and 28.   55 56

DS   [2]Irvin Y. Hashimoto, Barry M. Kroll, and John C. Schafer,   57
Strategies of Academic Writing: A Guide for College Students   58
(Ann Arbor: The University of Michigan Press, 1982), p. 1.   59 60

1″ (6 lines)   61
bottom margin   62 63 64 65 66

---

elite   formats as discussed by Guffey and Erickson[1] (business reports) and Hashimoto,   48

Kroll, and Schafer[2] (academic reports).   49 50

SS   _____   51

DS   [1]Mary Ellen Guffey and Lawrence W. Erickson, Business Office Practices   52 53
Involving the Typewriter with Implications for Business Education Curricula,   54
Monograph 136 (Cincinnati: South-Western Publishing Co., 1981), pp. 17, 27,   55
and 28.   56

DS   [2]Irvin Y. Hashimoto, Barry M. Kroll, and John C. Schafer, Strategies of   57 58
Academic Writing: A Guide for College Students (Ann Arbor: The University of   59
Michigan Press, 1982), p. 1.   60

1″ (6 lines)   61
bottom margin   62 63 64 65 66

25b ▶ 12
Learn new keyreaches
( )

Follow the "Standard procedure for learning new keyreaches" on page 10 (Lines 1–4 twice; Lines 5–8 once; repeat 5–8 if time permits.)

\# = number/pounds
( ) = parentheses

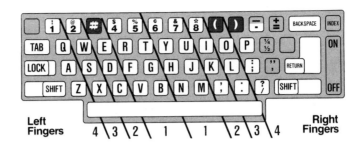

Left Fingers 4 \ 3 \ 2 \ 1 \ 1 \ 2 \ 3 \ 4 **Right Fingers**

Reach technique for #

Shift; then reach *up* to # with *left second* finger.

Reach technique for (

Shift; then reach *up* to (with *right third* finger.

Reach technique for)

Shift; then reach *up* to) with *right little* finger.

#	1 # # #3 #33 Card #3, File #3, Car #33, #3 grade. Try #3 now.
	2 Memo #169 says to load Car #3758 with 470# of #2 grade sand.
( )	3 (1 (1);); (90) two (2); type (1) and (2); see (8) and (9).
	4 He (John) and his cousin (Lynne) are both the same age (17).
#/( )	5 Pay the May (#34) and June (#54) bills soon (before July 1).
	6 We lease Car #84 (a white sedan) and Car #86 (a blue coupe).
all figures/ new symbols	7 Our Check #230 for $259 paid Owen & Cobb (auditors) in full.
	8 Deliver the $78 order (collect) to Fox & Tucker (Room #416).

| 1 | 2 | 3 | 4 | 5 | 6 | 7 | 8 | 9 | 10 | 11 | 12 |

25c ▶ 8
Proofread/revise
as you keyboard

each line twice SS; DS between 2-line groups; correct circled errors as you type

1 I saw them fill the (Baskets) full of (appels) (form) the orchard.

2 None of (use) took that (specal) train to Cincinnati (adn) Dayton.

3 They (paln) an intensive (campaing) for television and/or (raido).

4 (Teh) two leaders (Betty and Luis) left at 2--not 1:30 today.

5 (put) a fork, knife and (sppon) at each informal place setting.

**Format/type a report
with a footnote**

full sheet; refer to pages
96 and 98 for format
guidelines if necessary

F O O T N O T E S

TS

	words
	4

Formal reports are usually written to put forward some point of view, to | 18

convince readers, and/or to convey information in such a way that it will be | 34

relied upon, accepted, or believed. To substantiate the contents of a report and | 50

to give it greater weight of authority, a writer often cites evidence that other | 66

people support his or her conclusions. Sources for such support are then shown | 82

as footnotes at appropriate places within the report. | 93

Citations for all such opinions or statements of fact spoken or written by | 108

someone other than the writer should be documented. This procedure is simply | 124

a matter of fair play, of "giving credit where credit is due." Whenever a writer | 140

paraphrases or quotes directly from the work of someone else, credit should be | 156

given. | 158

Footnotes are also frequently used to clarify points, provide additional | 172

information, or add other forms of editorial comment that the writer may wish | 188

to make. For whatever reason a footnote is included, it must be done with the | 204

idea of assisting a reader. | 209

Footnotes may be placed at the end of a report, or they may be placed at the | 224

foot of the page on which reference to them is made.* In either case, the | 239

footnotes are typed in sequential order and numbered consecutively throughout | 255

the report. Footnotes on a partially filled page may immediately follow the last | 271

line of the text, or they may be placed to end one inch from the bottom of the | 287

page. | 288

1½" underline ——————— SS | 291

DS

* Footnotes at the foot of the page are usually preferred for academic | 305

writing. | 307

**Preparatory
practice**

each line 3 times SS
(work for fewer than 3
errors per group); DS
between 3-line
groups; repeat
selected lines as time
permits

55

alphabet	1	The objective of the tax quiz was clarified by checking samples of it.
fig/sym	2	Ship the $567 order for 29 1/3 grams of X8-D40 (8% solution) tomorrow.
shift	3	Will Pamela Forsman be quite happy visiting Kansas and Alaska in July?
easy	4	In the land of enchantment, the fox and the lamb sit down by the bush.

| 1 | 2 | 3 | 4 | 5 | 6 | 7 | 8 | 9 | 10 | 11 | 12 | 13 | 14 |

25d ▶ 8
Improve keyboarding continuity

1 Practice the ¶ once for orientation.

2 Take three 30″ writings and three 1′ writings.

Goal: At least 14 *gwam*.

all letters/ figures/ symbols learned

Difficulty index			
E	1.2 si	5.1 awl	90% hfw

```
               .       2       .       4       .       6       .       8       .      10      .
Issue #27 of a recent (1/9/85) magazine told how an ex-
       12      .      14       .      16       .      18       .      20       .      22       .
ecutive got her first job with a top-level firm (Roe & Roe):
       24      .      26       .      28       .      30       .      32       .      34       .
She knew how to keyboard.  Paid merely $140 a week at first,
       36      .      38       .      40       .      42       .      44       .      46       .
she moved up quickly; now she is making about $1,360 a week.
```

25e ▶ 15
Review centering an announcement on special-size paper

half sheet; insert short side first; DS; center vertically in reading position; center each line horizontally; proofread/ circle errors

Calculation checks:

The page is 8½″ long. There are 6 lines in one vertical inch. 8½ × 6 = 51 available lines.

Lines in problem: 14
Exact top margin: 18
Reading position
    top margin: 16

Add right paper edge reading to left paper edge reading; divide by 2. The result is the center point of the page.

Members of THE CHORALIERS
TS

Arvid Badger

Muriel Ann Bressuyt

Bertram Garrett, Jr.

Wayne L. Jewell

Phillip R. Runyun

Bette Lee Yamasake

26a ▶ 7
Preparatory practice

each line twice SS (slowly, faster); as many 30″ writings on Line 4 as time permits

Goal: Complete Line 4 in 30″.

alphabet	1	Jewel quickly explained to me the big fire hazards involved.
space bar	2	is by it do in be of am my go me an us so if to or ad on and
figure symbol	3	Silva & Stuart checked Items #2346 and 789 (for a $150 fee).
easy	4	The auditor did the rush work right, so he risks no penalty.

```
| 1 | 2 | 3 | 4 | 5 | 6 | 7 | 8 | 9 | 10 | 11 | 12 |
```

53c, continued

Problem 2

half sheet; 2″ top margin; center each heading at the far right as a spread heading, as shown in the first heading.

Center spread headings

1 To center a spread heading, backspace from the center point once for each letter, character, and space except for the last letter or character in the heading.

2 From this point, type the heading, spacing once after each letter or character and 3 times between words.

	words
S P R E A D H E A D I N G S	6
SIMPLE REPORT FORMAT	10
SOURCE FOOTNOTES	14
PREPARING AN OUTLINE	18

Problem 3

full sheet; refer to page 98 for for-mat directions if necessary

Repeat the report in Problem 1 page 98. Use a spread heading.

54a ▶ 6
Preparatory practice

each line 3 times SS (work for fewer than 3 errors per group); DS between 3-line groups; repeat selected lines if time permits

alphabet 1 We have printed just sixty dozen meal tickets for the banquet meeting.

fig/sym 2 Room #476 is $39 a day, but call 615-2890 (before 2 p.m.) for 7% less.

hyphen/dash 3 Hyphenate a multiword modifier preceding a noun--a hard-and-fast rule.

easy 4 The town may wish to blame us for the auditory problems in the chapel.

| 1 | 2 | 3 | 4 | 5 | 6 | 7 | 8 | 9 | 10 | 11 | 12 | 13 | 14 |

54b ▶ 12
Improve concentration

1 Prepare a copy of the ¶ DS. Where a blank space occurs, insert either the word **that** or **your**.

2 Take 1′ writings as time permits. Use your corrected copy.

Difficulty index

all letters used	A	1.5 si	5.7 awl	80% hfw

gwam 1′

When _____ job requires you to use the telephone, use it well. A 13

caller cannot see you; so you should realize _____ _____ words have to 27

express the same cordiality, sincerity, and interest _____ you would show 41

if you were talking to the caller face to face. You can project a posi- 56

tive image for _____ company with polite answers and a helpful, consider- 70

ate attitude. 73

gwam 1′ | 1 | 2 | 3 | 4 | 5 | 6 | 7 | 8 | 9 | 10 | 11 | 12 | 13 | 14 |

54c ▶ 5
Keystroke the * (asterisk)

The * (asterisk) may be used to refer to a footnote. Find the loca-tion of the * on your machine; watch your finger practice the reach; then type the drill line twice.

* ** * I may use * and ** to indicate the first and second footnotes.

26b ▶ 12
Learn new keyreaches:
% ' !

% = percent
' = apostrophe/single quote
! = exclamation point

Note: If you are using a nonelectric machine, refer to page 3; see directions for reach to '.

Reach technique for %

Shift; then reach *up* to % with *left first* finger.

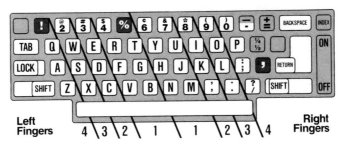

Left Fingers 4 3 2 1 1 2 3 4 **Right Fingers**

Apostrophe (')

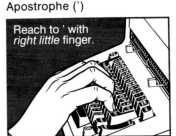

Reach to ' with *right little* finger.

Follow the "Standard procedure for learning new keyreaches" on page 10 (Lines 1–4 twice; Lines 5–8 once; repeat 5–8 if time permits).

Exclamation point:

If your machine has an exclamation point key, strike it with the nearest little finger. If it does not, refer to page 3. Space twice after an exclamation point when used after an emphatic interjection or as end–of–sentence punctuation.

%
1 % % 5%, off 5%, if 5%, save 15%, ask 15%, less 50%, 5% force
2 Mark prices down 15% on coats, 5% on hats, and 10% on shoes.

,
3 ' ' 10's, it's, Bob's, Sec'y, Ok'd; It's summer. I'm going.
4 It's time for Ann's party. I don't have Melanie's notebook.

!
5 Fire! Ouch! Oh wow! Keep out! They offer a big discount!
6 Their slogan reads THINK! They used the headline OOPS SALE!

%/'/!
7 Don't give up! Keep on! We're over the top! We have $950!
8 Uhl & Co. had a 16% profit! Their third quarter showed 20%!

| 1 | 2 | 3 | 4 | 5 | 6 | 7 | 8 | 9 | 10 | 11 | 12 |

26c ▶ 10
Proofread/revise as you keyboard

Errors are often circled in copy that is to be retyped. More fre–quently, perhaps, the copy is marked with special symbols called "proofreader's marks" which indicate changes desired by an editor.

Some commonly used proof–reader's marks are shown at the right. Study them; then type each drill line at least twice, SS; DS between 2–line groups.

Concentrate on copy content as you keyboard.

Proofreader's marks

Symbol	Meaning	Symbol	Meaning
Cap or ≡	Capitalize	#	Add horizontal space
∧	Insert	/ or lc	Lowercase letters
ℓ	Delete (remove)	⊂	Close up space
⊏	Move to left	∪	Transpose
⊐	Move to right	stet	Leave as originally written

1 patience pays; the espert's goalis 1% every day improvement.
2 do today's work today; tomdorrow's work will be 100% lighter.
3 One's best isusually enough; Few are expected to give 101%.
4 It's easier to risk 10% than, but return depends on risk.
5 We miss life's pleasures I know because we refuse to sample.
6 I'll be lucky if at anytime I can solve 50% of my problems.

Improve concentration

1 Keyboard a copy of the ¶ DS. Where a blank space occurs, insert either the word **they** or **that**.

2 Using your corrected copy, take as many 1' writings as time permits.

Difficulty index

| all letters used | A | 1.5 si | 5.7 awl | 80% hfw |

gwam 1'

Typically, women and men who are successful give the best ———can	13
give. ——— do not do this just because ———have the personality makeup	28
——— demands it; ——— do so because ——— are seemingly oriented to be	42
achievers. Quite simply, ——— expect to succeed; and ——— refuse to	56
recognize any effort, including theirs, ——— is not top rated.	68

gwam 1' | 1 | 2 | 3 | 4 | 5 | 6 | 7 | 8 | 9 | 10 | 11 | 12 | 13 | 14 |

53c ▶ 32

Format/type reports/ spread headings

Problem 1

full sheet; DS; 1" side margins; 5-space ¶ indention.

1 Read carefully the guides for preparing reports.

2 Follow these guidelines as you keyboard.

Preparing reports

Before you prepare any report, determine whether or not there are specific instructions for its format. In the absence of such instructions, the guides given here are generally accepted for reports that are not to be bound. Follow these guidelines for the reports in Section 12.

• Use a 1½" top margin (pica) or 2" (elite) for the first page; otherwise, use 1" margins for all four sides.

• Use double spacing.
• Do not number the first page.
• Number the second and all subsequent pages in the upper right corner, ½" (Line 4) from the top of the page.
• Enclose short quotations in quotation marks. Indent longer quotations 5 spaces from each margin; omit quotation marks, and use single spacing.

words

SIMPLE REPORT FORMAT — 4
TS

It is important that students who prepare term papers, themes, and other — 19
forms of academic writing know the procedures for typing reports. — 32

In the previous sections, your typed work has been set to a stated line — 46
length of 50, 60, or 70 spaces, regardless of whether your machine was equipped — 62
with pica- or elite-size type. Here in Section 12 you will be asked to prepare formal — 79
reports that require placement in accordance to the number of inches in top, — 95
bottom, and side margins rather than to the number of spaces in the writing — 110
line. — 111

Because of the difference in type size, pica and elite solutions will differ — 127
somewhat. When 1-inch side margins are used, a pica line will contain 65 — 141
spaces; an elite line will contain 78 spaces. Both sizes of type, of course, will — 158
accommodate 6 line spaces to a vertical inch. — 167

When side margins of 1 inch are used, 10 pica spaces should be allowed in — 182
each margin; on the other hand, users of elite type should allow 12 spaces. — 197

26d ▶ 11
Reach for new goals

1 Take a 1' writing on Line 1.

2 Take a 1' writing on Line 2, try-ing to type as many lines as on Line 1.

3 Practice each of the other pairs of lines in the same way to im-prove figure/symbol keyboarding speed.

words
in line

		words in line
1	Did the girls make soap in a handy clay bowl?	9
2	They spent $85 on a visit to Field & Co.	8
3	Did the men visit the dismal shanty on the island?	10
4	Form #72 is title to the island (their half).	9
5	I turn the dials on the panel a half turn to the right.	11
6	She may pay me for my work, and I make 40% profit.	10
7	It is a shame he spent the endowment on a visit to the city.	12
8	She paid 20% down for the $18 formal tie; it's apricot.	11

| 1 | 2 | 3 | 4 | 5 | 6 | 7 | 8 | 9 | 10 | 11 | 12 |

26e ▶ 10
Improve keyboarding continuity

1 Practice the ¶ for orientation.

2 Take three 30" writings and three 1' writings.

3 Proofread/circle errors after each writing.

Goal: At least 14 gwam.

Avoid looking at the keyboard when you encounter figures and symbols.

Difficulty index

| all letters/symbols learned | E | 1.2 si | 5.1 awl | 90% hfw |

Sales Report #38/39 of the modern firm of Wenz & Jelkes states that, if they are to remain in business, they are re-quired to clear a profit of 10% on all sales (net)--or $1 on each $10. They don't expect the figure to change very soon.

27

27a ▶ 7
Preparatory practice

each line twice SS (slowly, then faster); DS between 2-line groups; take a 1' writ-ing on Line 4 if time per-mits

alphabet	1	Jacky Few's strange, quiet behavior amazed and perplexed us.
shift	2	Lily read BLITHE SPIRIT by Noel Coward. I read VANITY FAIR.
fig/sym	3	Invoice #38 went from $102.74 to $97.60 after a 5% discount.
easy	4	They may go to a town social when they visit the big island.

| 1 | 2 | 3 | 4 | 5 | 6 | 7 | 8 | 9 | 10 | 11 | 12 |

27b ▶ 8
Practice long reaches

each line twice SS; DS be-tween 2-line groups; repeat lines you find most difficult

Keep eyes on copy as you strike figures and symbols.

$	1	He spent $25 for gifts, $13 for dinner, and $7 for cab fare.
()	2	We (my uncle and I) watched his sons (my cousins) play golf.
%	3	If I add 3% to the company discount of 8%, I can deduct 11%.
&	4	Send the posters to Bow & Held, Mans & Tow, and Wick & Jens.
'	5	It's time to send Hale's credit application to Land's Store.

| 1 | 2 | 3 | 4 | 5 | 6 | 7 | 8 | 9 | 10 | 11 | 12 |

Lessons **26, 27** | Section **5** | Learning symbol keyreaches

52

52c ▶ 30
Format/type outlines

Problem 1

full sheet; 1½" top margin

1 Set a line length that will accommodate the longest line.

2 Set tab stops at 4-space intervals.

3 Center the heading and type the outline.

Problem 2

full sheet; 1½" top margin; reset margins to accommodate longest line

1 Type the second part (II) of Problem 1 as a total outline.

2 Change the first division **FORMAT ADAPTATIONS** to a centered heading.

3 Adapt all other parts of the outline to a form appropriate to their division.

	words
LETTER FORMATS AND ADAPTATIONS	6

I. LETTER FORMATS · 10

  A. Line Length (for Average Length Letter): 60 Spaces · 21

  B. Date Placement: Approximately Line 15 (2 1/2 Inches) · 33

  C. Common Formats (or Styles): · 39

    1. Block · 41

      a. All lines flush left · 46

      b. SS; DS between paragraphs · 52

    2. Modified Block · 56

      a. Most lines flush left · 61

      b. Certain lines begin at center point · 69

        (1) Date · 71

        (2) Closing lines · 75

          (a) Complimentary close · 79

          (b) Typed name · 82

          (c) Official title (when used) · 88

      c. SS; DS between paragraphs · 94

II. FORMAT ADAPTATIONS · 99

  A. Personal Letter · 103

    1. Return address above date · 109

    2. Reference initials usually omitted · 117

    3. Enclosure notation usually omitted · 125

  B. Business Letter · 129

    1. Return address usually printed (letterhead) · 139

    2. Reference initials used · 144

    3. Enclosure notation used when appropriate · 153

  C. Personal Business Letter · 159

    1. Address typed above date · 165

    2. Reference initials usually omitted · 173

    3. Enclosure notation used when appropriate · 182

53a ▶ 6
Preparatory practice

each line 3 times SS (work for fewer than 3 errors per group); DS between 3-line groups; repeat selected lines if time permits

alphabet 1 With a fixed goal in mind, quickly size up a job before making a move.

fig/sym 2 Items 318-325 cost $690, which is 75% (or 3/4) of the $920 sale price.

double letters 3 Three little batters slugged a ball across the deep and narrow valley.

easy 4 Did the men fight a duel, or did they go to the chapel and sign a vow?

| 1 | 2 | 3 | 4 | 5 | 6 | 7 | 8 | 9 | 10 | 11 | 12 | 13 | 14 |

27c ▶ 20
Learn new keyreaches:
" __

" = quotation marks
__ = underline

Quotation ('')

Shift; then reach to " with *right little* finger.

Underline (__)

Shift; then reach *up* to __ with *right little* finger.

Left Fingers 4 3 2 1 1 2 3 4 Right Fingers

Follow the "Standard procedure for learning new keyreaches" on page 10 (Lines 1–6 twice; the ¶ once, then again if time permits).

Note: If you are using a non–electric machine, see page 3 directions for reach to ".

To underline: Type the word, backspace to first letter, then strike underline once for each letter in the word.

" 1 ; "; "; James was "Jim"; Mary was "Mo"; and Janis was "Jan."
  2 "We are," he said, "alone." "Wrong," said I, "Lee is here."

__ 3 There is a right way and a wrong way; then there is her way.
  4 I ordered hose, not hoes, and soda for baking, not drinking.

"/__ 5 "This," she stated, "is the antique; that is the facsimile."
  6 She said, "I know that I should go, but I cannot do it now."

Wenz & Jelkes tell us too (in their Report #3) that the margin figure, 10%, is not "very high" for what a major firm makes. The profit this year ($1.5 million) isn't so high as it could have been, but the firm hopes to improve next year.

| 1 | 2 | 3 | 4 | 5 | 6 | 7 | 8 | 9 | 10 | 11 | 12 |

27d ▶ 15
Type a short report

full sheet; DS; 60-space line; 2" top margin; make corrections as you type; proofread/circle errors

words

SOME FACTS TO REMEMBER (Center) ... 4
TS

There are 10 pica and 12 elite spaces to an inch. With *one horizontal* ... 18

either *size* style of type, six lines comprise a vertical inch. ... 30

To find the center point of a given *horizontal* area *sheet,* add the readings ... 44

for *its* the left and right *edges* limits from the line of writing scale; ... 56

divide the *sum* total by 2. ... 61

determine *for vertical centering* to set top and bottom margins, subtract the number of ... 79

lines needed *to format* for the problem from the number available *on* of the ... 91

the remaining lines page; divide by 2 to find exact top margin. Subtract 12 if ... 107

you desire reading position. After computing lines to be left ... 120

in the top margin, space down *one line* once more and begin the first ... 133

line of the problem. ... 137

**Format/type
an outline**

full sheet; 1½" top margin; 70-space line; center heading

words

UNBOUND REPORTS
TS

	words
I. MARGINS	3
	6
A. Top Margins	9
1. First page: pica, 1 1/2"; elite, 2"	17
2. Other pages: 1"	21
B. Side and Bottom Margins	27
1. Left and right margins: 1"	33
2. Bottom margin: 1"	38
II. SPACING	40
A. Body of Manuscript: Double	47
B. Paragraph Indentions: 5 or 10 Spaces Uniformly	57
C. Quoted Paragraphs	62
1. Four or more lines	66
a. Single-spaced	70
b. Indented 5 spaces from each margin	78
c. Quotation marks not required	84
2. Fewer than 4 lines	89
a. Quotation marks used	94
b. Not separated from text or indented from text margins	105
III. PAGINATION	109
A. Page 1: Usually Not Numbered, but Number May Be Centered 1/2" from Bottom Edge	122 / 125
B. Other Pages: Number Typed at Right Margin, 1/2" from Top Edge of Paper Followed by a Triple Space	139 / 146

52

**Preparatory
practice**

each line 3 times SS; (concentrate on copy); DS between 3-line groups; repeat selected lines if time permits

alphabet	1	Our unexpected freezing weather quickly killed Joann's massive shrubs.
figures	2	Invoices 625, 740, and 318 were dated June 5, 1984; and all were paid.
br	3	Brad's brother, Bruce, broke my bronze brooches and brass bric-a-brac.
easy	4	Did the roan foal buck, and did it cut the right elbow of the cowhand?

| 1 | 2 | 3 | 4 | 5 | 6 | 7 | 8 | 9 | 10 | 11 | 12 | 13 | 14 |

Align at the right

half sheet; 40-space line; exact vertical center; SS

1 Space forward from left margin 20 spaces; set tab; space forward 20 more spaces; set second tab.

2 Keyboard first column at left margin; backspace from tab stops to type second and third columns.

words

			words
1.	I.	one	2
2.	II.	two	4
3.	III.	three	7
4.	IV.	four	9
5.	V.	five	12
6.	VI.	six	14
7.	VII.	seven	17
8.	VIII.	eight	20
9.	IX.	nine	22
10.	X.	ten	24

28

Learning goals

1 To achieve smooth, continuous keystroking.

2 To improve ability to concentrate on copy.

3 To improve proofreading skills.

4 To improve facility with figure and symbol reaches.

5 To type script and rough–draft copy smoothly.

Machine adjustments

1 Set paper guide at 0.

2 Set ribbon control to type on upper half of ribbon.

3 Use 60–space line throughout.

4 SS drills; DS paragraphs.

28a ▶ 7

Preparatory practice

each line three times SS (slowly, faster, still faster); DS between 3-line groups; repeat selected lines if time permits

alphabet	1	My wife helped fix a frozen lock on Jacque's vegetable bins.
difficult reaches	2	Beverly sneezed even though she ate a dozen square lozenges.
figures	3	Do Problems 6 to 19 on page 275 before class at 8:30, May 4.
easy	4	Did the form entitle Jay to the land at the end of the lane?

| 1 | 2 | 3 | 4 | 5 | 6 | 7 | 8 | 9 | 10 | 11 | 12 |

28b ▶ 10

Control machine parts

once as shown DS; repeat if time permits

Lines 1-4: Clear all tabs; set tab at center point; tab and type. Keep eyes on book copy.

Line 5: Supply appropriate spacing after punctuation.

Line 6: Release margin; backspace 5 spaces into left margin to begin.

Line 7: Depress shift/lock keys firmly.

center ↓

1 ——————————→ The tab key should be operated

tab and return 2 quickly. ——————————→ One quick flick of your finger

3 should suffice. ——————————→ Avoid pauses; do not slow down

4 or look up when you tab.

space bar 5 Was it Mary? Judy? Pam? It was a woman; she wore a big hat.

margin release/ backspacer 6 When you type from copy, elevate the copy to make reading easier.

shift/lock 7 Al read A TALE OF TWO CITIES; Vi read THE MILL ON THE FLOSS.

28c ▶ 10

Improve response patterns

1 Once as shown; checkmark the three most difficult lines.

2 Repeat the lines you checked as difficult.

3 Take a 1' writing on Line 2, next on Line 4, and then on Line 6. Determine *gwam* on each writing.

word	1	Did the antique map of the world also hang by the oak shelf?
	2	Did they pay the auditor the duty on eighty bushels of corn?
stroke	3	Holly tests fast race cars; we get oil at my garage in Juno.
	4	Johnny erected a vast water cascade on my acreage in Joplin.
combination	5	She paid the extra debt and the taxes on their land in Ohio.
	6	Lynn sewed the nylon flaps on the six burlap bags with care.

| 1 | 2 | 3 | 4 | 5 | 6 | 7 | 8 | 9 | 10 | 11 | 12 |

Learning goals

1 To prepare topical outlines.
2 To prepare unbound reports.
3 To prepare a data sheet.
4 To keyboard spread headings.
5 To develop greater awareness of copy content.
6 To improve ability to think and compose at the keyboard.

Machine adjustments

1 Set paper guide at 0; remove all tab stops.
2 Set ribbon control to type on upper half of ribbon.
3 Use a 70-space line unless otherwise directed.

51a ▶ 6
Preparatory practice

each line 3 times SS
(concentrate on copy); DS between 3-line groups; repeat selected lines if time permits

alphabet	1	Dixie Vaughn acquired the prize job with a large firm just like yours.
figures	2	The ad said to call 964-5781 before 3 p.m. to order 20 sheets on sale.
shift	3	Rosa and Lazaro spent April in Connecticut and May and June in Hawaii.
easy	4	The eight auto firms may pay for a formal field audit of their profit.

| 1 | 2 | 3 | 4 | 5 | 6 | 7 | 8 | 9 | 10 | 11 | 12 | 13 | 14 |

51b ▶ 14
Compose at the keyboard

2 full sheets; 1½" top margin; DS

1 Compose a four- or five-line paragraph in which you describe yourself.

2 Proofread the ¶; make changes with proofreader's marks.

3 Make a final copy. Center the title **A SELF PORTRAIT** over the ¶.

51c ▶ 14
Preapplication drill: format/type an outline

1 Study the information and the sample outline at the right.

2 Because the lines of the outline are short, set for a 40-space line (center point −20/center point +20); SS; 4-space indentions; 1½" top margin.

3 Use **PREPARING OUTLINES** as a main heading; TS; prepare a copy of the outline.

Preparing outlines

It is important that students and others interested in organizing data be able to use a standard form of outline. As you study and keyboard the example at right, note:

• that 4-space indentions separate divisions and subdivisions of various orders.

• that first-order divisions are typed in all capitals; second-order divisions have main words capitalized; third- and subsequent-order divisions have only the first word capitalized.

• that single spacing is used except before and after first-order divisions.

• that there must be at least two parts to any division.

• that all Roman numerals other than I, V, and X necessitate the use of the margin release and backspacer.

• that the line length used must accommodate the longest line in the outline but not exceed a 70-space line.

I. FIRST-ORDER DIVISION
                               DS

  A. Second-Order Division
  B. Second-Order Division
    1. Third-order division
    2. Third-order division
  C. Second-Order Division
                             DS

II. FIRST-ORDER DIVISION

  A. Second-Order Division
    1. Third-order division
    2. Third-order division
      a. Fourth-order division
      b. Fourth-order division
    3. Third-order division
  B. Second-Order Division

29

28d ▶ 23
Improve keyboarding continuity

full sheet; DS; 60-space line;
1½" top margin

1 Prepare the report once, making the corrections designated by the proofreading symbols.
2 Correct any new errors using proofreader's marks.
3 Prepare a final copy from your marked paragraphs; proofread; circle errors.

words

my ARIZONA HIDEAWAY
                                    TS   4

    In arizona, there is a small hotel that is locatd near   15

six high green and white mountains. I like ~~it~~ there, for A   27

enjoy the quite of that palce. The morningview is special,   40

and each day there i feel better that I felt the day before.   52

The six mountains are quite high, green just so far up;   63

then they turn white. They reach into the azure beyond like   75

human hands; and when a cloud appears, it seems as if one of   88

the hands has flung a small piece of vapor into the heavens.   100

    Rates are excellent. The hotel provides two (2) large-   111

size rooms and a tasty dinner for just $65 daily. The hotel   123

has only 134 rooms; therefore, I call early for reservations   136

when I visit this area--as I did last April 7, 8, 9, and 10.   148

29a ▶ 7
Preparatory practice

each line twice SS (slowly, then faster); DS between 2-line groups; 1' writings on Line 4 as time permits

alphabet	1	Bob realized very quickly that jumping was excellent for us.
fig/sym	2	Ann's 7% note (dated May 23, 1985) was paid at 4690 J Drive.
double letters	3	Will Buzz and Lee carry the supplies across the street soon?
easy	4	He paid for the endowment, and he owns the giant coal field.

| 1 | 2 | 3 | 4 | 5 | 6 | 7 | 8 | 9 | 10 | 11 | 12 |

29b ▶ 10
Improve symbol keyreaches

each line twice SS; DS between 2-line groups; repeat lines that seemed difficult

Keep eyes on copy; keep keystroking smooth and continuous.

'	1	Ray's brother didn't plan for the day's work; it's not done.
-	2	A pay-freeze plan on so-called full-time jobs is well-known.
( )	3	All of us (including Vera) went to the game (and it rained).
"	4	They read the poems "September Rain" and "The Lower Branch."
$	5	His weekly checks totaled $128.35, $96.20, $114.80, and $77.
/	6	The Sr/C Club walked and/or ran 15 1/2 miles in 6 3/4 hours.

50c ▶ 15
Review/improve communication skills: spelling

70-space line; decide size of paper, top margin, and spacing

1 Clear tab stops; set two new tab stops, one 30 spaces from left margin and one 59 spaces from left margin.

2 Keyboard the first word at the left margin; tab and type the word again; then tab and type it a third time, this time without looking at the word in the book or on the paper.

3 Repeat this procedure for each word on the list.

4 Study your completed copy. Correct errors. Note your comments about placement at the bottom of the copy.

SPELLING DEMONS

accessible	accessible	accessible
achieve		
analyze		
comparative		
definitely		
disappoint		
forty		
harass		
leisure		
maintenance		
occurrence		
privilege		
recommend		
separate		
truly		
weird		

50d ▶ 15
Proofread/revise as you keyboard

1 Cover the answer key at the bottom of the column. After keyboarding, check your answers.

2 As you keyboard each line, decide whether each circled word or figure follows the rules of form, spelling, or capitalization. If an item is incorrect, make the correction.

Key:
1. accessible, achieve, disappoint
2. privilege, eight, nine, 2d
3. Plaza, Cinema, recommended, 40
4. 50, Chapter, achievement
5. 40, truly, weird, leisure
6. comparatively, 3
7. 100, ten-cent, 1245—125th
8. recommend, analyze, separate, maintenance
9. Harass, definitely, five
10. 30, percent

1 The goal was (accessable) I did not (achieve) it. Did I (disappoint) you?

2 It was a (privilege) to meet (8) or (nine) students on the (second) of August.

3 The (plaza) (cinema) (reccommended) that we sit in the (forty) reserved seats.

4 The (50) questions from (chapter) 9 were included on the (acheivement) test.

5 They walked (forty) miles--(truly) a (weird) way to use their (liesure) hours.

6 It was (comparitvely) simple to find a place to sit at the May (3rd) meet.

7 Send the (100) (ten-cent) gifts to 125 Fifth Avenue or (1245--125th) Street.

8 I (recommend) that you (analyze) costs and (seperate) (maintenance) from rent.

9 (Harras) me no further; I (definitely) will not set places for (five) of us.

10 Approximately (thirty) (percent) of the profit is designated for salaries.

29c ▶ 5

Develop concentration with fill-ins

each line once DS; proofread and mark with proofreader's marks any errors you make; retype from your edited copy

1 Rent in the amount of $185 is payable the 5th of each month.

2 In response, refer to Invoice #187-3 and the date, April 21.

3 Plant seedlings 3 inches deep, 12 inches apart, after May 1.

4 On 3-17-85 Bands 7746-7789 were used to band Canadian geese.

5 Shipments left Dock 15 via Atlantic Express May 29 at 3 p.m.

29d ▶ 6

Improve response patterns

once as shown; repeat if time permits

Lines 1-2: Say and type each word as a unit.

Lines 3-4: Spell each word as you type it letter by letter at a steady pace.

Lines 5-6: Say and type short, easy words as units; spell and type longer words letter by letter.

word
1 Their goal is to do social work downtown for a city auditor.
2 Did the men cut the eight bushels of corn down by the field?

stroke
3 He acts, in my opinion, as if my cards gave him greater joy.
4 Jimmy deserves my extra reward; few cars ever tested better.

combination
5 Based on my theory, she decreased that quantity of protozoa.
6 They sign with great care several of their formal abstracts.

| 1 | 2 | 3 | 4 | 5 | 6 | 7 | 8 | 9 | 10 | 11 | 12 |

29e ▶ 9

Improve keystroking technique

each line twice SS; DS between 2-line groups; keep wrists low, eyes on copy

bottom row
1 Did six brave, zany exhibitors and/or bakers climb Mt. Zemb?

home row
2 Sada and Jake had a dish of salad; Gail had a glass of soda.

3d row
3 At her party, a quiet waiter poured tea as I wrote a letter.

figures
4 On June 24, Flight 89 left at 1:30 with 47 men and 65 women.

| 1 | 2 | 3 | 4 | 5 | 6 | 7 | 8 | 9 | 10 | 11 | 12 |

29f ▶ 13

Measure skill growth: straight copy

60-space line; DS

three 1' writings
three 3' writings

Goal:

1'—25 or more *gwam*
3'—21 or more *gwam*

Difficulty index

| all letters used | E | 1.2 si | 5.1 awl | 90% hfw |

gwam 3'

Do we care about how people judge us? Most of us do. 4 26

We hope and expect that other people will recognize quality 8 30

in what we do, what we say, and the way we act. Is it not 12 34

true, though, that what others think of us results from some 16 38

image that we have created in their minds? In other words, 20 42

are we not really our own creation? 22 44

gwam 3' | 1 | 2 | 3 | 4 |

49d ▶ 13
Measure straight-copy skill

1 Keyboard the ¶s once for orientation. Pay attention to spelling and usage.
2 Take two 3′ writings.
Goal: 26 or more *gwam*.

Difficulty index

all letters used | LA | 1.4 si | 5.4 awl | 85% hfw

	gwam 1′	3′
Being able to communicate can truly help us to realize success in	13	4	51
both our private and business lives. We can write, and we can quickly	29	9	56
read what is written. We can speak, and we can hear what is said; but	42	14	61
hearing is not exactly the same as listening. Hearing means using the	56	19	65
ears and sound waves; listening is using the mind and making judgments.	70	23	70
Listening requires an active mind, not a lazy, closed one. Those	13	28	74
of us who want to be good listeners must work for it, not just expect	29	32	79
that it will come. Good listening always begins with a real desire to	42	37	84
understand what others are trying to tell us; it increases when we are	56	42	89
patient and objective while they explain to us their thoughts and ideas.	70	47	93

gwam 1′ | 1 | 2 | 3 | 4 | 5 | 6 | 7 | 8 | 9 | 10 | 11 | 12 | 13 | 14 |
3′ | 1 | | 2 | | 3 | | 4 | | 5 |

49e ▶ 12
Make decisions: keyboarding a personal letter

1 plain full sheet

1 Make decisions about the line length and appropriate placement of the personal letter, and then type it.
2 Examine the letter carefully when you have finished it, and correct errors. Note your comments about it at the bottom of the page.
If necessary, refer to page 57 for assistance.

words

1225 Seventh Street | Bakersfield, CA 93304-9012 | February 2, 19-- | Mr. Bertram 15
B. Heck | 2521--112th Street, W. | Kansas City, MO 64131-7144 | Dear Bert 29

(¶) Good news! I found your copy of <u>Analyses</u>. It was behind a drape where you 46
often sat by the window to read. You may have set the book on the floor, and the 62
wheel of your chair pushed it behind the drape. 72

(¶) I shall mail the book back to you in four or five days. Why the delay? I must 88
confess that when I reexamined the book and discovered it was written by an 103
ex-worker with the Peace Corps, I became fascinated with it. Forgive me, good 119
friend; but I must read it before I return it. I shall have it in your hands, though, 136
before the 14th, when I know you are leaving for Chicago. 148

(¶) I hope your trip home was a pleasant one, Bert. 157

Cordially | Lu Chi 160

50a ▶ 7
Preparatory practice

each line twice SS (slowly, faster, still faster); DS between 2-line groups; then take a 1′ writing on Line 4; repeat if time permits

alphabet 1 Some obviously deaf, unknown organists composed the six jazz quartets.

fig/sym 2 Interest accumulated to $270.56 in 1984 (when the rate increased 13%).

long words 3 Their accumulated analyses provided reliable estimates of probability.

easy 4 Did the visitor to the city handle the authentic enamel dish and bowl?

| 1 | 2 | 3 | 4 | 5 | 6 | 7 | 8 | 9 | 10 | 11 | 12 | 13 | 14 |

50b ▶ 13
Measure straight-copy skill

Repeat 49d, above.

Learning goals

1 To prepare personal letters in block and modified block styles.
2 To correct keyboarding errors.
3 To improve ability to keyboard unedited copy.
4 To address envelopes.
5 To align and type over words.

Machine adjustments

1 Position desk and chair at com—fortable heights.
2 Elevate book.
3 Set ribbon control to type on upper half of ribbon.
4 Use 60–space line for drills; 50–space line for letters.
5 SS drills; DS paragraphs.
Materials: monarch–size sheets and envelopes; plain sheets; supplies for correcting errors.

30a ▶ 7
Preparatory practice

each line 3 times SS (slowly, faster, slower); DS between 3-line groups; re-peat if time permits

alphabet	1	Jayne Coxx puzzled over the workbooks required for geometry.
a/s	2	This essay says it is easy to save us from disaster in Asia.
figures	3	The box is 6 5/8 by 9 1/2 feet and weighs 375 to 400 pounds.
easy	4	The city auditor paid the proficient man for the fine signs.

| 1 | 2 | 3 | 4 | 5 | 6 | 7 | 8 | 9 | 10 | 11 | 12 |

30b ▶ 43
Prepare personal letters in block style

7¼″ × 10½″ personal station-ery [Laboratory Materials pp. 17-19]; 50-space line; 2″ top margin; proofread/circle errors

If personal–size stationery or plain paper cut to size is not available, use full sheets (8½″ × 11″); 50–space line; 2½″ top margin.

1 Study the explanatory para–graphs at the right. Refer to the style letter on page 58 for further illustration.
2 Prepare the letter illustrating the block style shown on page 58. Follow spacing directions given on the letter.
3 On a plain full sheet, do two 1′ writings on the opening lines (return address through saluta-tion) and two 2′ writings on the closing lines (last 2 ¶s through complimentary close).
4 Retype the letter; omit ¶3.

Letter placement information

Many personal letters are prepared on personal-size stationery; and Style Letter 1, page 58, is shown with pica (10-pitch) type on that size stationery.

Good letter placement results from the ability to make judgments based on the length of letter, style of stationery, and size of type. Therefore, while it is suggested that letters in Section 7 be started on Line 13 when personal stationery is used (which al-lows approximately a 2″ top margin) or on Line 16 if full sheets are used (approxi-mately a 2½″ top margin), the starting point can be raised for a longer letter or lowered for a shorter one if you believe it is wise to do so.

Every letter must have a return address. On business stationery, the return address is part of the letterhead. When personal stationery is used, a return address must be typed as part of the letter. The most appro-priate place for this address, according to common usage, is on the two lines imme-diately above and aligned with the date.

It is standard procedure to operate the return 4 times, leaving 3 blank line spaces between the date and the letter recipient's address. This procedure is repeated after the complimentary close, leaving 3 blank line spaces for the signature to be written between the complimentary close and the writer's typed name. (For a personal letter, a typed name is not necessary.) These placement procedures should be followed with all letters in Section 7.

For smaller personal stationery, side margins should be no less than 1″ and no more than 1½″. A 50-space line, pica or elite, fits within this standard. It is recom-mended, therefore, that a 50-space line be used with Section 7 letters regardless of type size.

Preparatory practice

each line twice SS
(slowly, then faster);
DS between 2-line
groups; then 1′ writ-
ings on Line 4; repeat
if time permits

alphabet 1 Put my five boxes in with the dozen jugs of quick-drying blue lacquer.

fig/sym 2 Hunt & Carte's $623.75 check (Check 1489) was delivered on January 10.

1st/2nd
fingers 3 As Frederick Vertman hinted, they were regarded as tame but untrained.

easy 4 Did a city auditor handle the formal audit of both firms for a profit?

| 1 | 2 | 3 | 4 | 5 | 6 | 7 | 8 | 9 | 10 | 11 | 12 | 13 | 14 |

49b ▶ 8

Review/improve communication skills: number usage

Follow directions given in 48b.

Key: 1b. 40 percent 1c. 37 percent, 15% 2c. 75 cents

Express as figures

1. Definite numbers with a (%) sign; percent (spelled) is used with formal writing and with approximations.

2. Large round numbers in the millions or higher with their word modifiers, such as 25 *million* or 63 *billion*; use with or without a dollar sign. Use the word *cents* after figure amounts of less than one dollar.

Note

To avoid confusion or error, businesses commonly use figures for all numbers except those which begin a sentence.

review 1a. Attendance is about 97 percent. The interest rate soared to 17%.
apply   b. Nearly 40% of the 86% increase came from charitable donations.
apply   c. The firm reinvested close to 37% of last year's 15 percent profit.

review 2a. They budgeted $12 million for highways and $10 million for parks.
review   b. She took $25 from her savings account; now she has only 14 cents.
apply   c. The group collected $1 million; some donations were only 75¢.

49c ▶ 10

Proofread/revise as you keyboard

half sheet; 74-space line; 1″
top margin; DS

1 Cover the answer key at the bottom of the column. When you have finished keyboarding, check your answers.

2 Keyboard the guide number (with period), space twice, and type the sentence.

3 As you keyboard each line, decide if the sentence is correct according to the guides for number usage. If the sentence is not correct, make the appropriate correction as you keyboard.

Key: 1. 2 **2.** seven **3** cents **4.** three, eight **5.** $25 million **6.** forty–six, 3d **7.** 9 **8.** One, 231–– 18th **9.** correct **10.** ¼, ½

1. A recipe containing two lbs. of veal won Al the 20th annual contest.

2. About 7 20-ounce containers of milk were on the counter yesterday.

3. He gave the clerk $5 and waited for the 25¢ change.

4. Yoko stacked 3 books and 8 magazines on the shelf.

5. Nearly two thirds of the $25,000,000 was spent on medical research.

6. Six hundred forty six graduates receive diplomas on the third of June.

7. Julio read Rule nine and then applied the principle to the problem.

8. We sent the gifts to 1 Laurel Avenue and 231 18th Street.

9. The company increased productivity by approximately 20 percent in May.

10. What is the sum of 2 1/8, one fourth, and one half?

**Return
address
Dateline**

101 Kensington Place   Line 13
Brockton, MA ⌃ 02401-5372
August 3, 19-⌄—— 2 spaces

Operate return
4 times

**Letter
address**

Ms. Viola Bargas
6776 Heidelberg Street
Durham, NC 27704-4329
                    DS

Salutation

Dear Viola
         DS

**Body
of
letter**

It will be great to have you living in Brockton
again. Your promotion to vice-president of the
marketing division is certainly well deserved.

You will find that our town has changed considerably since your last visit three years ago. It is
still a small, close-knit community; but the newly
established Arts Commission has begun to promote
the efforts of many local artists. As a result,
our little village has taken on a bohemian air.

Let me show you one way that Brockton has changed.
I should like you to be my guest on August 23 when
the local theater group presents SCHOOL FOR SCANDAL
at the Whitmore Playhouse. Two of our sorority
members are directing the production.

As you requested, I shall meet you at the airport
(Gate 11) on August 23 at 8:25 a.m. You can spend
the afternoon apartment hunting, and you can relax
in the evening during dinner and the play.

I am very eager to see you, Viola!
                                 DS

**Complimentary
close
Signature**

Cordially

Amanda

This letter is typed with
"open" punctuation; that is,
no punctuation follows the
salutation or complimentary
close.

gwam 1' (total words)	gwam 2'
4	
9	
12	
15	
20	
25	
27	
36	
46	
55	
65	
75	
86	
95	
105	
115	
125	5
135	10
146	15
155	20
163	24
173	29
183	34
193	39
202	44
209	47
211	48

Style letter 1: personal letter in block style

Review/improve communication skills: number usage

Follow directions given in 48b.

Key: 1b. 43 2c. One 3b. 18 4d. 9 4e. 23d 5b. correct 6b. 1/8

review 1a. The Treaty of Ghent is covered in Chapter 9 of the history text.
apply   b. Cesar went to Room forty-three and delivered his application.

review 2a. Pick up the parcel at One Elm Way and take it to 4729 Fifth Avenue.
review   b. The new address of the Museum of Modern Art is 2647--56th Street.
apply   c. The taxi stopped at 1 Sixth Street and 234--42d Street.

review 3a. At 8 a.m. the chef simmered the 3 lbs. of beef in the kettle.
apply   b. Their carton (14 in. × 14 in. × eighteen in.) was mailed.

review 4a. She will arrive in Boston between the 2d and the 4th of January.
review   b. On May 13 we shall attend the opening of the art exhibit in Richmond.
review   c. I shall arrive on the 15th. He will leave Mexico on the 12th.
apply   d. Victoria arrived on the 12th of April, and she left on June 9th.
apply   e. The cast had a rehearsal on the twenty-third.

review 5a. Maxine earned $68 last week for her work at the local garden store.
apply   b. This antique vase, which is made of porcelain, is valued at $400.

review 6a. What is the sum of 1/2, 3/4, and 4 2/3?
apply   b. The tailor cut 2 2/3, 1 1/4, one-eighth, and 4 5/8 yards of fabric.

Improve keyboarding continuity: statistical copy

1 Keyboard the ¶ once for orientation. Be especially aware of number usage as you prepare the copy.

2 Take two 3' writings; determine *gwam*.

Goal: at least 22 *gwam*.

Difficulty index

all letters/figures used	LA	1.4 si	5.4 awl	85% hfw

gwam 3'

We started to manufacture Dixie Real Tractors in the back of a small   5
plant at 3720 First Avenue in Quantico, Virginia; and in that first year   9
of 1968, we actually completed only five or six of these small-size 9 hp.   14
machines. Today, in our big, modern factory at One 45th Avenue, we find   19
it hard to realize that we turn out about seventy of our machines in just   24
one day and that our profit for last year was over $1 million.   28

gwam 3' | 1 | 2 | 3 | 4 | 5 |

31a ▶ 7
Preparatory practice

each line twice SS (slowly, faster, slower); DS between 2-line groups; then as many 30″ writings on Line 4 as time permits

alphabet	1	Max Jurez worked to improve the quality of his basic typing.
adjacent reaches	2	Bert quickly pointed to where onions grew in the sandy soil.
fig/sym	3	Veronica bought 16 7/8 yards of #240 cotton at $3.59 a yard.
easy	4	The formal gowns worn by the girls hang in the civic chapel.

| 1 | 2 | 3 | 4 | 5 | 6 | 7 | 8 | 9 | 10 | 11 | 12 |

31b ▶ 15
Correct errors

1 Read the information at the right.

2 Keyboard the lines below the information exactly as they appear DS; correct the errors *after* you have typed each line.

Truly finished work contains no errors. Most individuals rely upon an "inner sense" to tell them when they have made an error, and they stop keyboarding at once and correct it. This "inner sense," however, is fallible; and even an expert typist should carefully proofread completed work for undetected mistakes while the paper is still in the machine. Correcting errors before the paper is removed is easier than reinserting paper and trying to realign lines of copy.

There are several acceptable methods that can be used to correct errors, and they are explained below. Whichever one of them is used, one should keep in mind that an error must be repaired skillfully enough so that neither the error nor evidence of the correction can be observed.

Automatic correction

If your machine is equipped with an automatic correcting ribbon, consult with your instructor or the manufacturer's manual for operating instructions.

Correction paper ("white carbon")

1 Backspace to the error.

2 Place the correction paper in front of the error, coated side toward the paper.

3 Retype the error. The substance on the correction paper will cover the error.

4 Remove the correction paper; backspace; type the correction.

Correction fluid ("liquid paper")

1 Be sure the color of the fluid matches the color of the paper.

2 Turn the paper forward or backward to ease the correction process.

3 Brush the fluid on sparingly; cover only the error, and it lightly.

4 The fluid dries quickly. Return to correction point and make the correction.

Rubber eraser

1 Use a plastic shield (to protect surrounding type) and a typewriter (hard) eraser.

2 Turn the paper forward or backward in the typewriter to position the error for easier correction.

3 To keep bits of rubber out of the mechanism, move the carrier away from the error (or move carriage to the extreme left or right).

4 With a sharp edge of the eraser, erase ink from the paper. Move the eraser in one direction only to avoid cutting the paper.

1 Concentrate when you type; fongers can "telegraph" an error.

2 Just as soon as a mistade is made, it ought to be corrected.

3 It pays to be sure that you find evrey error and correct it.

4 Proofread carefully; then remove your work from the nachine.

Learning goals

1 To improve use of numbers in data.

2 To strengthen ability to spell.

3 To improve ability to make decisions.

Machine adjustments

1 Set paper guide at 0.

2 Set ribbon control to type on upper half of ribbon.

3 Use a 70-space line unless otherwise instructed.

48a ▶ 7

Preparatory practice

each line twice DS (slowly, then faster); DS between 2-line groups; then 1' writings on Line 4; repeat if time permits

alphabet 1 Why did an oval jet-black onyx ring blaze on the queen's plump finger?

figures 2 Bob moved 395 cardboard boxes, 146 of which went to Rooms 270 and 188.

home row 3 Hals had half a glass of soda as Jihad had half a dish of fresh salad.

easy 4 A cow, six roan foals, six turkeys, and a duck amble to the cornfield.

| 1 | 2 | 3 | 4 | 5 | 6 | 7 | 8 | 9 | 10 | 11 | 12 | 13 | 14 |

48b ▶ 13

Review/improve communication skills: number usage

half sheet; 74-space line; 1" top margin; SS sentences; DS between groups

1 Cover the answer key at the bottom of the column. When you have finished keyboarding, check your answers.

2 Study guides for number usage.

3 Keyboard guide number 1a. (with period), space twice, and keyboard review sentence(s), noting guide applications.

4 Keyboard apply sentence(s), correcting errors in number usage as you prepare the copy.

Key: 1b. Eight 2c. three, seven 2d. 7 3b. four, 20, two, four 4b. forty, two thirds 5b. Eighty–five 5c. thirty–one

Express as words

1. A number which begins a sentence even if figures are used later in the sentence.

2. Numbers ten and lower unless they are used in close proximity to numbers higher than ten, which are expressed as figures.

3. One of two adjacent numbers. Preferably the smaller number should be spelled for efficiency.

4. Isolated fractions and indefinite numbers.

5. Use a hyphen to separate compound numbers between twenty-one and ninety-nine that are spelled out, whether they stand alone or as a part of a number over one hundred.

review 1a. Six players were cut from the 37-member team.

apply b. 8 altos and 21 sopranos filled the front row of the stage.

review 2a. We saw five or six wild ducks swim away; three were mallards.

review b. All but 5 of the 15 lamps were turned on.

apply c. Andrew took 3 sweaters and 7 shirts to the cleaning service.

apply d. The librarian repaired the loose bindings on seven of the 25 books.

review 3a. The six 200-gallon drums are in the truck.

apply b. Cora bought 4 twenty-cent stamps; she used only 2 of the 4 stamps.

review 4a. About fifty women registered, but only one half stayed for the meal.

apply b. Close to 40 attended the meeting; 2/3 offered to help.

review 5a. Seventy-two of the four hundred fifty-eight pages were about Brahms.

apply b. Eighty five of the one hundred forty-six entry forms were submitted.

apply c. Out of the one hundred thirty one varieties, sixty-two were hybrids.

31c ▶ 28
Personal letters in block style

3 personal-size sheets [LM pp. 21-25] or plain paper; see pages 57 and 58 for guides to letter placement; proofread/correct errors

Postal authorities recommend using 2–letter state abbreviations (always with ZIP Code). For a complete list of such abbrevia–tions, see the Reference Guide, p. iv at the back of this book.

Personal titles

As a courtesy to the person to whom a letter is addressed, a letter writer may use a personal or professional title—Miss, Mr., Dr., etc.—with the name in the letter address and on the envelope.

A letter writer, if male, does not ordinarily give himself a title in the signature lines. A female writer, however, may properly use a title before her typed name or, when she writes it, in parentheses before her signature to indicate her preference.

Problem 1

	words
900 Beecher Street	Montgomery, AL 36108-4473	May 18, 19--		12
(Operate return 4 times)	Mr. Lymon S. Bohn	890 Crestview	18
Drive	Rockford, IL 61107-2317	DS	Dear Lymon	DS	26

(¶) This morning I talked with Debra Tredsaw, a member of the 38
school reunion committee; and I heard a bit of great news--that 51
you plan to attend our class reunion next month. 61

(¶) More great news! Herb Dobynski will also be here, and he 72
and I want to play a little golf that afternoon. Can you arrange 85
to be in town early enough to join us? Maybe I can persuade 98
Jimmy Geddes or Ted Oxward to make it a foursome. 108

(¶) Let me know when you are arriving, Lymon. I'll be glad to 120
pick you up at the airport or to make any other arrangements for 133
you. 133

Cordially | (Operate return 4 times) | Mike Stavros 138

Problem 2

890 Crestview Drive | Rockford, IL 61107-2317 | May 25, 19-- | Mr. 12
Michael Stavros | 900 Beecher Street | Montgomery, AL 36108- 24
4473 | Dear Mike 26

(¶) I do indeed plan to attend the Monroe High reunion of the 38
Class of '78. I wouldn't miss it--nor would I pass up a chance to 51
give you and Herb a drubbing on the golf course. 61

(¶) The trip to Montgomery will also involve taking care of some 74
business. I shall drive down, arriving there during the late 86
afternoon or early evening of the 16th. I have made reserva- 98
tions at the Graymoor for three days. I'll call you when I get in. 112

(¶) I'm really looking forward to this trip, Mike, and to the oppor- 125
tunity to visit many old friends. 131

Cordially | Lymon Bohn 135

Problem 3

900 Beecher Street | Montgomery, AL 36108-4473 | May 27, 19-- | 11
Mr. Herbert Dobynski | 8098 Fairwater Drive | Norfolk, VA 23
23508-6172 | Dear Herb 27

(¶) I have tried to reach you several times by phone, but I have 39
not been successful; hence, this brief note. 48

(¶) Lymon Bohn has confirmed that he'll be in town for the re- 60
union on June 17, and he has agreed to join us for golf that after- 73
noon. Ted Oxward will also join us. 81

(¶) Because I expect things might be hectic at my club that day, 93
I called the pro, Jill Nyles, today and asked her to save us a 105
tee-off time of 1 p.m. If for any reason this time is not good 118
for you, let me know. 123

Cordially | Mike Stavros 127

---

words

Problem 1
block style

(Current date) | Mr. Lonny L. Johnson, Director | The House by the Side of the 15
Road | 679 Truman Street | Abilene, TX 79601-5739 | Dear Mr. Johnson 28

(¶) The Executive Board of The House by the Side of the Road has instructed me 43
to express to you how deeply it regrets your resignation as House Director. 58
(¶) The Board recognizes that you have served as Director for 18 years. Your 73
leadership, loyalty, and perseverance will be missed; and finding another Direc- 89
tor to take your place will not be easy. 97
(¶) Therefore, the Board also asks me to express its special thanks for your 112
willingness to continue to serve as Director until we find a replacement. 126
(¶) We shall, of course, begin a search for a new Director right away; but, in the 142
meantime, please let us know of any assistance we can provide. 155
Sincerely yours | Dale L. Berger | Secretary | xx 163/**184**

Problem 2
modified block style

(Current date) | Mr. Byung Chung, Manager | Nikki's Paris Shop | 1890 San Luis 15
Street | Las Vegas, NV 89110-7241 | Dear Mr. Chung 24

(¶) This letter introduces Gale Senter, our Nevada representative for Cleo 38
Sportswear. Gale will stop at your shop in a day or two to show you samples of 54
our new spring line. 59
(¶) One of the features you should look for in Cleo clothes--and stress to your 74
customers--is the basic, uncluttered look of each style. Our designers fashion 90
clothes that do not have faddish elements that outdate them after one or two 105
seasons. 107
(¶) Also, examine carefully the fine cloth used to make our Cleo line. All our 122
fabrics are washable and do not need ironing. Easy care and long wear are Cleo 138
hallmarks. Notice our wide range of color choices, which allows customers to 154
pick colors that complement personality as well as please the eye. 167
(¶) Gale will be happy to discuss availability and terms of purchase with you. 181
You'll be glad she called. 187
Sincerely yours | Miss Celia Murtagh | Sales Manager | xx 197/**215**

Problem 3
style of your choice

(Current date) | Miss Molly Bester | 3724 Mumford Road | Macon, GA 31204-4493 | 15
Dear Miss Bester 18

(¶) It is difficult for us to express adequately our regret for the recent error we 34
made in your telephone order. Mistakes like this rarely occur; when they do, it 50
is not easy to make them right. 57
(¶) We understand that you ordered a pound box of chocolates to be sent gift 71
wrapped for your mother's birthday. All our records confirm this. We do not 87
know why a box of cigars was sent. 94
(¶) We can understand your acute embarrassment when your mother opened 108
your gift and found a box of cigars. Immediately upon hearing of our error, we 124
sent by special messenger a 5-pound box of our deluxe chocolates with a note of 140
apology to your mother. We hope she will understand. 150
(¶) We do not ask that you pay for the chocolates. We do not ask that you return 166
the cigars. We do ask you to forgive us. 174
Sincerely yours | Leonard J. Anhut | Vice President | xx 184/**196**

32a ▶ 7
Preparatory practice

each line three times SS
(slowly, faster, slower); DS
between 3-line groups; repeat if time permits

alphabet 1 Jim Kable won a second prize for his very quixotic drawings.

shift 2 Zora and Donald Pace flew over Byrd Peak six times in March.

fig/sym 3 I said, "My check for $739.50 (#184) is not dated April 26."

easy 4 The ancient oak on the quay is visible to an island visitor.

| 1 | 2 | 3 | 4 | 5 | 6 | 7 | 8 | 9 | 10 | 11 | 12 |

32b ▶ 10
Improve concentration:
typing from unedited copy

60-space line; DS

1 Find and correct errors in the
copy as you type the paragraph.

2 Proofread/correct final copy
while it is still in the machine.

words

What causes you eraser to erase? There is no thing spe-   11
cial about it. When you type, the element forses ink into the   24
fibers of the paper. If you type some thing wrong, therefore,   36
the fibers under the error must be remover. Such removal is   48
best accomplished by confining the erasing to a small area   60
and by moving the eraser in just one direction, an action that   73
removes just one layer of inked fibbers.   81

32c ▶ 13
Personal letter
in block style

1 personal-size sheet [LM p.
27] or plain paper; SS ¶s; DS
between ¶s; proofread/correct
errors

1 Format the letter at the right,
making corrections as marked.

2 For special parts, use:

Return address and date

334 Pittman Street
Olathe, KS 66061-1678

March 22, 19--

Letter address

Miss Evelyn Guione
1352 Pilgrim Place
Pasadena, CA 91108-3307

Salutation **Dear Evelyn**

Closing lines

Sincerely

(Return 4 times)

Trevor Hunter

Save your typed letter to
use in 33c, p. 63.

words

opening lines   26

¶ As I told you I might, I have changed my plans. I shall be   38

taking three morning classes, there at the Univeristy during   52

July and august.   55

¶ My expenses would be eased considerably if I could find a   67

part-time job, where I might work afternoons or evenings.   78

So, would you be kind enough tolet me know if you would   89

learn of such a position? May I use your name if I make the   104

application?   106

¶ I valeu you friendship, Evelyn; and I shall be very gratful 119

for any assistnce that you may provide.   127

closing lines   129

47a ▶ 6
Preparatory practice

each line 3 times 33 (slowly, faster, still faster); DS between 3-line groups; repeat if time permits

alphabet	1	Does Frank expect to solve the jigsaw puzzle more quickly than before?
fig/sym	2	Model #S6-713 (20″ screen) sells for $359; with a 27″ screen, $468.20.
long words	3	Automatic typewriters are highly effective with repetitive procedures.
easy	4	Pay the right girl to work with them as a tutor with the ancient maps.

| 1 | 2 | 3 | 4 | 5 | 6 | 7 | 8 | 9 | 10 | 11 | 12 | 13 | 14 |

47b ▶ 11
Measure skill growth: straight copy

a 3′ and a 5′ writing; determine gwam; proofread and circle errors

Difficulty index

all letters used	A	1.5 si	5.7 awl	80% hfw

gwam 3′ | 5′

Diogenes, quaint little light in hand, journeyed out night after   4 | 3
night looking for an honest man. We don't know exactly how Diogenes   9 | 5
intended to recognize honesty, but he was very serious about his effort.   14 | 8
He really thought he would know such a person when he met one.   18 | 11

Just as a matter of conjecture, do you wonder whether Diogenes, if   22 | 13
he were living today, might look for an educated person? If he were   27 | 16
to undertake such a search, would an educated person be recognizable?   32 | 19
If so, how? What qualities might you expect an educated person to have?   37 | 22

The idea poses interesting questions. Just what is education? Is   41 | 25
it a mental thing? Can it be recognized in the actions or reactions of   46 | 28
a person? Is it backed up by a diploma? Or is it more? Does it perhaps   51 | 30
include such unscholarly elements as experience and observation?   55 | 33

Diogenes might find that an educated person is one, for example,   59 | 36
who has more questions than answers, is more puzzled than positive, is   64 | 38
aware that more is not known than is known, yet is better able to solve   69 | 41
problems with value judgments than with memorized formulas.   73 | 44

gwam 3′ | 1 | 2 | 3 | 4 | 5 |
5′ | 1 | 2 | 3 |

47c ▶ 33
Measure skill application: business letters

Time schedule:

Assembling materials	2′
Timed production	25′
Final check; proofread; compute *g–pram*	6′

Materials needed:

3 letterheads and envelopes [LM pp. 63–67] or plain paper
60–space line; begin on Line 15

When the signal to begin is given, insert paper and begin typing Problem 1. Keyboard the problems in sequence until the signal to stop is given. Prepare a large envelope for each letter. Do Problem 1 again on a plain sheet if you have finished Problem 3 and time has not been called. Proofread all problems; circle errors. Calculate *g–pram*.

$$g\text{–}pram = \frac{\text{total words typed}}{\text{time (25')}}$$

32d ▶ 12
Address envelopes

1 Addressing envelopes is entirely a matter of visual placement. Read the following guides and study the illustrations to help you with the placement of addresses.

2 Type in United States Postal Service (U.S.P.S.) style a Monarch envelope (No. 9) and in standard style a small envelope (No. 6¾) for each address [LM pp. 29–33]. Use your own return address; proof-read/circle errors.

Letter address

Vertically: Visualize a line drawn from side to side across the vertical center of the envelope. Begin the first line of the address just below such an imaginary line.

Horizontally: Visualize a line drawn from top to bottom across the horizontal center of the envelope. Align an address from 5 (for larger envelopes) to 10 (for smaller envelopes) spaces to the left of such an imaginary line.

Return address

Type the writer's name and address SS in block style in the upper left corner. Start about 3 spaces from the left edge on Line 2.

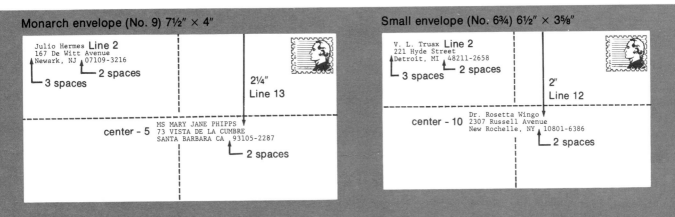

The envelope above is typed in ALL CAPS with no punctuation, the form recommended by the U.S. Postal Service.

Mrs. Arthur T. Werther
1321 Fairbanks Road
Concord, NH 03301-1789

Miss Grace Carveck
35 Fox Mill Lane
Springfield, IL 62707-7133

Mr. Brett Reymer
94 Mercer Street
Paterson, NJ 07524-5447

32e ▶ 8
Fold and insert letters

Study the illustrations below. Practice folding 8½″ × 11″ paper for small envelopes and 7¼″ × 10½″ paper for Monarch envelopes.

The folding procedure for Monarch envelopes is also used for large (No. 10) business envelopes.

Folding and inserting letters into small envelopes

Folding and inserting letters into Monarch envelopes

Step 1
With letter face up, fold bottom up to ½ inch from top.

Step 2
Fold right third to left.

Step 3
Fold left third to ½ inch from last crease.

Step 4
Insert last creased edge first.

Step 1
With letter face up, fold slightly less than ⅓ of sheet up toward top.

Step 2
Fold down top of sheet to within ½ inch of bottom fold.

Step 3
Insert letter into envelope with last crease toward bottom of envelope.

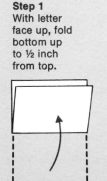

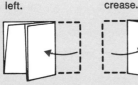

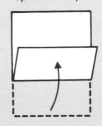
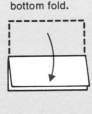

46a ▶ 6
Preparatory practice

each line 3 times SS (slowly, faster, still faster); repeat if time permits

alphabet	1	Gwendolyn Post lives in a quiet area just six blocks from the old zoo.
figures	2	The 1983 edition of this book had 5 parts, 40 chapters, and 672 pages.
hyphen	3	Here is an up-to-date reference for those out-of-this-world questions.
easy	4	The rich man paid half of the endowment, and this firm also paid half.

| 1 | 2 | 3 | 4 | 5 | 6 | 7 | 8 | 9 | 10 | 11 | 12 | 13 | 14 |

46b ▶ 10
Improve concentration

1 Cover the answer key at the bottom of the column. When you have finished, check your answers.

2 Prepare a copy of the ¶ DS. Unscramble the underlined words as you keyboard.

3 Using your corrected copy, take 1′ writings as time permits.

Key: make, been, good, very, read, with, more

Difficulty index

all letters used	A	1.5 si	5.7 awl	80% hfw

gwam 1′

Many people <u>mkae</u> fast work of their letter writing. They com- 12
pose letters on their typewriters. Such a letter has not always <u>bene</u> 26
considered <u>doog</u> form; but now even etiquette experts, whose judgments 40
are accepted by some, recognize and accept typed letters--and for <u>ervy</u> 55
good reasons. A typed letter is easier to <u>rade</u> than a handwritten one; 69
and, as a typist can more easily keep pace <u>hitw</u> his or her thoughts, a 83
typed letter seems to be <u>erom</u> coherent, interesting, and conversational. 98

gwam 1′ | 1 | 2 | 3 | 4 | 5 | 6 | 7 | 8 | 9 | 10 | 11 | 12 | 13 | 14 |

46c ▶ 10
Compose at the keyboard

2 full sheets; 2½″ top margin; 70-space line

1 Compose three brief ¶s, each beginning with the words shown at the right.

2 Make pencil corrections; retype edited copy.

¶ 1 One of my favorite

¶ 2 However, I must say that I dislike

¶ 3 Therefore, whenever I can I

46d ▶ 24
Improve production skill

2 plain full sheets

1 Using Style Letter 4, p. 84, take a 10′ writing. Proofread and circle errors. Calculate g–pram.

2 Take a second 10′ writing. Proofread; circle errors. Calculate g–pram. Work to improve either speed or accuracy on the second writing.

> Use the following formula to calculate *g–pram* (gross production rate a minute):
>
> $$g\text{–}pram = \frac{\text{total words typed}}{\text{time (10′)}}$$

33a ▶ 7
Preparatory practice

each line 3 times SS
(slowly, faster, still faster);
DS between 3-line groups;
repeat if time permits

alphabet 1 Perry might know I feel jinxed because I have missed a quiz.

figures 2 Buy 147 fish, 25 geese, 10 ponies, 39 lambs, and 68 kittens.

hyphen 3 He won the first-class ribbon; it was a now-or-never effort.

easy 4 The neighbor owns a fox, six foals, six ducks, and six hens.

| 1 | 2 | 3 | 4 | 5 | 6 | 7 | 8 | 9 | 10 | 11 | 12 |

33b ▶ 10
Align and type

It is sometimes necessary to reinsert the paper to correct an error. The following steps will help you learn to do so correctly.

1 Type this sentence, but do not make the return:

I can align this copy.

2 Locate aligning scale (16), variable line spacer (2), and paper release lever (13) on your machine.

3 Move the carrier (carriage) so that a word containing an i (such as align) is above the align-

ing scale. Note that a vertical line points to the center of i.

4 Study the relation between top of aligning scale and bottoms of letters with downstems (g,p,y).

Get an exact eye picture of the relation of typed line to top of scale so you will be able to adjust the paper correctly to type over a character with exactness.

5 Remove paper; reinsert it. Gauge the line so bottoms of letters are in correct relation to top of aligning scale. Operate the variable line spacer, if necessary, to move paper up or down. Operate paper release lever to move paper left or right, if necessary, when centering the letter i over one of the lines on the aligning scale.

6 Check accuracy of alignment by setting the ribbon control (28) in stencil position and by typing over one of the letters. If necessary, make further alignment adjustments.

7 Return ribbon control to normal position (to type on upper half of ribbon).

8 Type over the characters in the sentence, moving paper up or down, to left or right, as necessary to correct alignment.

33c ▶ 10
Address envelopes; fold letters

1 sheet plain paper

Refer to page 62 as needed.

Use your letter from 32c, page 61, or plain paper cut to size.

NOTE: If you typed the letter of 32c on standard typing paper, fold it for insertion into a large envelope in the same way the personal-size letter is folded for a Monarch envelope.

1 Address a Monarch envelope to the address below right; use your return address.

2 Fold the letter you typed in 32c, p. 61, for insertion into the envelope.

3 Open the folded paper. Is the typed side facing you?

4 Mark an X at the top edge of a plain sheet, then fold for insertion into a small envelope.

5 Open the folded paper. Is the X facing you?

MISS EVELYN GUIONE
1352 PILGRIM PLACE
PASADENA CA   91108-3307

33d ▶ 23
Prepare personal-business letters in modified block style

1 sheet personal-size paper [LM p. 35] or plain paper; envelope

*From this point on, the last figure in the word count column includes the envelope address.

Study the letter in modified block style illustrated on page 64. Notice the change in position of the return address, date, complimentary close, and typed name.

2 Clear tab stops; set a new stop at center point.

3 Type the letter. Proofread/correct errors.

4 Type an envelope; correct errors.

5 Fold the letter for insertion into envelope.

Review business letters in modified block style

2 letterheads and envelopes [LM pp. 59-61]; carbon paper; copy sheets

60-space line; begin on Line 15

Problem 1

Prepare the letter; make one carbon copy. Proofread and correct your copy before re–moving it from the machine. Address an envelope.

words

August 28, 19-- | Miss Noriko Harada | 9580 Evelyn Way | Reno, NV 89502-4839 | 14
Dear Miss Harada   18

(¶) Thank you for your recent letter inquiring about admission to our School of   33
Graduate Studies. I hope the following information will be helpful.   47

(¶) Admission here depends upon several factors. The applicant, for example,   62
must have completed an appropriate undergraduate degree at an accredited   76
institution with a cumulative grade point average of 2.75 or better on a 4-point   93
scale.   94

(¶) Further, each applicant's transcript is examined to determine whether   108
additional background courses will be required. The background courses   123
necessary for admission are set by each of the various areas of study. The   138
applicant must also complete satisfactorily any admission test that may be   153
required by the area of study for which admission is sought.   165

(¶) I am enclosing an application form for your use. Please let me know if I can   181
help you again.   184

Sincerely | Derek J. Wertz, Ph.D. | Dean, Graduate Studies | xx | Enclosure   197/**208**

Problem 2

Follow directions given for Problem 1.

July 29, 19-- | Mr. Hyman J. Greathouse | President, Apex Motors | 5600 El Avado   15
Avenue | Lincoln, NE 68504-3976 | Dear Mr. Greathouse   25

(¶) Thank you for your kind comments about my presentation before the Lincoln   40
Chamber of Commerce. It was a pleasure for me to be there to describe our   55
company's fringe benefits program.   62

(¶) You asked about my allusion to our company's physical fitness program. We   77
have a good one, I believe. Each year in March, for example, every employee is   93
encouraged to have a complete physical examination by a personal physician at   108
our expense.   111

(¶) We maintain a company membership in a fitness facility, which we urge our   126
employees to use for swimming, racquetball, and other forms of exercise.   141

(¶) We engage in team and league sponsorship when a substantial number of our   156
employees are involved.   161

(¶) As you can see, we are strong advocates of healthy minds and bodies for   175
people who work for us. This program is mutually advantageous and makes   190
very good business sense to us.   196

Cordially yours | Mrs. Frances Trewes Baxter | Executive Vice President | xx   210
  228

Shown in pica type
50–space line

Tabulate to center to type
return address, date, and
closing lines.

	gwam 2'	total words

Return
address

Dateline

Line 13 4885 Crescent Avenue, N.   3   5
Chicago, IL 60656-3781   5   10
April 6, 19--   6   13

Operate return
4 times

Letter
address

Ms. Alice Trent-Rockler   9   17
Personnel Manager   11   21
Leisure Life Inns   12   25
1000 East Lynn Street   15   29
Seattle, WA 98102-4268   17   34
                 DS

Salutation

Dear Ms. Trent-Rockler   19   38
                 DS

Body
of
letter

The Placement Office at Great Lakes College tells   5   48
me that your company has employment available this   10   58
summer for students.   12   63

I am now in my junior year as an economics major.   17   73
Although my educational background has been mostly   22   83
in the liberal arts, I have learned to keyboard;   27   93
and I have taken two accounting courses. In past   32   103
summers I have worked successfully at a variety of   37   113
jobs; in fact, I have accepted responsibility for   42   123
most of my college expenses. I travel as much as   47   133
I can; I like to meet new friends; and I have a   52   143
friendly, outgoing personality.   56   149

Your interest in providing summer employment for   5   159
students is much appreciated, Ms. Trent-Rockler.   10   169
I am sure I would enjoy working at Leisure Life   15   178
Inns. May I send you a complete resume and a list   20   189
of my references?   21   192
          DS

Complimentary
close

Sincerely yours   23   195

Operate return
4 times

Lance J. Mykins

Typed name

Lance J. Mykins   25   198
                     232

Style letter 2: personal-business letter in modified block style,
                      open punctuation

45a ▶ 6
Preparatory practice

each line 3 times SS (slowly, faster, still faster); DS between 3-line groups; repeat if time permits

alphabet 1 Douglas quickly won several junior prizes at the Foxburgh swim trials.

figures 2 Flight 372 will leave at 9:58 a.m. and arrive in Buffalo at 10:46 a.m.

left shift 3 Jenny and I are going to Maryland in May, but Jane is going to Norway.

easy 4 They may also dismantle the eight authentic antique autos in the town.

| 1 | 2 | 3 | 4 | 5 | 6 | 7 | 8 | 9 | 10 | 11 | 12 | 13 | 14 |

45b ▶ 6
Proofread/revise as you keyboard

1 Cover the answer key at the bottom of the column. When you have finished keyboarding, check your answers.

2 Provide needed capitals for each of the five sentences.

Key: **1** Lee, Room, He, Chapter **2** You, New York **3** They, Thursday's **4** Jan, Mo, I, Chicago, Thanksgiving **5** Did, Shaw, Caesar, Cleopatra, I, Memphis

1 lee left his history book in room 27. he must study chapter 15 today.

2 you will reach the new york state line if you drive east for 21 miles.

3 they announced their fall hosiery sale on page 15 of thursday's paper.

4 jan said, "mo and i should arrive in chicago on thanksgiving evening."

5 did shaw write "caesar and cleopatra"? i saw it at a memphis theater.

45c ▶ 18
Keyboard letter parts

Lines 1-3: Take three 1' writings on each line. Try to finish each line at least once in the time allotted.

Lines 4-6: Take two 45" writings on Lines 4–6, arranging them in 3–line address format.

Goal: To complete each address in Lines 4–6 in 45".

> **Technique hint:**
> Type at a controlled, but constant rate. Do not pause before typing figures.

1 123 Brandy Street; 459 Reynolds Drive; 650 River Road; 78 Osage Avenue

2 Erie, PA 16511-4478; Brooklyn, NY 11227-2785; Dayton, OH 45410-3367

3 April 29, 19--; May 18, 19--; June 27, 19--; July 26, 19--; January 17

4 Ms. Deirdre Ann Beebe | 262 Orient Boulevard | Wichita, KS 67213-4976

5 Mrs. Rosetta Hayman | 595 Singingwood Drive | Torrance, CA 90505-3047

6 Mr. Angelo Ybarra | 341 Demunda Avenue | Niagara Falls, NY 14304-8259

| 1 | 2 | 3 | 4 | 5 | 6 | 7 | 8 | 9 | 10 | 11 | 12 | 13 | 14 |

34a ▶ 7
Preparatory practice

each line twice SS (slowly, then faster); DS between 2-line groups; then 30″ writings on Line 4; repeat if time permits

Goal:
Finish Line 4 in 30″.

alphabet 1 Buddy Jackson is saving the prize money for wax and lacquer.

figures 2 He moved from 823 West 150th Street to 794 East 66th Street.

space bar 3 Mr. Han may go to Cape Cod on the bus, or he may go by auto.

easy 4 Do throw a bit of light on their theory of dual entitlement.

| 1 | 2 | 3 | 4 | 5 | 6 | 7 | 8 | 9 | 10 | 11 | 12 |

34b ▶ 10
Improve concentration: typing from unedited copy

60-space line; DS

1 Correct errors in the copy as you type the paragraph.

2 Proofread/make final corrections before you remove paper from the machine.

words

Two kinds of erasers can be help ful to a typist: A   10

soft eraser, like the one on a pencil, is use to remove ink from   24

hard-surfaced, erasable paper; to take off carbon smudges; and   36

fro erasing carbon copies. The harder, more abrasive typing   49

erase is used to rcmove ink that is embedded in paper. Typing   61

erasers are abailable in both "wheel" and "pencil" forms and   74

with or without a brushh.   78

34c ▶ 33
Personal-business letters in modified block style

Problem 1

personal–size sheet [LM p. 37]; address envelope; proofread/correct errors

5601 Sharp Lane | Denver, CO 80239-3618 | October 15, 19-- | 11
Mrs. Barbara Arbee | 4445 George Drive | Lubbock, TX 79416-   23
6841 | Dear Barbara | 26

(¶) I am delighted to hear that you have finished your courses   38
and are ready to accept that "just right" position. All of   50
your friends are, I know, proud of you; and they all say that   62
you will be a great asset to any company that hires you.   74

(¶) Might you consider moving to a new location? If so, I hope   86
you'll consider moving to Colorado--maybe even to Denver. I   98
know of several places where your talents would match what I   110
consider genuine opportunities.   117

(¶) I shall, of course, be very pleased to have you use my name   129
as one of your references. Thank you for asking. Please let   141
me know if I can be helpful in other ways.   149

Sincerely | Ms. Fusako L. Kimura   155/179*

*From this point on, the last figure in the word count column includes the envelope address.

Communications Design
Associates

348 INDIANA AVENUE
WASHINGTON, DC 20001-1438
Tel: 1-800-432-5739

Tabulate to center to type
date and closing lines

total words

Dateline   Line 15 November 28, 19--   4

Operate return 4 times

Letter   Mr. Otto B. Bates, President   9
address Third Bank and Trust Company   15
         9080 Reservoir Avenue   20
         New Brunswick, NJ 08901-4476   26
                                          DS

Salutation Dear Mr. Bates   28
                        DS

Body of This letter is written in what is called the "modified block   41
letter   style." It is the style we recommend for use in your office   53
         for reasons I shall detail for you in the paragraphs below.   65

         First, the style is a fairly efficient one that requires only   77
         one tab setting--at center point--for positioning the current   90
         date, the complimentary close, and the typed signature lines.   102
         All other lines begin at left margin.   110

         Second, the style is quite easy to learn. New employees will   123
         have little difficulty learning it, and your present staff can   135
         adjust to it without unnecessary confusion.   144

         Third, the style is a familiar one; it is used by more busi-   156
         ness firms than any other. It is conservative, and customers   168
         and companies alike feel comfortable with it.   178

         I am happy to enclose our booklet on the subject of letter   189
         styles and special features of business letters.   199
                                                          DS

Complimentary   Sincerely yours   202
close   Operate return 4 times

                                         Kathryn E. Bowers

Typed name   Ms. Kathryn E. Bowers   206
Official title   Senior Consultant   210
                                                        DS

Reference xx   211
initials   DS
Enclosure Enclosure   213
notation

Shown in pica type
60—space line

Style letter 4: modified block style, block paragraphs, open punctuation

34c, continued

Problem 2

personal–size sheet [LM p. 39]; SS
¶s; DS between ¶s; address en–
velope; proofread/correct errors

4445 George Drive | Lubbock, TX 79416-6841 | October 27, 19--   12

Ms. Fusako Kimura | 5601 Sharp Lane | Denver, CO   21

80239-3618 | Dear Fusako | (¶) Thank you for your   30

kind ... filled with words of praise and   38

enco... You teased me just enough   46

with ... bout opportunities in   55

Col ... upon more   62

in ... move. Yes, I   71

... under the right   78

circu... me more. (¶) You   86

know me ... Fusako, to give   94

me the kind ... I need; and I'm   101

going to rely on you to be frank about   109

such a move. | Sincerely | Mrs. Barbara Arbee   117

141

35

35a ▶ 7
Preparatory practice

each line twice SS (slowly,
then faster); DS between
2-line groups; then type 30″
writings on Line 4; repeat if
time permits

Goal: Finish Line 4 in 30″.

alphabet 1   Loquacious, breezy Hank forgot to jump over the waxed floor.

figures 2   Must he add the fractions 2/3, 3/4, 4/5, 5/6, 7/8, and 9/10?

shift keys 3   Ready to cross the Pacific, Commander Law boarded HMS JAMES.

easy 4   It is a shame to make such emblems of authentic whale ivory.

| 1 | 2 | 3 | 4 | 5 | 6 | 7 | 8 | 9 | 10 | 11 | 12 |

35b ▶ 10
Build speed on problems

Use Style Letter 2, page 64. Take five 1′ writings on the opening lines of the letter. At the signal to begin a 1′ writing, insert the paper to the point where the return ad–dress is to be placed. Type it and the date, and then space forward and type the letter address and salutation. Make completion of the salutation your goal; ignore all errors temporarily.

35c ▶ 33
Personal-business letters

3 personal-size sheets; [LM pp. 45-49]; envelopes; proof-read/correct errors

1 Format/type each of the letters on page 67 in the style indicated.
2 Prepare an envelope for each letter; use the appropriate address and return address.
3 Fold each letter for insertion into an envelope.

44b ▶ 12
Improve concentration

1 Cover the answer key at the bottom of the column. When you have finished keyboarding, check your answers.

2 Prepare a copy of the ¶ DS. Unscramble the underlined words as you keyboard.

3 Using your corrected copy, take 1' writings as time permits.

Key: down, what, will, this, them, Then

Difficulty index

all letters used	A	1.5 si	5.7 awl	80% hfw

gwam 1'

When you sit <u>donw</u> at your typewriter to compose, the first problem   13
to be conquered is deciding <u>waht</u> to write about. For a school paper,   27
however, this problem does not exist; the subject <u>lliw</u> likely have been   42
assigned. Therefore, the primary need in <u>hist</u> situation is to organize   56
mentally your facts and ideas and type <u>mhet</u> in somewhat logical order   70
as they occur to you. <u>Tehn,</u> the process is one of continual refinement.   85

gwam 1' | 1 | 2 | 3 | 4 | 5 | 6 | 7 | 8 | 9 | 10 | 11 | 12 | 13 | 14 |

44c ▶ 12
Use carbon paper
Materials needed:

1 original sheet
2 second sheets
2 carbon paper sheets
1 firm (5"×3") card

70–space line; DS; 2½" top margin; correct errors

1 Study the information and illustrations at the right.

2 Assemble a carbon pack and make an original and 2 carbon copies of the ¶ shown below the illustrations.

Assembling a carbon pack

1 Assemble letterhead, carbon sheets (uncarboned side up), and second sheets as illustrated below. Use one carbon and one second sheet for each copy desired.

2 Grasp the carbon pack at the sides. Turn it so that the letterhead faces away from you, the carbon sides of the carbon paper are toward you, and the top edge of the pack is face down. Tap the sheets gently on the desk to straighten.

3 Hold the sheets firmly to prevent slipping; insert pack into typewriter. Hold pack with one hand; turn platen with the other.

Many companies no longer make carbon copies; of those that do, some do not erase errors on them. If you need to do so, pull the original forward and place a firm card in front of the carbon sheet. Erase the error on the original with a typewriter eraser; erase the carbon copy with a soft pencil eraser. For additional carbon copies, use the card to protect them by placing it between the sheet being erased and the next sheet of carbon paper.

44d ▶ 20
Format business letters in modified block style

2 plain full sheets; copy sheets

1 Study the special information at the right, then study Style Letter 4 on page 84.

2 Type a copy of the letter; proofread; correct errors.

3 Type another copy of letter. Make one carbon copy.

As you study Style Letter 4, page 84, note that the block style has been "modified" by moving the dateline and the closing lines from block position at the left margin. In the modified block style, these lines begin at the center point of the page.

Because stationery with printed letterhead is either used or assumed, the dateline will be the first item typed in these letters. As all letters in Section 10 are of average length, it is correct to type the dateline on about Line 15 and to use a 60–space line for all of them.

Spacing between letter parts is the same as was used with the block style. This spacing is standard for all business letters.

Problem 1

modified block style

Goal: 9 minutes

words

778 Diamond Street | Wilkes Barre, PA 18704-8121 | February | 11
10, 19-- | Mr. Marvyn Hyatt | 303 King Edward Trail, SW | Atlanta, | 24
GA 30331-5749 | Dear Marv | | 28

(¶) I'm sorry my memory was so nonfunctional when I spoke to | 40
you Saturday about my current stock holdings. | 49

(¶) As soon as I returned to Wilkes Barre, I checked my files; the | 62
stock I wanted to mention to you was Allied Plastics common | 74
stock. Its present quotation, I see, is 16 3/8. | 84

(¶) I enjoyed having lunch with you and wish we could have | 95
arranged to have more time to talk about your portfolio. | 106

(¶) I'll call you again next month when I am in Atlanta. | 117

Sincerely yours | Brad Bruhnsen | 124/**148**

Problem 2

block style

Goal: 12 minutes

248 Brooklyn Avenue | Salt Lake City, UT 84101-6112 | September | 12
12, 19-- | Ms. Cluny Lee Brinks | 465 Fulkerson Street | St. Joseph, | 25
MO 64504-3783 | Dear Ms. Brinks | | 31

(¶) I have read with much interest the manuscript you propose to | 43
submit to AMERICAN TECHNOLOGY. I think it is a very fine | 55
piece of writing, and I encourage you to submit it right away. | 68

(¶) Your approach to methods for gradual changeover to word | 79
processing by small companies will be helpful, I am sure, to | 91
many readers. I commend especially your nontechnical ap- | 102
proach to what can be a very technical problem. | 112

(¶) Your manuscript will be returned in a few days; my few | 123
criticisms will accompany it. Should you believe it might be | 135
helpful, mention to Adele Abt, the editor, that you sent the manu- | 148
script to me to read. | 153

Cordially | Miss Joyce Ashmyre | 158/**185**

Problem 3

style of your choice

Goal: 9 minutes

2120 Uhle Street, S. | Arlington, VA 22204-4961 | May 24, 19-- | Ms. | 13
Cara Ann Babbett | 42 Quebec Street, S. | Arlington, VA 22204- | 25
4975 | Dear Cara Ann | | 29

(¶) Thank you for your note reminding me that the Lilac Valley | 41
Golf League is making plans for the opening of league play next | 53
month. | 55

(¶) Unfortunately (or, on the other hand, fortunately), I have | 67
accepted a position as research assistant during the summer | 79
months with Dr. Eunice Guzman; therefore, I shall not be able | 91
to participate in league play this year. | 99

(¶) I shall miss playing. Perhaps I can join you again next year, | 112
Cara Ann. Please keep my name on your list just in case. | 123

Cordially | Miss June Dupois | 129/**154**

43d ▶ 22
Format business letters in block style

2 plain full sheets; 60-space line; date on Line 15

Problem 1

Make a corrected copy of the letter at right. Insert longer changes as numbered.

Problem 2

Follow the directions for Problem 1, but address the letter to

Mr. George B. Glackmun
406 Rathbun Avenue
White Plains, NY 10606-3642

Use an appropriate salutation. In ¶2, change office layout to office hours.

---

① for consideration
② has been accepted by them,
③ adoption and
④ amount of money

total words

June 16, 19--   3

Mr. Olin N. Werger   7
1640 Barnes Lande   10
¿Whate Plains, NY 10604-3719   16

Dear Mr. Werger   19

                                                          inform ①
It is my happy opportunity to ~~tell~~ you that the sug-   30
gestion you recently submitted ~~has been studied~~ by   40
our Management Board, and they have recommended to me   56
its immediate implementation. ②   65

                                          your ③
I (, too,) have studied ~~the~~ suggestion, and I must tell   74
you that I am extremely enthusiastic about it. Your   85
explanations makes it quite obvious that by making   95
the changes in office layout you recommend our com-   105
pany should be able to save a substantial ~~expense~~.   117
                                                          ④
Will you attend a brief ceremony to be held in my   127
office next Friday morning at 13? At that time it   137
will be my pleasure to award to you a check in the   147
amount of $4500 in appreciation of your excellent   157
money-saving recommendation.   163

Accept my sincere congratulations.   170

Sincerely yours   173

Mrs. Cecelia P. Barbette   178
President   180

xx   181

44a ▶ 6
Preparatory practice

each line 3 times SS (slower, faster, slower); DS between 3-line groups; repeat if time permits

alphabet	1	The explorer questioned Jack's amazing story about unknown lava flows.
figures	2	I am sending 2,795 of the 4,680 sets now and the remainder on June 13.
capitali–zation	3	Is the notation on this memorandum Bob's, Edna's, Ralph's, or Myrna's?
easy	4	Work with vigor to shape a theory to make visible and audible signals.

| 1 | 2 | 3 | 4 | 5 | 6 | 7 | 8 | 9 | 10 | 11 | 12 | 13 | 14 |

Learning goals

1 To evaluate problem formatting and keyboarding skills.

2 To measure statistical–copy keyboarding speed.

3 To measure straight–copy keyboarding speed.

Machine adjustments

1 Set paper guide at 0.

2 Set ribbon control to type on upper half of ribbon.

3 Use a 60–space line for drills and writings; a 50–space line for letters.

4 SS drills: DS paragraphs.

Materials: Monarch–size sheets and envelopes; plain sheets.

36a ▶ 7
Preparatory practice

each line three times SS (slowly, faster, slower); DS between 3-line groups; repeat selected lines as time permits

alphabet 1 Jim was able to liquify frozen oxygen; he kept it very cold.

figure 2 Sue moved 720 boxes, 395 of which went to Rooms 146 and 188.

i/e 3 Neither friend believes she received benefits from the diet.

easy 4 Do they blame us for their dismal social and civic problems?

| 1 | 2 | 3 | 4 | 5 | 6 | 7 | 8 | 9 | 10 | 11 | 12 |

36b ▶ 12
Measure skill growth: statistical copy

three 3′ writings; determine *gwam*; circle errors

Difficulty index

all letters/figures used | E | 1.2 si | 5.1 awl | 90% hfw |

gwam 3′ | 5′

As you might know, the size of the liability to which a — 4 | 2

car insurance firm limits itself is expressed in three fig- — 8 | 5

ures; as, 10/20/5. The first figure in this group, 10, means — 12 | 7

that a limit of $10,000 has been set for one person hurt in — 16 | 9

one accident; the 20 means that $20,000 has been set for all — 20 | 12

persons who are hurt in one accident--subject, of course, to — 24 | 14

the limit of $10,000 a person--and the last figure (5 here) — 28 | 17

is for loss due to other damage up to $5,000 in value. What — 32 | 19

you might not know is that if you were to look at 70 or 80 — 36 | 22

car insurance contracts of the kind that were used 20 years — 40 | 24

ago in the 1960's, you might find that just 3 out of 4 had a — 44 | 26

liability clause in them. Such clauses are now required in — 48 | 29

each of the 50 states. — 49 | 30

36c ▶ 31
Measure skill application

Materials needed:
2 half sheets
1 full sheet

Time schedule:

Assembling materials .... 2′
Timed production .... 25′
Proofread; circle errors ..... 4′

43b ▶ 10
Compose at the keyboard

2 full sheets; decide top margin and spacing

1 Read the questions at the right.

2 Compose an answer for each question in one or two sentences. Join the sentences into para-graphs to make a short essay. Center the title **MY CAREER** over the paragraphs.

3 Proofread; mark errors. If time permits, retype the copy in final form.

1 What is your career goal as you now see it?

2 What led you to make this career choice?

3 In what part of the world do you think you would like to live and work?

4 Why do you want to live and work there?

5 Do you see yourself following any other career path in the years ahead?

43c ▶ 12
Address large envelopes

3 large (No. 10) envelopes [LM pp. 55-57]

1 Read carefully the special placement information.

2 Address a large envelope to each addressee listed below; proofread; circle errors.

3 Fold a sheet of blank 8½" × 11" paper for insertion into a large envelope. Use the fold-ing procedure shown for the Monarch envelope on page 62.

Placement information

Some businesses use small envelopes for 1-page letters and large envelopes for letters of 2 or more pages or letters with enclosures. Many firms, however, use large envelopes for all correspondence.

Study the placement of the letter address on the large en-velope illustrated below. Set a tab stop about 5 spaces to the left of center or about 4" from the left edge of the envelope. Space down about 14 lines from the top edge of the en-velope and begin typing at the tab stop, thus positioning the address in approximately ver-tical center and slightly below the horizontal center. Learn to visualize this position so that you can type envelope ad-dresses without special set-tings or measurements.

Type special messages for the addressee (*Please for-ward, Hold for arrival, Per-sonal,* etc.) a TS below the re-turn address and 3 spaces from the left edge of the en-velope. Underline or type in ALL CAPS.

Type special mailing nota-tions (such as REGISTERED, SPECIAL DELIVERY, etc.) in ALL CAPS below the stamp posi-tion.

MR MILO K DECKER PRESIDENT
POPULAR TOOL COMPANY
528 ESSEX LANE
DAVENPORT IA 52803-4163

BERA WALLPAPERS INC
7747 MC ARTHUR CIRCLE
EVANSVILLE IN 47714-3821

Ms. Barbara B. Treece
Breummer & Joyner
6234 Reynolds Avenue
Columbus, OH 43201-6822

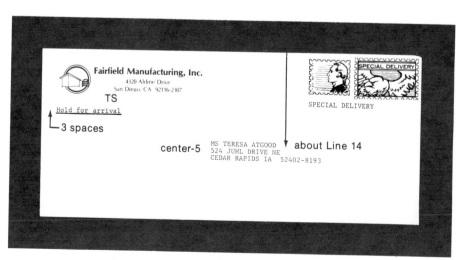

36c, continued

When the signal to begin is given, begin with Problem 1. Prepare the problems in sequence until the signal to stop is given. Do Problem 1 again if you have finished Problem 3 and time has not been called.

Problem 1

half sheet (insert long side up); DS; exact center

Problem 2

half sheet (insert long side up); DS; center the problem in exact vertical center; center each line horizontally

Problem 3

Repeat Problem 1 in reading position on full sheet; DS.

	words
The committee	3
for the reelection of	7
JOAN E. SHEARD	10
as county commissioner	15
respectfully solicits your support	22
on election day	25
Tuesday, November 7	29

Mr. J. Drew Munger	4
cordially requests your presence	10
at dinner	12
Saturday evening, March 23	18
at eight o'clock	21
One Hunter Cross, Sturgis	26

37

37a ▶ 7
Preparatory practice

each line 3 times SS (slowly, faster, still faster); DS between 3-line groups; repeat selected lines as time permits

alphabet 1 Avoid lazy punches; expert fighters jab with a quick motion.
fig/sym 2 Hunt & Moya's $623.75 check (#1489) was delivered on May 10.
adjacent reaches 3 We sat talking by ruined columns prior to an opera overture.
easy 4 The big men paid their own firms for the eight enamel signs.

| 1 | 2 | 3 | 4 | 5 | 6 | 7 | 8 | 9 | 10 | 11 | 12 |

37b ▶ 12
Measure skill growth: straight copy

three 3' writings; determine *gwam*; circle errors

Difficulty index

all letters used	E	1.2 si	5.1 awl	90% hfw

gwam 3'

How easy it is to become discouraged, especially after   4 | 35
we did what we thought was the best we could do with a job;   8 | 39
and we still did not quite win the specific prize we had in   12 | 43
mind. It is often difficult for us to realize that what we   16 | 47
think is our best is not really our best at all. Few of us   20 | 51
ever approach our maximum potential at what we do. There's   24 | 55
always another path to try, another step that can be taken.   28 | 59
The wise among us just knuckle down and take that next step.   32 | 63

gwam 3' | 1 | 2 | 3 | 4 |

42d ▶ 22
Format business letters in block style

2 plain full sheets; 60-space line; begin on Line 15

Problem 1

Prepare the letter; proofread and correct your copy before removing it from the machine.

words

(Current date) | Mr. Herbert B. Wymore, Jr. | Millikin & Descartes, Inc. | 800   15
Hazel Court | Denver, CO 80204-1192 | Dear Mr. Wymore | 25

(¶) In answer to his request, I am very happy to write a letter of recommenda-   40
tion for Mehti K. Boromand, who worked with our company for about fourteen   55
months.   56

(¶) Mr. Boromand's responsibilities, while he was employed here with us, in-   71
volved carrying important documents and packages from building to building.   86
He was responsible, prompt, and virtually tireless; cheerful, polite, and very   102
friendly; and above all, discreet and reliable. He was absolutely trustworthy.   118

(¶) He left our employ at the end of last summer to begin college studies, but he   134
will be welcomed back to our staff at any time that we have an opening in which   150
he might be interested and for which he might be qualified.   161

Sincerely | Miss Kim L. Schuyler | Assistant Vice President | xx   173

Problem 2

Follow directions given for Problem 1.

(Current date) | Mrs. Lynn Martinez | 431 Poplar Lane | Annapolis, MD 21403-2261   15
| Dear Mrs. Martinez | 19

(¶) Our Credit Department informs me that you recently returned to us for   33
credit a Wilcox Model 24 toaster. It appears from the report that some question   49
was raised about the condition of the toaster when it was returned and that you   65
objected to certain statements made at the credit counter.   77

(¶) I apologize if in any way the routine return of this toaster was questioned. As   93
you know if you are a longtime shopper in our store, we guarantee our mer-   108
chandise to be satisfactory in every way. If you, the customer, are not satisfied,   125
then we, the store, are not satisfied either.   134

(¶) I assure you, Mrs. Martinez, that we have properly adjusted your account to   150
reflect credit for the return. If you have any further questions about this mat-   166
ter, please contact me personally.   173

Sincerely yours | Myles J. Longano, Head | Customer Relations | xx   185

43

43a ▶ 6
Preparatory practice

each line 3 times SS (slowly, faster, slower); DS between 3-line groups; repeat if time permits

alphabet 1 Ben Jackson will save the money required for your next big cash prize.

fig/sym 2 The 7 1/2% interest of $18.68 on my $249.05 note (dated May 3) is due.

double letters 3 Dell was puzzled by the letter that followed the offer of a free book.

easy 4 In Dubuque, they may work the rich field for the profit paid for corn.

| 1 | 2 | 3 | 4 | 5 | 6 | 7 | 8 | 9 | 10 | 11 | 12 | 13 | 14 |

37c ▶ 31
Measure skill application

2 Monarch sheets [LM pp. 51-53]
2 Monarch envelopes

Reference pages

Block style letter, p. 58
Modified block style
letter, p. 64
Envelopes, p. 62

Time schedule:

Assembling materials .... 2'
Timed production .... 25'
Proofread; circle errors ..... 4'

When the signal to begin is given, insert paper and begin with Problem 1. Prepare the problems in sequence until the signal to stop is given.

Begin Problem 1 again if you have finished Problem 2 and time has not been called.

You are not necessarily expected to finish all problems within the time limit. Do your best, not your most; and you will have better results.

words

Problem 1
Personal-business letter

modified block style; address envelope

890 Congress Street | Stamford, CT 06902-6417 | November 6, ⟶ 11
19--| Mr. Ezra M. Rhyne, Jr. | 6331 Shell Point Place | Tampa, ⟶ 23
FL 33611-5121 | Dear Mr. Rhyne ⟶ 29

(¶) Thank you for your note about the rental of your condo- ⟶ 40
minium. My husband and I plan to be in Tampa on December 1 ⟶ 52
and should like to take occupancy then. As I have done in past ⟶ 65
years, I shall give you the full rental amount for two months ⟶ 77
($1,200) as soon as wc arrive. ⟶ 83

(¶) Thank you, too, for inquiring about our daughter, Katren. She ⟶ 96
will visit with us only during the holidays this year. Katren has ⟶ 109
accepted a position as consultant with the Bowers, Roos, & ⟶ 121
Arensberg investment firm and is their first unsighted em- ⟶ 133
ployee. They seem to be pleased with her work, for she was ⟶ 145
promoted in October. ⟶ 149

(¶) Fred and I are looking forward to our annual visit to Florida ⟶ 161
and the renewal of old friendships. ⟶ 168

Very sincerely | Mrs. Kate Murphy ⟶ 175/**200**

Problem 2
Personal-business letter

block style; center the speech topic on a separate line with a DS above and below it; address envelope

2452 Shadetree Drive | Cincinnati, OH 45242-4377 | January 24, ⟶ 12
19-- | Mrs. Lucia Bravo | 1551 Geranium Avenue, E. | St. Paul, MN ⟶ 24
55106-1721 | Dear Lucia ⟶ 29

(¶) I have a note from my good friend, Theresa Ogden, the noted ⟶ 41
ornithologist from Cleveland, saying that she will be in St. Paul ⟶ 54
during the entire first week of June. She has been invited to ⟶ 67
speak before the combined Kiwanis Clubs on the subject | (DS) ⟶ 78
ECOLOGY: WHERE NOW? (DS) | ⟶ 82

(¶) This is exciting news, because her visit coincides with our ⟶ 94
national convention that week. If you think there might be a ⟶ 106
place on our program for Tess, I'll be happy to make the request. ⟶ 120

Cordially | Edward T. Baer ⟶ 124/**150**

42a ▶ 6
Preparatory practice

each line 3 times SS (slowly, faster, still faster); DS between 3-line groups; repeat if time permits

alphabet 1 Jim Bond quickly realized that we could fix the pretty girl's vehicle.

fig/sym 2 Serial #815-47 was stamped on the engine; Model #209(36) was below it.

combina- 3 Look for the fastest racer to get a big treat at the end of the races.
tion

easy 4 Both of the towns bid for the giant quantity of coal down by the dock.

| 1 | 2 | 3 | 4 | 5 | 6 | 7 | 8 | 9 | 10 | 11 | 12 | 13 | 14 |

42b ▶ 10
Compose at the keyboard

2 full sheets; 2″ top margin; DS

1 Center your name horizontally, then TS.

2 Answer the questions at the right in complete sentences.

3 Make pencil corrections on your copy, then retype it. Proofread; correct errors.

1 What is the name and address of the high school from which you were graduated?

2 In what year were you graduated from high school?

3 How long have you been studying at your present school?

4 Have you attended any other postsecondary schools?

5 When do you plan to complete your formal schooling?

42c ▶ 12
Determine line endings

2 half sheets; insert long edge first; 2″ top margin; divide words as needed; proofread; correct errors

1 Type ¶ SS, 60–space line.
2 Type ¶ DS, 70–space line.

words

Composing at the typewriter can be helpful   9
to you, for you should be able to get your thoughts   19
and ideas onto paper more quickly with a typewriter   29
than with a pencil or pen. Concentrate on your sub-   40
ject and let ideas flow to the page; ignore for the   50
present any typographical mistakes. Use double   60
spacing so that proofreader's marks can be easily   70
used. Rewrite your composition as many times as   80
you think necessary.   84

LEVEL TWO
Formatting/typing basic communications

Let's be elemental. A keyboard is made up of several rows of buttons, or keys, which, when struck, operate your machine. This activity of striking is called keyboarding.

Keyboarding certainly seems commonplace enough. It takes on added meaning when you consider that your keyboard is identical to those used to operate an increasingly large number and variety of technical machines, such

as computers, microcomputers, word processors, and electronic typewriters. As part of such equipment, the keyboard becomes the instrument through which are transmitted thoughts and ideas, facts and figures, and all sorts of business, academic, social, and scientific data.

How efficiently any machine functions, of course, depends directly upon how skillfully the operator uses it. Its utility increases in ratio to a user's knowledge about it and ability to operate it rapidly and accurately.

By successfully completing Level 1 work, you have gained ability to keyboard by touch and to enter data attractively on a page. Now you are ready to begin a new level of learning, one in

which you will learn to put these important skills to professional use.

You will learn, for example, to format and input business correspondence, tables, data sheets, and reports; and you will gain more experience using printed, rough-draft, and handwritten input materials.

In addition, as you enter the practice and problem data, your keyboarding speed should increase; and, with concentrated effort, your accuracy should also improve.

Learning to keyboard and format with skill is a significant accomplishment. From now on, you should realize that future output from equipment you use depends on the input abilities you develop now.

Communications Design Associates

348 INDIANA AVENUE
WASHINGTON, DC 20001-1438
Tel: 1-800-432-5739

		total words	gwam 2'

Dateline **February 14, 19--** Line 15

Operate return 4 times

	total words	gwam 2'

Letter address **Mr. Harvey B. Barber** — 8 | 4
Sunstructures, Inc. — 12 | 6
2214 Brantford Place — 16 | 8
Buffalo, NY 14222-5147 — 21 | 10
DS

Salutation **Dear Mr. Barber** — 24 | 12
DS

Body of letter **This letter is written in what is called "block style." It** — 36 | 18
is the style we recommend for use in your business office for — 48 | 24
reasons I shall detail for you in the following paragraphs. — 61 | 30

First, the style is a very efficient one. Because all lines — 73 | 6
(including the date) begin at the left margin, time is not — 85 | 12
consumed in positioning special parts of each letter. — 96 | 18

Second, this style is an easy one to learn. New employees — 107 | 23
should have little difficulty learning it, and your present — 119 | 29
staff should adjust to it without unnecessary confusion. — 131 | 35

Third, the style is sufficiently different from most other — 143 | 41
styles that it can suggest to clients that your company is a — 155 | 47
creative one. The style is interesting. It gains attention. — 168 | 54

I am pleased to enclose our booklet on the subject of letter — 180 | 6
styles and special features of business letters. — 190 | 11
DS

Complimentary close **Sincerely yours** — 193 | 13

Operate return 4 times

Kathryn E. Bowers

Typed name **Ms. Kathryn E. Bowers** — 197 | 15
Official title **Senior Consultant** — 201 | 17
DS

Reference initials **xx** — 202 | 17
DS

Enclosure notation **Enclosure** — 203 | 18

Shown in pica type
60—space line

Style letter 3: business letter in block style, open punctuation

Learning goals

1 To improve understanding of the place and function of capital letters.
2 To strengthen ability to spell.
3 To improve decision making.
4 To increase keystroking skill.

Machine adjustments

1 Set chair and desk adjustment and placement.
2 Set paper guide at *0*.
3 Set ribbon control to type on upper half of ribbon.
4 Use a 70–space line unless otherwise instructed.

38a ▶ 7

Preparatory practice

each line 3 times SS (slowly, faster, slower); DS between 3-line groups; repeat if time permits

alphabet 1 Would a lazy executive manage to finish his job quickly and properly?

figures 2 Polly Wertze moved from 479 East 125th Street to 328 West 60th Street.

adjacent keys 3 We condemn her notion that we can buy rewards with excellent behavior.

easy 4 The sorority did work with vigor for the goals of the big civic corps.

| 1 | 2 | 3 | 4 | 5 | 6 | 7 | 8 | 9 | 10 | 11 | 12 | 13 | 14 |

38b ▶ 14

Review/improve communication skills: capitalization

full sheet; DS; 1½" top margin; set a tab 5 spaces to right of center point

1 Keyboard the data as shown; tab to type each example.
2 Proofread carefully and correct errors.
3 Study each line and its example from your copy.
Note: Some literary titles may be underlined or shown in all capital letters.

words

USING CAPITAL LETTERS   4
TS

Capitalize   9

		words
the first word of a complete sentence:	She put the car in the garage.	23
the first word of a direct quotation:	Tio said, "That is my valise."	37
titles that precede personal names:	Introduce me to Senator Reese.	50
main words in literary titles:	I saw Anne of a Thousand Days.	67
adjectives derived from proper nouns:	We always enjoy Italian opera.	81
weekdays, months, and holidays:	Sunday, April 1, isn't Easter.	94
political and military organizations:	The Democrat left by Navy jet.	109
names of specific persons or places:	Jo jogs daily in Central Park.	123
nouns followed by identifying numbers:	They were assigned to Room 14.	137

TS   144

Do not capitalize

compass directions not part of a name:	I drive due north to Leesport.	158
a page if followed by a number:	Did he quote Milton on page 9?	171
a title that follows a name:	LeCare is captain of the ship.	183
commonly accepted derivatives:	Put french toast on the china.	196
geographic names made plural:	I sail on Moon and Fish lakes.	209
seasons (unless personified):	Sweet Summer gave way to fall.	221
generic names of products:	Try Magic Mugg instant coffee.	232

Learning goals

1 To prepare business letters in block and modified block styles.
2 To address large envelopes.
3 To develop composing skills.
4 To make carbon copies.

Machine adjustments

1 Check desk/chair adjustments.
2 Set ribbon control to type on upper half of ribbon.
3 Check placement of copy.
4 Set paper guide on 0.
5 Use a 70–space line unless otherwise directed.
6 SS drills; DS paragraphs.

41a ▶ 6
Preparatory practice

each line 3 times
SS (slowly, faster, slower);DS between 3-line groups; repeat if time permits

alphabet 1 One gray antique zinc box was the most favored object kept on display.

figures 2 Please turn to page 350 and answer Questions 2, 4, 6, 7, 8, 9, and 17.

hyphen 3 Pam thinks we have an up-to-the-minute plan for our out-of-town sales.

easy 4 When risk is taken by a giant firm, signs of visible profit may ensue.

| 1 | 2 | 3 | 4 | 5 | 6 | 7 | 8 | 9 | 10 | 11 | 12 | 13 | 14 |

41b ▶ 10
Compose at the keyboard

2 half sheets; 1" top margin; 5-space ¶ indention; DS

1 Keyboard the sentences in ¶ form, inserting the needed information. Do not correct errors.

2 Remove the paper and make pencil corrections. Retype the ¶s. Proofread; correct errors.

(¶ 1) **My name is** (your name). **My home address is** (your complete home address, including ZIP Code). **I am a student at** (name of your school) **in** (city and state), **where I am majoring in** (major area of study). **My school address is** (street address, dormitory name, or other). (¶ 2) **The brand name of the typewriter I use is** (brand name). **I type at approximately** (state the rate in figures) **gwam. My greatest difficulty now seems to be** (name one, as: too many errors, not enough speed, poor techniques, lack of confidence).

41c ▶ 34
Format business letters in block style

plain full sheets

1 Read the special information–tion at the right; then study the style letter on page 78.

2 Prepare a copy of the letter, following directions given on the letter. Correct errors.

3 Take three 2' writings on opening lines and ¶1. Begin with paper out of the machine. Estimate placement of the date; move quickly from part to part to improve your speed.

Business letter placement information

Letter styles used for business letters are similar to styles used for personal letters, but note the following differences.

When letterhead paper (with a printed return address) is used, the return address is not typed above the date; begin the letter by typing the date.

If the letter is signed by a woman, the personal title she prefers (Ms., Miss, or Mrs.) may be included on the typed signature line. No title, personal or professional, is

needed if the writer is male.

The writer's official title may be typed directly beneath the typed signature line.

The initials of the typist may be shown at the left margin a DS below the typed name or title. (In Section 10 letters, reference initials are indicated by xx; you should substitute your own initials.)

If an enclosure notation is used, type it a DS beneath the reference initials.

An attractive appearance is

as essential for business letters as for personal letters. Proofreading and correcting must be done well if a letter is to have its desired effect.

The business letters in Section 10 are of average length; such letters fit well on a 60-space line. The date is usually typed on about Line 15, or 2½" from the top of the page. This placement is recommended for all letters to be typed in Section 10.

**Review/improve
communication skills:
forming plurals**

full sheet; SS, DS between ¶s,
listed items, and examples; 1"
top margin; 5-space ¶ indention; set a tab 10 spaces to left
of center point to type examples

1 Prepare the data as shown; tab
to type each example.

2 Proofread and correct errors.

3 Study the rules from your typed
copy.

Note: The abbreviation e.g. may
be used in place of the phrase *for
example*.

FORMING PLURALS
                                    TS
    To achieve the regular plural form for most nouns, simply add s to the
singular form; e.g., hats. Some nouns, such as men and oxen, take an irregular
plural form. These nouns have to be memorized. A few nouns, such as deer
and sheep, have no plural form at all. To achieve the plural form for still other
groups of nouns, certain guidelines, some of which are given below with examples, should be followed. In every instance of doubt, of course, consult a dictionary.
                                    DS
    1. To form the plural of a noun ending in y preceded by a consonant sound
or a consonant (any letter except a, e, i, o, or u), change the y to i and add es.

        husky--huskies
        hobby--hobbies
        colloquy--colloquies

    2. To form the plural of a noun ending in y preceded by a vowel, just add s.

        attorney--attorneys
        decoy--decoys
        holiday--holidays

    3. To form the plural of most nouns ending in o, add es.

        tomato--tomatoes
        hero--heroes
        mosquito--mosquitoes

    4. To form the plural of nouns ending in o preceded by a vowel, add s to
the singular.

        cameo--cameos
        ratio--ratios
        taboo--taboos

    5. For singular nouns ending in sis, change the sis to ses to form the
plural.

        basis--bases
        analysis--analyses
        crisis--crises

    6. To form the plural of most nouns ending in s, ss, ch, sh, or x, add es.

        kiss--kisses
        box--boxes
        lash--lashes
        match--matches

40c ▶ 13
Review/improve communication skills: spelling

70-space line; decide size of paper (full or half sheet), top margin (1″, 1½″, or 2″), and spacing (SS or DS)

1 Clear tab stops; set two new tab stops, one 29 spaces from left margin and one 58 spaces from left margin.

2 Type the first word at left margin as shown; tab and type the word again; then tab and type it a third time, this time without looking at the word in the book or on the paper.

3 Repeat this procedure for each word on the list. Proofread carefully; correct errors.

4 Use the completed copy as a study list and for future reference.

5 Make comments about your placement decisions on the bottom of your typed copy.

absence	absence	absence
accumulate		
already		
benefited		
convenience		
develop		
embarrass		
guarantee		
judgment		
likable		
noticeable		
parallel		
receive		
seize		
surprise		
vacuum		
yield		

40d ▶ 13
Proofread/revise as you keyboard

half sheet; 1″ top margin; DS

1 Cover the answer key at the bottom of the column. After keyboarding, check your answers.

2 As you keyboard each line, decide whether each circled word is correct according to rules of form, spelling, or capitalization. If it is not correct, make the correction.

Key: 1 and, china **2** analyses, hobbies **3** huskies, winter, north, parks **4** already, seize, yield **5** parties, attorneys, Room, Hall **6** convenient, vacuum, lobbies **7** judgment, embarrass, absence **8** Fall, Winter's, December **9** Put, tomatoes, potato, holidays **10** accumulate, receive, surprise

1 Lay my copy of The King and I on the shelf beside the old china bowls.

2 Dr. Thu gave several analysis of why a person needs some good hobbies.

3 To see huskeys at work in winter, go North to Whaler or Glacier parks.

4 The enemy had already tried to sieze the tower; Kroma would not yield.

5 The partys will meet with their attornies in Room 27 of Yorkton Hall.

6 When it is convient, please vacuum the carpets in the front lobbies.

7 In my judgment, I did not embarass her; her abscence spoke for itself.

8 Demure fall trembled before winter's icy breath. It was now december.

9 He said, "put a few tomatoes in your potatoe salad for these Holidays."

10 If we accumulate enough points, we shall receive three surprise gifts.

38d ▶ 12

Improve keyboarding continuity

1 Type the ¶ once for orientation. Be aware of spelling and word usage.
2 Take two 3' writings.
Goal: 22 or more *gwam*

Difficulty index

all letters used | LA | 1.4 si | 5.4 awl | 85% hfw

	gwam 1'	3'
Just where does responsibility lie? I recall a day last fall when	13	4 | 39
I had a date to meet with two attorneys to discuss a crisis our firm	27	9 | 43
was having. It was in October. The night before my meeting, my young	41	14 | 48
nephew called to remind me that I had said I would go to his school's	55	18 | 53
Halloween party the next day. I apologized and told him why I could	69	23 | 58
not be there. While he said he understood, I learned quickly that re-	83	27 | 62
sponsibility has two bases--emotional and economical--and that it is	97	32 | 67
sometimes hard to separate the two.	104	35 | 69

gwam 1' | 1 | 2 | 3 | 4 | 5 | 6 | 7 | 8 | 9 | 10 | 11 | 12 | 13 | 14 |
    3' | 1 | 2 | 3 | 4 | 5 |

39a ▶ 7

Preparatory practice

each line three times SS (slowly, faster, still faster); DS between 3-line groups; repeat if time permits

alphabet 1 We have begun our quiz in journalism; do not make a copy for the exam.

fig/sym 2 Han's Policy #718426 for $49,300 has been renewed for another 5 years.

third row 3 We were quite ready to prepare a report for our quiet trio of workers.

easy 4 Hand me a bit of cocoa, a pan of cod, an apricot, and a bowl of clams.

| 1 | 2 | 3 | 4 | 5 | 6 | 7 | 8 | 9 | 10 | 11 | 12 | 13 | 14 |

39b ▶ 11

Improve keystroking technique

60-space line; type 2 times SS; DS between 3-line groups

Technique hint:

Concentrate on each word as you type it.

direct reaches

1 ice cede gun herb deck mute nut shy grunt hunt hymn jump sun
2 Cecelia Haynes and John Lunce hunt in Greece every December.
3 A group of shy, hungry gnus munched on green jungle grasses.

adjacent reaches

4 folk three lion sort trite quit pods ankle oil yule were art
5 Opal is prepared to buy gas and oil for her sporty roadster.
6 Tio has a new poncho for sale; it has beading and silk trim.

double letters

7 door veer err skiing lass committee odd off all success inns
8 Ella successfully crossed the creek at the foot of the hill.
9 Deer need access to green grass, welds, and trees in summer.

Reach for new goals

1 Take a 1' writing on ¶1. Note your *gwam* base rate.

2 Add 4 words to base rate to set a new goal. Note your ¼' subgoals below.

3 Take a ½' writing on ¶1, guided by ¼' guide call. Try to reach your ¼' goal as each guide is called.

4 Take a 1' writing on ¶1, guided by ¼' guide call. Try to reach your ¼' goal as each guide is called.

5 Take two more ½' and two more 1' writings as directed above. If you reach your 1' goal, set a new one.

6 Type ¶2 as directed in 1–5.

7 Take a 3' writing on both ¶s without the call of the guide.

gwam	¼'	½'	¾'	Time
16	4	8	12	16
20	5	10	15	20
24	6	12	18	24
28	7	14	21	28
32	8	16	24	32
36	9	18	27	36
40	10	20	30	40
44	11	22	33	44
48	12	24	36	48

Difficulty Index

all letters used | LA | 1.4 si | 5.4 awl | 85% hfw

gwam 3'

Who is happier, a person with much education or one with little? 4

Which of the two is better adjusted, more satisfied, and better able to 9

realize goals? These are not easy questions. Education is no magic 14

elixir. It is only a tool that can help us to use knowledge to win out 19

over problems. The answer lies in how we use that tool. 22

Education will not bring about happiness any more than a hammer will 27

bring about a house. Yet we can use what we learn, through experience as 32

well as through school, to build the kind of lifestyle that will enable 37

us to recognize those values that have great significance for us. We can 41

use them in our best judgment to find the satisfaction we all seek. 46

gwam 3' | 1 | 2 | 3 | 4 | 5 |

Make decisions

1 Decide what size paper to use and how to place the announce–ment attractively on the page; then prepare the copy.

2 Check the appearance of your completed copy. Note your com–ments on the bottom of your typed copy.

THE WAREHAM GRADUATE SCHOOL OF BUSINESS

announces its winter graduation ceremonies

to be held January 5

in the Bristol-Callister Memorial Auditorium

Processional begins promptly at 2 p.m.

40

Preparatory practice

each line three times SS (slowly, faster, still faster); DS between 3-line groups; repeat if time permits

alphabet 1 Two exit signs jutted obliquely above the beams of a razed skyscraper.

figures 2 The test on March 26 will cover the contents of pages 14-59 and 70-83.

capitali-zation 3 Do Max and Kay Pasco expect to be in breezy Vera Cruz, Mexico, in May?

easy 4 Did the visitor on the bicycle signal and turn right at the cornfield?

| 1 | 2 | 3 | 4 | 5 | 6 | 7 | 8 | 9 | 10 | 11 | 12 | 13 | 14 |

Reach for new goals:

Repeat 39c, above.

Capitalize

1 The first word of a complete sentence.

I have the final page of the report.

2 The first word of a direct quotation.

She said, "Let's work together."

3 The first and main words in titles or headings in books, poems, reports, songs, etc.

I read portions of Leaves of Grass.

4 Titles that precede personal names.

I met Major Busby and Mayor Lopez.

5 Titles of distinction that follow a personal name.

Ms. Chu is a U.S. Senator from Idaho.

6 Names of specific persons and places.

My friend Larry lives in Baltimore.

7 Words derived from the names of specific persons and places.

Barry, a Scot, wore an Edwardian costume.

8 Names of weekdays, months, holidays, and historic periods.

Thursday, November 27, is Thanksgiving.

9 Most nouns followed by identifying numbers.

Issue Check #7813 to pay Invoice 785–J.

10 The first word after a colon if it begins a complete sentence.

Notice: No running is permitted.

11 Seasons of the year if they are personified, and compass points if they designate definite regions.

The icy breath of Winter chilled the Midwest.

12 Trademarks, brand names, and names of commercial products.

My Peerless radio uses Rayovac batteries.

Do not capitalize

1 Compass points when they indicate direction.

We drove north to South Brunswick.

2 *Page* and *verse*, even when followed by a number.

The quotation is in verse 72 on page 512.

3 A title following a name that is not a title of distinction.

Rana was elected secretary of our club.

4 Commonly accepted derivatives of proper nouns.

Why not go dutch treat tonight?

5 The common noun following the name of a product.

I have a Silvertone radio; Jan has an SRE tape deck.

6 Generic terms when they appear in the plural to describe two or more names.

Meet me where Oak and Maple roads cross.

Numbers: Type as words

1 A figure that begins a sentence.

Three of the runners were disqualified.

2 Numbers ten and lower, unless used as part of a series of figures, some of which are above ten.

I carried five books with me today.
Only 9 of the 27 ducks had been banded.

3 Expressions of time with the word *o'clock*.

Dinner will be served at seven o'clock.

4 The smaller of two numbers used together.

Buy two 5–gallon containers of gasoline.

5 Isolated fractions or indefinite amounts.

Only one third of almost six hundred members attended.

6 Names of small-numbered (ten and under) streets.

He moved from First Street to Seventh Avenue.

7 Large even numbers.

My chances of winning are one in a million.

Numbers: Type as figures

1 Numbers preceded by most nouns.

Check Column 3 of the Volume 2 appendix.

2 Expressions of time followed by *a.m.* or *p.m.* and days and years used as part of a date.

We will meet again at 2 p.m., May 5, 1989.

3 House numbers (except One) and high-numbered street names (with *d* and *th*).

Deliver the flowers to 45 East 72d Street.
My temporary address is 340––39th Street.

4 Numbers used with abbreviations, symbols, or dimensions.

For a 2% solution, add 4 tsp. salt to 4 qts. of water.

5 Dates (with *d* and *th*) that precede the month and are separated from it by words.

We signed a lease on the 23d or 24th of April.

Use a comma (followed by a single space, unless it is used internally in a large figure)

1 After introductory words, phrases, or dependent clauses.

```
No, I cannot answer the phone now.
If you don't answer, we may miss a call.
```

2 Between words or groups of words that comprise a series.

```
The flag is red, white, and blue.
We left home, drove to town, and saw a show.
```

3 To set off explanatory and descriptive words, phrases, and clauses used in a sentence.

```
Today, Friday, is my day off.
You did not, I know, leave early.
```

4 To set off words in direct address.

```
If you can, Betsy, write to Joan tonight.
```

5 To set off nonrestrictive adjective clauses (not necessary to the meaning of the sentence), but not restrictive adjective clauses (needed for meaning).

```
The books, some of which I read, are missing.
The guests who were late missed dinner.
```

6 To set off (a) a year that is used as part of a date and (b) the state when it follows a city.

```
On July 4, 1985, I left for Richmond, Virginia.
I saw her in Topeka, Kansas, on May 1, 1986.
```

7 To separate two or more parallel adjectives (adjectives that could be separated by the word *and* instead of the comma). Do not use commas to separate adjectives so closely related that they appear to form a single element with the noun they modify.

```
It was a frosty, windy day in March.
She sat under a green linden tree.
```

8 To separate (a) unrelated groups of figures that come together and (b) whole numbers into groups of three digits each (however, numbers that identify rather than enumerate are usually typed without commas).

```
At 5:15, 1,250 papers were sent to Room 4085.
```

9 To set off contrasting phrases and clauses.

```
People, not machines, make decisions.
```

Use an apostrophe (followed by a single space unless a letter, figure, or mark of punctuation immediately follows it)

1 As a symbol for *feet* and *minutes*.

```
Take a 3' writing.
The crate measured 2' by 2' by 6'.
```

2 With *s* to form the plural of most figures, figures written as words, and letters. In market quotations, the apostrophe is not used.

```
2's  two's  C's  Fourstar Fund 8s
```

3 To show omission of letters or figures.

```
Rob't  Sec'y  Class of '89
```

4 To show possession: Add the apostrophe and *s* to a singular noun not ending in *s*. If a singular noun ends in an *s* or *z* sound, add *'s* to form the possessive if the ending *s* is to be pronounced as a syllable; add the apostrophe only if the ending *s* would be awkward to pronounce.

```
book's cover  horse's hoof  Bess's crown
box's lid  species' peculiarities
```

5 To show possession: Add the apostrophe and *s* to a plural noun that does not end in *s*.

```
men's hats  women's coats  children's toys
```

6 To show possession: Add only the apostrophe after (a) plural nouns ending in *s* and (b) a proper noun of more than one syllable ending in *s* or *z*.

```
workers' cards  Cortez' trip  Lois' wish
```

7 To show possession: Add *'s* after the last noun in a series to indicate joint or common possession of two or more persons; however, show separate possession of two or more persons by adding *'s* to each noun.

```
Alice and Bill's anniversary
Rita's and Trevor's birthdays
```

Use an exclamation point (followed by 2 spaces)

1 After emotional words or phrases.

```
Wow!  Watch it!  Hurray!  Look out!
```

2 After exclamatory sentences.

```
You spilled the chemicals!
```

Use a hyphen (with no space before or after it)

1 To join compound numbers typed as words.

```
sixty-two   forty-eight   two hundred fifty-six
```

2 To join compound adjectives written *before* a noun they modify as a unit.

```
first-rate lunch   up-to-date information
```

3 After words or figures in a series that have a common ending (suspended hyphenation).

```
two-, three-, and five-minute writings
```

Use a dash (two consecutive hyphens with no space before or after them)

1 For emphasis, clarity, or change of thought.

```
The trees--very large trees--loomed ahead.
The trip--it was my idea--was great fun.
```

2 To show the source of a direct quotation.

```
A dash separates; a hyphen joins.--Anonymous
```

3 To indicate in written form verbal pauses.

```
Yes--er--no--oh, I don't know!
```

Use parentheses (with no space between them and the data they enclose)

1 To enclose explanatory, parenthetical, or nonessential material.

```
My roommate (my older sister) owns the car.
```

2 To enclose letters or figures in a listing.

```
Show your (a) name, (b) address, and (c) age.
```

3 To enclose figures that follow spelled-out amounts to give clarity or emphasis.

```
You must pay fifty dollars ($50) now.
```

Use a colon (followed by two spaces unless it is used with integrated figures)

1 To introduce a statement or listing.

```
Order these items:  a lamp, a cord, and a plug.
This is the question:  Where is Dan?
```

2 To separate integrated figures.

```
3:1 odds   2:45 a.m.   ratio of 5:2
```

Use a semicolon (followed by one space)

1 To separate two or more independent clauses in a compound sentence when the conjunction is omitted.

```
I came; I saw; I conquered.
```

2 To separate independent clauses joined by a conjunctive adverb (however, therefore, etc.).

```
He knows me well; however, we do not correspond.
```

3 To separate a series of word or figure groups if one or more of the groups contains a comma.

```
Bring a ball; a bat; and, of course, your mitt.
```

4 To precede an abbreviation or word(s) that introduce further explanation.

```
Myra was here; that is, I saw her earlier.
```

Use an underline (continuously, unless each word is to be considered separately)

1 With titles of complete literary works.

```
Hamlet   The Daily News   New England Magazine
```

2 To emphasize special words or phrases.

```
Can he spell convenience?  I know he can.
```

Use a period (followed by two spaces if it ends a sentence, one space if it ends an abbreviation)

1 To end a declaratory sentence or a request.

```
It is raining.  Will you hand me my umbrella.
```

2 With a variety of abbreviations.

```
Mr. R. E. Riaz, a CPA, called at 2 p.m.
```

Use quotation marks (after a comma or period, before a semicolon or colon, and after a question mark only if the quotation itself is a question)

1 To enclose a direct quotation.

```
She asked, "Who is in charge here?"
Did you hear her say, "Lex is a Gemini"?
```

2 To enclose titles and parts of publications.

```
"Storm Strikes Area"   "The Mikado"   "Trees"
```

3 To enclose special or coined words.

```
The child said he saw a "wabbit."
```

4 As a symbol for inches and seconds.

```
The board is 9" long.
The timer is set for 45".
```

Word-division guides

A word may correctly be divided between syllables as defined in a dictionary or word-division manual. In special cases, the guidelines below will be helpful.

Short words. Do not divide words of five or fewer letters, even if they have two or more syllables.

```
area  bonus  alien  aroma  truth  ideal
```

Double consonants. Divide between double consonants unless the division involves a word that ends in double consonants.

```
excel-lent  call-ing  win-ner  add-ing
```

One- or two-letter syllables. Do not divide a one-letter syllable at the beginning of a word.

```
enough  ideal  opened  aboard  ozone
```

Do not separate a two-letter syllable at the end of a word.

```
friendly  shaker  nickel  groggy  fluid
```

Divide after a one-letter syllable within a word; if two single-letter syllables occur together, divide between them.

```
tele-vision  ele-ment  gradu-ation  idi-omatic
```

Hyphenated words. Divide at the hyphens only.

```
self-centered  off-white  soft-spoken
```

Figures. Do not divide figures presented as a unit.

```
2,785,321  127,100  #3290533  150/371
```

Avoid if possible. Try to avoid dividing proper names, dates, and the last word on a page.

See also page 43 of the textbook.

ZIP Code abbreviations

Alabama, AL	Kentucky, KY	Ohio, OH
Alaska, AK	Louisiana, LA	Oklahoma, OK
Arizona, AZ	Maine, ME	Oregon, OR
Arkansas, AR	Maryland, MD	Pennsylvania, PA
California, CA	Massachusetts, MA	Puerto Rico, PR
Colorado, CO	Michigan, MI	Rhode Island, RI
Connecticut, CT	Minnesota, MN	South Carolina, SC
Delaware, DE	Mississippi, MS	South Dakota, SD
District of Columbia, DC	Missouri, MO	Tennessee, TN
Florida, FL	Montana, MT	Texas, TX
Georgia, GA	Nebraska, NE	Utah, UT
Guam, GU	Nevada, NV	Vermont, VT
Hawaii, HI	New Hampshire, NH	Virgin Islands, VI
Idaho, ID	New Jersey, NJ	Virginia, VA
Illinois, IL	New Mexico, NM	Washington, WA
Indiana, IN	New York, NY	West Virginia, WV
Iowa, IA	North Carolina, NC	Wisconsin, WI
Kansas, KS	North Dakota, ND	Wyoming, WY

Margins/Date Placement. The average letter, business or personal, fits well on an 8½″ × 11″ page if 1½″ side margins are used. When letterhead paper is not used, type a return address on Lines 14 and 15. Type the date on Line 16, just below the return address (or alone on letterhead paper). With a short or long letter, adjust the margins in or out ½″; lower or raise the return address and date as needed. (See also letter placement table on page 162.)

Horizontal placement of the date varies according to letter style. In block and AMS Simplified styles, type the date at left margin; in modified block style, begin the date at center point. Other letter parts, when they are used, are formatted at left margin, unless otherwise noted.

Mailing notation: on the second line space between the date and letter address. See Letter 2 below.

Letter address: on the fourth line space below the date. Type any official title on the same line as the name or below it, whichever gives better balance. A personal title (as *Ms.* or *Mr.*) precedes an individual's name.

Attention line: as the second line of the letter address. The salutation corresponds with the letter address, not the attention line. See Letter 1 below.

Subject line: a double space below the salutation. An introduction such as *Re.* or *SUBJECT:* is optional. See Letter 3 below.

Salutation: a double space below letter address or subject line. The salutation corresponds with the first line of the letter address. If the first line has no gender, use *Ladies and Gentlemen* or *Dear Sir or Madam.* See Letters 1 and 3 below.

Company name in closing: on the second line space below the complimentary close, in ALL CAPS, at center point for modified block style. See Letter 2 below.

Writer's typed name/official title: on the fourth line space below the complimentary close or company name. With the exception of the AMS style, the writer's title may go on either the same line as the name or below it—whichever gives better balance. A female signatory may indicate personal title preference; a male does not, as *Mr.* is always acceptable. See Letters 1–4 below.

Reference initials: a double space below the name and official title in lower case. See Letters 1–4 below.

Enclosure notation: a double space below the reference initials. See Letter 2 below.

Copy notation (cc, bcc, pc): a double space below the reference initials or enclosure notation, followed by the recipient's name. See Letter 1 below.

Postscript: a double space below the last letter item, in the same style as was used for other paragraphs. The letters P.S. are rarely used. See Letter 3 below.

Multiple pages: If a letter is too long for one page, at least 2 lines of the body of the letter should be carried to the second page. Begin the second and subsequent pages on Line 7; leave two blank line spaces below page headings. Use the same side margins as the first page.

Second-page headings

block form

```
Leslie Moll, Inc.
Page 2
October 23, 19--
            TS
1"   and it would seem appropriate for the remainder of the shipment   1"
     to be kept in storage at the Dubuque depot until the conditions
```

horizontal form

```
Leslie Moll, Inc.                    2                 October 23, 19--
                                                            TS
1"   and it would seem appropriate for the remainder of the shipment   1"
     to be kept in storage at the Dubuque depot until the conditions
```

1 Block, open

Communications Design Associates

348 INDIANA AVENUE
WASHINGTON, DC 20001-1438
Tel: 1-800-432-5739

February 14, 19--

Sunstructures, Inc.
Attention Mr. Harvey Bell
2214 Brantford Place
Buffalo, NY 14222-5147

Ladies and Gentlemen

This letter is written in what is called "block style."
It is the style we recommend for use in your business
office for reasons detailed in the following paragraphs.

First, the style is a very efficient one. All lines
(including date) begin at the left margin, and time is
not consumed in positioning special parts of letters.

Second, the style is easy to learn. New employees will
have little difficulty learning it, and your present
staff can adjust to it without unnecessary confusion.

Third, the style is sufficiently different from most
other styles that it can suggest to clients that your
company is creative. The style gains attention.

At the request of Thomas Wray, I am enclosing his booklet about business letter styles and special features.

Sincerely

Kathryn E. Bowers

Ms. Kathryn E. Bowers
Senior Consultant

xx

pc Mr. Thomas Wray

2 Modified block, open

Communications Design Associates

348 INDIANA AVENUE
WASHINGTON, DC 20001-1438
Tel: 1-800-432-5739

November 28, 19--

SPECIAL DELIVERY

Mr. Otto B. Bates, President
Third Bank and Trust Company
9080 Reservoir Avenue
New Brunswick, NJ 90901-4476

Dear Mr. Bates

This letter is written in the "modified block style."
It is the style we recommend for use in your office for
reasons detailed for you in the paragraphs below.

First, the style is an efficient one that requires only
one tab setting--at center point--for positioning the
date, complimentary close, and typed signature lines.

Second, the style is easy to learn. New employees will
have little difficulty learning it, and your present
staff can adjust to it without unnecessary confusion.

Third, the style is a familiar one; it is used by more
business firms than any other. It is conservative, and
customers and companies alike feel comfortable with it.

A booklet about business letter styles and special features is enclosed. Use the reply card, also enclosed,
if you need additional information.

Sincerely yours

COMMUNICATIONS DESIGN ASSOCIATES

Kathryn E. Bowers

Ms. Kathryn E. Bowers
Senior Consultant

xx

Enclosures: 2

3 Modified block, indented ¶s, mixed

Communications Design Associates

348 INDIANA AVENUE
WASHINGTON, DC 20001-1438
Tel: 1-800-432-5739

November 2, 19--

Office Manager
Ramsey Engineering, Inc.
4799 Hammer Drive
Amarillo, TX 79107-6359

Dear Sir or Madam:

Subject: Modified Block Style Letter

  . I am pleased to answer your letter. As you can
see, we use the modified block style, indented paragraphs, and mixed punctuation in our correspondence.
It is the style used in this letter.

    The spacing from the top of the page to the date
varies with the length of the letter. Other spacing in
the letter is standard. The date, complimentary close,
and name and official title of the writer are begun at
horizontal center.

    Please write to me again if I can help further.

Very truly yours,

Allen M. Woodside

Allen M. Woodside
Marketing Manager

xx

    Our new LETTER STYLE GUIDE will be sent to you as
soon as it comes from the printer.

4 AMS Simplified

Communications Design Associates

348 INDIANA AVENUE
WASHINGTON, DC 20001-1438
Tel: 1-800-432-5739

May 9, 19--

Dr. William S. Rapp
Rapp, Hedgson, & Emblatt
98 Clutter Mill Road
Great Neck, NY 11021-4527

AMS SIMPLIFIED LETTER STYLE

This letter is typed in the simplified style that is
recommended by the Administrative Management Society.
The letter features the following points which are de-
signed to save time:

1. Block format is used.

2. Salutation and complimentary close are omitted.

3. A subject heading is typed in ALL CAPS a triple
    space below the address; the first line of the body
    is typed a TS below the subject line.

4. Enumerated items begin flush with the left margin;
    unnumbered items are indented five spaces.

5. The writer's name and title are typed in ALL CAPS
    on the 4th line space below the last line of the
    body of the letter.

6. The reference initials (typist's only) are typed a
    double space below the writer's name.

Correspondents in your company may like the AMS Simplified letter style both for its eye appeal and for its
potential reduction in letter-writing costs.

Luella E. Draper

MRS. LUELLA E. DRAPER, PRESIDENT

xx

Ergonomics Consultants, Inc.

INTEROFFICE COMMUNICATION

TO: All Communication Processors

FROM: Rachel Darboro, Director

DATE: June 13, 19--

SUBJECT: Interoffice Memoranda

The exchange of information within a company is frequently typed on interoffice forms, either half or full sheets, depending upon the length of the message. The following points describe unique features of this form of memorandum.

1. Space twice after a printed heading; set the left margin stop for typing heading items and the body. Set the right margin stop an equal distance from the right edge. These margin adjustments will usually provide side margins of 1 inch.

2. Full addresses, the salutation, the complimentary close, and the signature are omitted.

3. Personal titles, such as Mr., are usually omitted from the memo heading. They are included on the envelope, however.

4. TS between the heading and the message; SS the paragraphs, but DS between them.

5. Reference initials, enclosure notation, and carbon copy notation are included if needed.

Special colored envelopes are often used for interoffice memos. Type the addressee's personal title, name, and business title or name of department for the address. Type COMPANY MAIL (in caps) in the postage location.

xx

pc Paul Glass, Assistant to the President

1 Interoffice memorandum

Communications Design Associates

348 INDIANA AVENUE
WASHINGTON, DC 20001-1438
Tel: 1-800-432-5739

January 11, 19--

Mr. Manuel D. Legallo
Office Manager, DGT, Inc.
4532 Mahood Drive
Huntington, WV 25705-8450

Dear Mr. Legallo

This letter is typed on executive-size stationery, a size preferred by some administrators, supervisors, and executives.

Executive-size stationery is smaller than the typical office stationery, for it measures only 7½" x 10½". It usually carries the company letterhead and a statement identifying the office from which it originates.

When typing letters on stationery narrower than the usual 8½" by 11" paper, margins of 1" are recommended. To center long or short letters requires adjustment of the date placement, which may vary from Line 10 to Line 16. Standard letter styles and punctuation forms are used.

We hope this example letter will help to answer the questions you asked in your recent letter about the use of this special stationery.

Very truly yours

Adelle Pruitt

Mrs. Adelle Pruitt
Communications Consultant

xx

2 Letter on executive-size paper

Fairfield Manufacturing, Inc.

MESSAGE	REPLY
TO:	DATE: January 23, 19--
Jonathan Kappel	The topics listed are timely and relevant to our long-range plans. I suggest that I attend the conference in New York in March and make a formal proposal to the corporate officers by April 1.
Director, Employee Development	
126 Hancock Tower	
DATE: January 22, 19--	
SUBJECT: Conference on Employee Development	

The attached brochure was received from the National Center for the Advancement of Business Practices. Since employee development will be a priority for us for some time, these conference topics may be relevant. Please let me know your opinion.

SIGNED: Maria Gonzalez, Vice President

SIGNED: Jonathan Kappel

3 Message/reply form

Sally Ann Dupois
123 Poinciana Road
Memphis, TN 38117-4121
(901-365-2775)

PRESENT CAREER OBJECTIVE

Eager to accept part-time position that provides opportunities for additional training and potential for full-time employment.

MAJOR QUALIFICATIONS

Knowledge of merchandising, management, inventory control, and related areas of a retail clothing store. Cheerful, outgoing personality and a dependable, cooperative worker.

EDUCATION

Junior at Memphis State University, Memphis, Tennessee, majoring in Marketing.

AA degree (associate degree/advertising; honors), State Technical Institute, Memphis, Tennessee.

Graduate (honors), East High School, Memphis, Tennessee.

EXPERIENCE

Assistant Manager, The Toggery, 100 Madison Avenue, Memphis, TN 38103-4219, June 1985 - Present.

Inventory Clerk and Cashier, Chobie's, 1700 Poplar Avenue, Memphis, TN 38104-2176, June 1984 - September 1984.

Clerk and Assistant to the Buyer, Todds, 1450 Union Avenue, Memphis, TN 38104-5417, June 1983 - September 1983.

REFERENCES

Mrs. Evelyn J. Quinell
Manager, Chobie's
1700 Poplar Avenue
Memphis, TN 38104-2176

Professor Aldo R. MacKenzie
Marketing Department
Memphis State University
Memphis, TN 38114-3285

Ms. Lanya Roover
The Toggery
100 Madison Avenue
Memphis, TN 38103-4219

Mr. Robert D. Tindall, Jr.
Attorney-at-Law
1045 Quin Avenue
Memphis, TN 38106-4792

4 Personal data sheet

Addressing procedure

Envelope address. Set a tab stop (or margin stop if a number of envelopes are to be addressed) 10 spaces left of center for a small envelope or 5 spaces for a large envelope. Start the address here on Line 12 from the top edge of a small envelope and on Line 14 of a large one.

Style. Type the address in *block style*, single-spaced, without punctuation at the ends of lines, except when an abbreviation ends a line. Type the city name, state name or abbreviation, and ZIP Code on the last address line. The ZIP Code is usually typed 2 spaces after the state name.

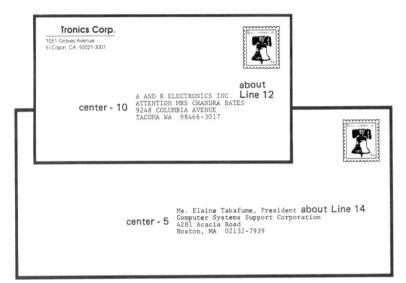

Addressee notations. Type addressee notations, such as *Hold for Arrival, Please Forward, Personal,* etc., a triple space below the return address and about 3 spaces from the left edge of the envelope. These notations may be underlined or typed in all capitals.

If an *attention line* is used, type it immediately below the company name in the address line.

Mailing notations. Type mailing notations, such as SPECIAL DELIVERY and REGISTERED, below the stamp and at least 3 line spaces above the envelope address. Type these notations in all capital letters.

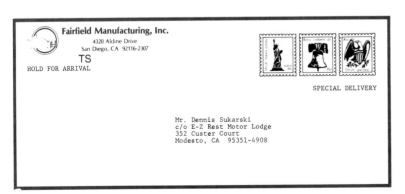

Folding and inserting procedure

Small envelopes (No. 6¾, 6¼)

Step 1
With letter face up, fold bottom up to ½ inch from top.

Step 2
Fold right third to left.

Step 3
Fold left third to ½ inch from last crease.

Step 4
Insert last creased edge first.

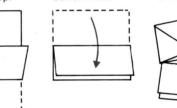
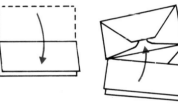

Large envelopes (No. 10, 9, 7¾)

Step 1
With letter face up, fold slightly less than ⅓ of sheet up toward top.

Step 2
Fold down top of sheet to within ½ inch of bottom fold.

Step 3
Insert letter into envelope with last crease toward bottom of envelope.

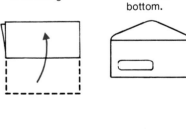

Window envelopes (letter)

Step 1
With sheet face down, top toward you, fold upper third down.

Step 2
Fold lower third up so address is showing.

Step 3
Insert sheet into envelope with last crease at bottom.

Window envelopes (invoices and other forms)

Step 1
Place sheet face down, top toward you.

Step 2
Fold back top so address shows.

Step 3
Insert into envelope with crease at bottom.

Formatting reports (See illustrations below)

Margins. Use 1" top, side, and bottom margins, except for the first page, which has a 1½" or 2" top margin.

Binding. Allow an extra ½" for side or top binding.

Spacing. Double spacing for the body of a report and 5-space paragraph indentions are usual.

Quotations. Single-space quotations of 4 or more lines and indent them 5 spaces from each margin; otherwise, enclose the quotations in quotation marks and include them double-spaced as part of the body of the report.

Ellipses. An ellipsis, an intentional omission of part of a quotation, is indicated by 3 periods with one space between each of the periods. If the omission ends a sentence, use 4 periods.

Leaders. If the report contains tabular copy, the columns may be separated by leaders. Leaders (spaced periods) can help a reader to move from one column to another. After typing the first item in the first column, space once and then alternate a period and a space to a point 2 or 3 spaces short of the next column. Note whether you type the periods on odd or even line-of-writing numbers; align subsequent rows by starting on an odd or even number as you did in the first line.

Justifying the right margin (manually). A preliminary copy must be typed to determine how many extra spaces must be added between words to insure an even right margin in a final copy. The normal procedure for the preliminary typing is to type as close to the end of each line as possible and then fill the remaining spaces with diagonals until the machine locks. Interpret diagonals as spaces to be added to each line in the final copy.

Footnotes. Footnotes may be placed at the end of a report, or they may be placed at the foot of the page on which reference to them is made.

Use a superior figure or symbol in the text of the report as reference to a footnote. Repeat the reference with the footnote.

Separate footnotes from the body of a report with a single underline 1½" long; single-space below the last line of the report to type the underline, type the underline, and double-space below the underline to begin the first line of the footnotes.

Single-space footnotes; double-space between them.

Calculate footnote placement to insure a 1" bottom margin.

Formatting outlines

Data may be reduced to a more functional form through the use of an outline. Use the following suggestions.

Separate divisions and subdivisions of various orders with 4-space indentions.

Type first order divisions in ALL CAPS: capitalize main words only in second-order divisions; capitalize only the first word in third- and subsequent-order divisions.

Use the margin release and backspacer to type all Roman numerals other than I, V, and X.

The line length chosen must accommodate the longest line but must not exceed 70 spaces.

There must be at least two parts to any division.

```
                         HEADING
                            TS
        I.  FIRST—ORDER DIVISION
                             DS
             A.  Second—Order Division
             B.  Second—Order Division
                  1.  Third—order division
                  2.  Third—order division
             C.  Second—Order Division
                             DS
       II.  FIRST—ORDER DIVISION
                             DS
             A.  Second—Order Division
                  1.  Third—order division
                  2.  Third—order division
                       a.  Fourth—order division
                       b.  Fourth—order division
                  3.  Third—order division
             B.  Second—Order Division
```

1 Unbound report, page 1

PREPARING REPORTS: THE PROFESSIONAL TOUCH

Both the writer and keyboard operator, or compositor, share concern for the preparation and ultimate success of a report, but usually the writer must accept final accountability. The compositor's contribution, however, is a vital one; and she or he should proceed cautiously. For example, before starting to prepare a final copy of a report, the compositor should determine

1. the specified purpose of the report and whether some particular format is required;

2. the number, kind, and grade of copies required;[1] and

3. deadlines for completion.

The keyboard operator should be prepared to work from script, rough-draft, or printed copy and yet give the report a final presentation that is as professional as it is functional.

"Tricks of the Trade"

Those with experience in preparing reports have found that there are special procedures they can use to simplify their tasks. The following paragraphs contain samples of some procedures that can be especially helpful to a person who has not previously keyboarded reports. (Anyone who plans to prepare more than a few reports, however, should read several good books on the subject.)

Right margins. Attractive right margins result when good judgment is exercised. Using the warning bell judiciously ensures right margins that approximate left margins in width.

---
[1]For further information, see The Chicago Manual of Style, 13th ed. (Chicago: The University of Chicago Press, 1982), p. 40.

1 Unbound report, page 1

2 Unbound report, page 2

2

Reference characters. To keystroke a superior figure, turn the platen back a half line and type the figure. Asterisks and other reference symbols require no such adjustment. Keyboards with special symbol keys for report writing are available.

Page endings. A few simple guides become important whenever a report has more than one page. For example, never end a page with a hyphenated word. Further, do not leave a single line of a paragraph at the bottom of a page or at the top of a page (unless the paragraph has only one line, of course).

Footnote content. Underline titles of complete publications; use quotation marks with parts of publications. Thus, the name of a magazine will be underlined, but the title of an article within the magazine will be placed in quotation marks. Months and locational words, such as volume and number, may be abbreviated.

Penciled guides. A light pencil mark can be helpful to mark approximate page endings, planned placement of page numbers, and potential footnote locations. When the report has been finished, erase any visible pencil marks.

Conclusion

With patience and skill, the keyboard operator can give a well-written report the professional appearance it deserves. Says Lesikar[2],

Even with the best typewriter available, the finished work is no better than the efforts of the typist. But this statement does not imply that only the most skilled typist can turn out good work. Even the inexperienced typist can produce acceptable manuscripts simply by exercising care.

---
[2]Raymond V. Lesikar, Basic Business Communication (Homewood: Richard D. Irwin, Inc., 1979), p. 364.

2 Unbound report, page 2

3 Title page

TRENDS IN OFFICE COMMUNICATION

Bernadette E. Blount

Northern Illinois University

January 11, 19--

3 Title page

4 Bibliography

BIBLIOGRAPHY

Blum, Lester. "Computer Generated Graphic Tutorials In Economics." Collegiate Microcomputer 4 (Winter 1983): 289-97.

Crawford, T. James, et al. Basic Keyboarding and Typewriting Applications. Cincinnati: South-Western Publishing Co., 1983.

Hess, M. Elizabeth. Printing Manager, Effective Office Systems, New Orleans, Louisiana. Interviewed by Lois Walker, March 20, 1985.

Ray, Patrick V. "Electronic Printing Applications." Class handout in BADM 487, Central University, 1985.

Toffler, Alvin. The Third Wave. New York: William Morrow and Company, Inc., 1980.

4 Bibliography

LENDING POLICY FOR COUNTY BANK
Limits of Authority

The President of the bank is authorized to make loans up to
$100,000 on a secured basis and up to $50,000 on an unsecured
basis. Any request for a line of credit in excess of the limit
specified for the President must be approved by at least two members of the Loan Committee other than the President. These lending
limits are in agreement with recommended standards (Burge, 1985).

The President shall delegate authority to make loans to the
senior officers of the bank. Senior officers may approve loans up
to $50,000 on a secured basis and up to $25,000 on an unsecured
basis. The President may delegate authority to make loans to other
officers. Authority delegated to officers other than the senior
officers shall not exceed $10,000 and shall be for secured loans
only. This policy is based on recommended guides (White, 1985).

REFERENCES

Burge, S. Michael. "General Lending Policy," South-Western Banking
Association Report. March 12, 1985, p. 8.

White, Deborah B. "Guides for Delegating Lending Authority." Class
handout in Bankers' School, Central University, 1985.

1 Reference citations

TABLE OF CONTENTS

Page

2 Table of contents

Cap or ≡	Capitalize
⌒	Close up
⌒ϩ	Delete
∧	Insert
⟨ϩ⟩	Insert comma
# or /#	Insert space
∨	Insert apostrophe
⟨ϩ⟩ ⟨ϩ⟩	Insert quotation marks
⎡‾‾⎤	Move right
⎣‾‾	Move left
⌐‾⌐	Move down; lower
‾⎤‾	Move up; raise
lc or /	Set in lowercase
¶	Paragraph
no new ¶	No new paragraph
‖	Set flush; align type
◯ sp	Spell out
stet	Let it stand; ignore correction
∿ or tr	Transpose
‾‾‾‾	Underline or italics

Proofreader's marks

Preliminary copy may be corrected with proofreader's marks.
The typist must be able to interpret correctly these marks
when retyping the corrected (rough-draft) copy. The most
commonly used marks are shown above.

Correcting errors

There are several methods that can be used to correct errors, and they are explained below.

Correction paper ("white carbon")

1 Backspace to the error.

2 Place the correction paper in front of the error, coated side toward the paper.

3 Retype the error. The substance on the correction paper will cover the error.

4 Remove the correction paper; backspace; type the correction.

Rubber eraser

1 Use a plastic shield to protect surrounding and a typewriter (hard) eraser.

2 Turn the paper forward or backward in the machine to position the error for easier correction.

3 To keep bits of eraser out of the mechanism, move the carrier away from the error (or move carrier to the extreme left or right).

4 Move the eraser in one direction only to avoid cutting the paper.

Correction fluid ("liquid paper")

1 Be sure the color of the fluid matches the color of the paper.

2 Turn the paper forward or backward to ease the correction process.

3 Brush the fluid on sparingly; cover only the error, and it lightly.

4 The fluid dries quickly. Return to correction point and make the correction.

Automatic correction

If your machine is equipped with an automatic correcting ribbon, consult with your instructor or with the manufacturer's manual for operating instructions.

Horizontal centering

1 Move the margin stops to extreme ends of the scale.

2 Clear tab stops; then set a tab stop at center of paper.

3 Tabulate to the center of the paper.

4 From center, backspace once for each 2 letters, spaces, figures, or punctuation marks in the line.

5 Do not backspace for an odd or leftover stroke at the end of the line.

6 Begin to type where backspacing ends.

	Example
Scale reading at left edge of paper	0
+Scale reading at right edge of paper	102
Total ÷ 2 = Center point	102 ÷ 2 = 51

Spread headings

1 Backspace from center once for each letter, character, and space except the last letter or character in the heading. Start typing where the backspacing ends.

2 When typing a spread heading, space once after each letter or character and three times between words.

Vertical centering

Roll-back-from-center method

From vertical center of paper, roll platen (cylinder) back once for each 2 lines, 2 blank spaces, or line and blank line space. Ignore odd or leftover line.

Steps to follow:

1 To move paper to vertical center, start spacing down from top edge of paper:

a half sheet
  down 6 TS (triple spaces)
    −1 SS (Line 17)

b full sheet
  down 11 TS
    +1 SS (Line 34)

2 From vertical center:

a half sheet, SS or DS; follow basic rule, back 1 for 2.

b full sheet, SS or DS; follow basic rule, back 1 for 2; then back 2 SS for reading position.

Mathematical method

1 Count lines and blank line spaces needed to type problem.

2 Subtract lines to be used from lines available (66 for full sheet and 33 for half sheet).

3 Divide by 2 to get top and bottom margins. If fraction results, disregard it. Space down from top edge of paper 1 more than number of lines to be left in top margin.

For reading position, which is above exact vertical center, subtract 2 from exact top margin.

Formula for vertical mathematical placement:

$$\frac{\text{Lines available} - \text{lines used}}{2} = \text{top margin}$$

Prepare

1 Insert and align paper.

2 Clear margin stops by moving them to extreme ends of the scale.

3 Clear all tab stops.

4 Decide the number of spaces to be left between columns (for intercolumns).

Plan vertical placement

Follow either of the vertical centering methods explained on page xi.

Headings. Double-space (count 1 blank line space) between main and secondary headings, when both are used. Triple-space (count 2 blank line spaces) between the last heading (either main or secondary) and the first horizontal line of column items or column headings. Double-space between column headings (when used) and the first line of the columns.

Plan horizontal placement

Backspace from center of paper 1 space for each 2 letters, figures, symbols, and spaces in the *longest item* of each column and for each 2 spaces between columns. Set the left margin stop of the longest item when backspacing, carry it forward to the next column. Ignore an extra space at the end of the last column. (See illustration below).

An easy alternate method is to backspace for the longest item in each column first, *then* for the spaces to be left between columns.

Note. If a column heading is longer than the longest item in the column, it may be treated as the longest item in determining placement. The longest column item must then be centered under the heading, and the tab stop set accordingly.

Set tab stops. From the left margin stop, space forward 1 space for each letter, figure, symbol, and space in the longest item in the first column and for each space in the first intercolumn. Set a tab stop. Follow this procedure for each additional column to be typed.

To center column headings

Backspace-from-column-center method

From the point at which the column begins (tab or margin stop), space forward (→) once for each 2 letters, figures, or spaces in the longest item in the column. This leads to the column center point; from it, backspace (←) once for each 2 spaces in the column heading. Ignore an odd or leftover space. Type the heading at this point; it will be centered over the column.

Mathematical method

1 To the number of the cylinder (platen) or line-of-writing scale immediately under the first letter, figure, or symbol of the longest item of the column, add the number shown under the space following the last stroke of the item. Divide this sum by 2; the result will be the center point of the column. From this point on the scale, backspace to center the column heading.

—or—

2 From the number of spaces in the longest item, subtract the number of spaces in the heading. Divide this number by 2; ignore fractions. Space forward this number from the tab or margin stop and type the heading.

To type horizontal lines

Depress the shift lock; strike the underline key.

To draw vertical lines

Operate the automatic line finder. Place a pencil or pen point through the cardholder (or the type bar guide above the ribbon or carrier). Roll the paper up until you have a line of the desired length. Remove the pencil or pen and reset the line finder.

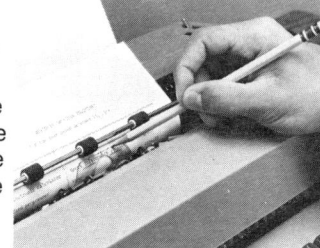

```
              MAIN HEADING

           Secondary Heading


   These        Are       Column        Heads

 xxxxxx       longest     xxxx         xxxxx
 xxxx         item        longest      xxx
 xxxxx        xxxxx       item         longest
 longest      xxxxxx      xxxxx        item
 item         xxxx        xxx          xxx
```